Prison is
not supposed to
be fun - and Dwight B Barera
tells you. He didn't have
many giggles during his 7
man confinement in a jail

Money only

Bribery

Swallowed his money
to Protect it

Rape -

effied on family

Claimed for stealing
from welfare

Mexican prisons wait
you to buy out
Six went on Hunger strike
psychic ward

"mayor" prisoner elected
King of the ward

Detailed description
of battles with
prisoners — mice, lice
Rats & bugs

CH
Son
Linda Son
Sara Edison
Judy Gibbon

ESCAPE

Dwight and Barbara Worker

SAN FRANCISCO BOOK COMPANY, INC.

San Francisco 1977

We are grateful for the help, advice, and support of the following: Alice LeVeen, Rick Klein, Stan and Bonnie Roth, Kenneth Worker, J.V.P., G. S. Daly, Patricia Holt, Skew and Pam, Dana, R.L.H., Congressman Fortney Stark, Edie Wilkie, Clifford and Anna Jane Brown, C.L.H., Erica Meyer, Ben and Lynn Marshall, Robert and Mary Coulter, Jerry Kamstra, Seymour Sommer, S. Gerstein, and A. H. Skinner.

Library of Congress Cataloging in Publication Data

Worker, Dwight, 1946–
  Escape!

  1. Escapes. 2. Worker, Dwight, 1946–
3. Worker, Barbara, 1954– 4. Fugitives from justice—Biography. I. Worker, Barbara, 1954– joint author. II. Title.
HV8657.W67 365'.641 [B] 77-78676
ISBN 0-913374-76-8

Printed in the United States of America 10 9 8 7 6 5 4 3 2 1

To our parents, Elmer and Eva Chilcoate, and

Fred and Dolores Worker

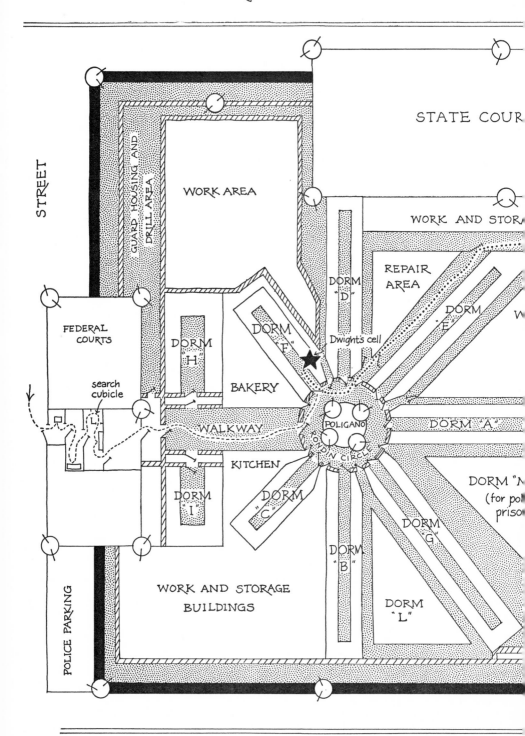

STREET

STREET

STATE COUR

STREET

GUARD HOUSING AND DRILL AREA

WORK AREA

WORK AND STOR

REPAIR AREA

FEDERAL COURTS

DORM "D"

DORM "F"

Dwight's cell

DORM "E"

W

search cubicle

DORM "H"

BAKERY

POLIGANO

DORM "A"

WALKWAY

ONION CIRCLE

KITCHEN

DORM "I"

DORM "C"

DORM "B"

DORM "N (for pol prisor

DORM "G"

POLICE PARKING

WORK AND STORAGE BUILDINGS

DORM "L"

STREET

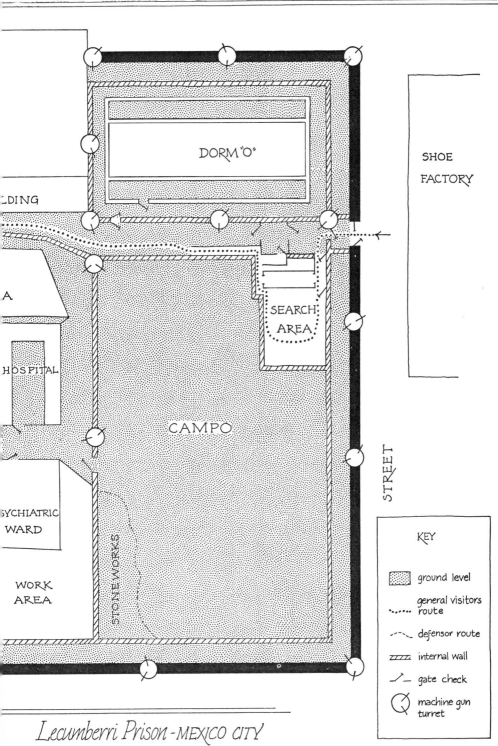

SHOE
FACTORY

DORM "O"

LDING

SEARCH
AREA

A

HOSPITAL

CAMPO

PSYCHIATRIC
WARD

STONE WORKS

STREET

WORK
AREA

KEY

ground level

general visitors
route

defensor route

internal wall

gate check

machine gun
turret

Lecumberri Prison -MEXICO CITY

ESCAPE

We would be getting married today. Barbara would arrive in the morning just like she always did, except this time there would be tears of fright in her eyes. We would first hide ourselves away and embrace. And then, if everything went right, today we would be married.

I stood at the door, peering down at the gate, waiting for my name to be called. Would she be late? Not because of anything she might do. We had talked about and planned on this day for nearly a year.

The kittens began to cry. I warmed up some milk and fed them with the eyedropper. In a few minutes their cries ceased. Bloated with milk, they began licking themselves. While I was putting away the milk, I dropped the dish. It shattered. My shaved hands were shaking uncontrollably. I busied myself by cleaning it up.

Today—my wedding day. A rite of passage. A year in the waiting, and now it was time. We should be happy. We had both wanted this so. But only the coldest dread rose up within me today. Trembling at the door, waiting waiting waiting for her, I had never been so afraid in all my life.

1 Limping to My Apocalypse

I went to Peru to smuggle cocaine in November 1973. I also planned to do some mountain climbing and take a boat ride down the Amazon. But the purpose of my journey was to make a lot of fast money.

I had sniffed enough cocaine to know that I liked it, despite my perpetually bloody nose, nervousness, and vague, lurking paranoia. I had the money to buy the cocaine, but I never seemed to have enough. Never enough. I also had the address and telephone number of a good, reliable source, so that I would not have to bother searching for a street connection. I would just buy the cocaine, hide it away, and then take it back to the U.S.A. Easy. Every detail had already been worked out.

I met René, my connection in Lima, and gave him the money. A week later he rapped softly on my hotel door and peered cautiously around the room before coming in. He looked careful but confident. He was well educated, spoke perfect English, and was honest. That last point was the most important, for had he wanted to, he could have already ripped me off. Trust like this was essential to good business.

We spoke briefly. Seeing that everything was safe with me, he quickly went back to his car. In a minute he returned with a bulge under his jacket.

The cocaine was pure, fine snowflake. With one small sniff

came the fresh, cool, numbing clarity—the fleeting crystal illusion that the lady fools you with every time. I loved it.

I told René about my smuggling plan. With the cocaine under a plaster body cast, I would take a bus to Ecuador. From Guayaquil I would fly directly to Guatemala City. There I would disembark and pass customs. From Guatemala I would cross the Mexican border by land and travel north to the U.S. border. Near the border I would remove the body cast and hide the cocaine in the desert. I would return later with a backpack and the necessary gear and hike the twenty miles through the mountains into the U.S.A. with the coke. Safely within the U.S., selling the cocaine would be the easiest part.

René, approving my plan, warned me about the customs at the Panama City airport and, especially, the Mexico City airport. A partner of his had been busted in Mexico City. I had already heard about the tight customs there, so I agreed with him.

But only when I showed René the X-ray of my broken shoulder did he become truly interested. He nodded as he looked over the false newspaper article that I had had printed in Spanish telling of how I had broken my shoulder while climbing Mount Chimborazo in Ecuador. The false hospital bill and phony doctor's letter, along with a suitcase full of mountain-climbing equipment, convinced René that any customs agent would believe that I had indeed been injured in a serious mountaineering accident.

René looked over the documents again and nodded. Then he asked if he could send several hundred grams of his own cocaine along with mine. We would split the profits fifty-fifty.

I thought it over for a moment. I had not planned to carry more than 600 grams of cocaine with me. Any more could create too big a bulge under my cast. René explained that there should be at least a $6,000 profit on the 200 extra grams of cocaine, $3,000 for each of us. And $3,000 was $3,000. Rushing on coke, wanting as much as possible, I went for it.

I reweighed the cocaine—800 grams in total. Not much, but then again, a lot. Enough to pay for my vacation, buy a complete camera system, and earn ten Gs on the side. I had made myself an offer I could not refuse.

We taped the three polyethylene bags of cocaine tightly onto my left arm. I then folded my arm against my body and told René how to apply the plaster rolls. At the time I was a licensed emergency medical technician in the state of New Mexico and I knew how to do such things. I showed René a xeroxed copy from a medical book of a Volpeau cast, and he applied the plaster rolls accordingly.

In thirty minutes I had a shoulder cast that covered my entire left arm and shoulder up to my neck and down to my lower abdomen, leaving no room to move my arm at all. The cast bulged slightly more than I had anticipated, but not too much more. René then took a pencil and pen and began writing inscriptions on the cast: *BUENA SUERTE*, BETTER LUCK NEXT TIME, GET BETTER, and a score of names in different handwritings and pen colors. We laughed heartily with each signature.

I deliberately cut my left hand with a razor blade and let it bleed for a while. Then I bandaged it and left some of the blood showing. As a final touch, I put a knee brace on my right leg. My injuries now appeared even more credible.

René and I discussed the plan. He felt the possibility of the customs agents breaking the cast off without prior information on me was too remote to consider. I felt good about René having a vested interest in the success of the scam, because he would now have no reason to turn me in. Of course I trusted him, but in matters such as these, with the stakes as high as they were, I should never trust anyone completely.

We sniffed more coke. Our optimism on the success of our smuggle fed our imaginations. We made arrangements to do more business in the future. We would both get rich. Then we gave each other an *abrazo* (hug), and said *adios*.

Two days later I caught a bus to Guayaquil, Ecuador. During the ride I sat next to a French girl. Since neither her English nor my French was adequate, we spoke in Spanish. She had arrived on a chartered Air France jet in La Paz, Bolivia, with several hundred other French students. When it was time for the jet to leave, she had decided to stay on in South America. In Cuzco, Peru, someone had stolen all of her identification and traveler's checks, forcing her to return to France.

In the course of our conversation, she mentioned that probably one-fourth of all the students on that chartered flight were carrying cocaine back to France with them.

Really? And where were they hiding it? She thought that most of the men had it in their platform shoes, but the *jeunes filles* had "special" places to hide things.

We laughed.

She looked at my feet and, seeing my sandals, smiled and shook her head. I looked at her and told her I had *no* way of knowing whether or not *she* was carrying cocaine. Her eyebrows lifted. We laughed some more. Then she rapped on my cast with her knuckles and laughed that I probably had a *kilogram of cocaine under there right now.*

That shocked me. Trying to keep my composure, I told her that I actually had ten kilos of pure heroin beneath it. She continued smiling mischievously. I sat there wondering if there was any possible way that she might know. No, not a chance. But still—I could be superstitious about such things.

When we came to the Ecuadorian border, everyone got a thorough personal baggage search. They had not done this to me three years ago at this border. Like a curious tourist, I asked the customs man if he was looking for guns.

"No. Cocaine."

The times had changed. He checked my luggage and then waved me through.

We rode into Guayaquil and I checked into the Hotel Boston. I would be staying there for several days, doing last-minute preparations before I flew to Guatemala. Just a few more days.

The next morning I said goodbye to the French girl and went downtown to a medical store. By now I was getting my act of being a cripple down perfectly. I was letting people carry my bags, allowing women to open doors, and even accepting minimal help when getting dressed. In my mind I was becoming what I was pretending to be. This was good. It would be important to be convincing when I passed the next customs points.

At the medical supplies store I bought a crutch. I planned to walk with a limp from then on, so I began practicing on the way back to the hotel. Never in my life had I needed or used a crutch. Now I had only a few days in which to cultivate a credible limp.

December 8, 1973. The route was clear and simple. That morning I would leave Guayaquil for Panama City. There I would purchase a previously reserved ticket for the flight to Guatemala City. That flight would be leaving fifty-five minutes after I arrived from Guayaquil. At the Panama City airport I would wait in the international zone without passing customs until my departure to Guatemala City. At Guatemala City I would disembark and pass customs, which was supposed to be especially easy for tourists. If I was approached by a customs agent, I would have him carry my suitcases. Simple as that.

But when I arrived at the Guayaquil airport that morning, something was wrong. There was an abnormally large crowd, and the place was swarming with military police. I walked up to a policeman who was cradling an Uzi machine gun and asked him what was happening. He replied that Princess Anne of England was arriving. She had just gotten married and was on her honeymoon. *Big Deal,* I thought, in the solid American tradition of disdain for royalty. But judging from the size of the crowds, the Ecuadorians were of a different opinion. The entire airport was decorated for the welcoming ceremony, including a red carpet stretched on the runway, which would later be lined with young girls carrying flowers.

I checked in with my airline and was told there would be a delay because of the arrival of the Princess. With the red-carpet ceremony prepared outside, no plane could take off until it was over.

Big Deal. All of this for one of George III's descendants. How long would I have to wait there? She would be arriving at any moment, they told me. No more than thirty minutes. Well, that would still give me time in Panama City to catch my flight to Guatemala City. I was getting nervous, so I took two Valiums that I had brought along with me expressly for that purpose. It was the first time in my life that I had taken Valium.

Two hours later the Princess finally arrived. She must have been sleeping late on her honeymoon—at my expense, for now I would miss my connecting flight to Guatemala City. I asked the airline's agents if there were any other flights from Panama City to Guatemala City that afternoon. There were none. But I could stay in Panama City overnight and catch a flight the next morning to Guatemala City. That would be no good, because I would have to pass Panama City customs. What other flights were there? To Miami, New Orleans, and Mexico City. I did not want to go directly to the United States, because I could easily be caught at the airports. If I stayed in Panama City overnight to catch the Guatemala City flight the next day, that would mean I'd have to pass both Panama City and Guatemala City airport customs, and then the Mexican border customs at the Guatemalan frontier.

By now I was feeling very calm. The Valium must have been coming on. I had to make a decision on the spot, while they were clearing away the red carpet preparations.—All right, I'll fly directly from Panama City to Mexico City and go through just one customs—Mexico City—instead of three. Less risk that way.

My plane to Panama City left moments later and I boarded it feeling tranquil. Very tranquil.

The flight to Panama City was uneventful, the way flights are supposed to be. In Panama City I discovered that I had to pass through customs anyway. There did not appear to be a delineated international zone at the airport. But the customs was easy. Cursory searches. If I wanted to, I could stay there and catch a flight to Guatemala City the next day with no additional risk.

But things had been going so smoothly and easily—and I was *so tranquil.* Everybody *knew* that I had been injured, so I decided to maintain momentum and get it over with—by staying with the flight. I played the slot machines until the plane was ready to go on to Mexico City.

On the flight to Mexico City I sat next to a young Chilean woman. A moustached American man of about thirty-five years then sat next to me. He was moddishly dressed and spoke fluent Spanish to the stewardess. He reminded me of a dapper Errol Flynn. When he pointed to my cast, I related my mountain-climbing accident. We talked some more and he told me he was coming from Bolivia, where he and some friends had just acquired a 15,000-acre plantation. He was very happy about having it *in reserve* for an early retirement later on.

It sounded suspicious to me. Where did a youngish man get the money to buy 15,000 acres of land in Bolivia, the Cocaine Capital of the world? Or was I just projecting my thoughts? Maybe he was completely legitimate. Most people are. *Why did he sit next to me? Did he know something? Of course not. Was I paranoid? Calm down.*

I ordered a gin and tonic. So did he and the Chilean woman. After finishing it, I ordered another. They did not. I kept thinking about René's warnings about Mexico City. Well, it was too late now. We were already aloft—there was no stopping now. Once I'd been through Mexico City customs I would be glad I had done it this way. The only alternative I had was to cut the cast off in the bathroom and dump the cocaine—and that *would* be suspicious, and also wasteful and stupid. But when I went to the bathroom I actually did think of cutting it off. By now I was urinating every few minutes, or so it seemed. Nerves. Wondering if the Valium had worn off, I took two more, believing they would be the magic pills that would make me so inconspicuous I would pass through customs as if I were invisible. I wanted to believe that.

When I returned to my seat, the American suggested that the three of us have a drink together in Mexico City that night. He knew some good night spots. The woman and I both agreed. Chummy.

The plane was flying by Mount Citlaltepetl, 150 miles east of Mexico City. At 18,700 feet, the mountain towered over everything else on the horizon, magnificently snowcapped against the backdrop.

I had a whole suitcase full of unused mountain-climbing gear in the plane. I wished I were climbing that mountain right then. Suddenly the idea of climbing a mountain made perfect sense to me—simple and direct. I would know what I was doing, and why, too. No moral questions about it. . . . And what was I doing now?

Stop thinking like this. Later.

By the time the plane landed in Mexico City, I was numbed to semiconsciousness. Events appeared to be moving on a slow, blank screen in front of me. Whatever Valium did do, it did not help my mind function.

I had once read a customs report on the smuggler profile. It said that customs agents were suspicious of anyone who was overly friendly with them, so I knew to be silent. It also stated that smugglers tended to stand at the ends of the customs lines, hoping that the customs agents would by then be so bored that they would give only cursory searches to the remaining people. Well then, I would use some reverse psychology on them. I would go through customs as soon as possible. So I lifted my suitcases off of the luggage retriever with my one good hand and then, while balancing on my right crutch, I pushed my luggage with my feet to the customs table. I was near the front of the line.

The agent opened my suitcases and carefully went through the contents, feeling the clothes, opening the bags, and then checking the suitcases for false sides and bottoms. He was thorough. Then he motioned me to pass by.

I had made it. I shut the suitcases and waved a porter over to carry them for me. The porter lifted them up and began walking to the front of the airport as I limped behind him.

We had almost left the customs zone when a clean-shaven, stocky, well-dressed Mexican man stopped the porter and took my suitcases from him. The tag on his sports jacket said Agente Valdez. Valdez motioned for me to follow him and I did. I was led into a small room in back of the airport customs area. There I saw another agent finishing up a body search of the American man I had sat next to on the plane. He was pulling up his trousers. He told me that he would be waiting in the lounge for me, and then walked out.

Valdez told me to take off my shirt. Before I could get it off, he was trying to stick his hand down the top of my cast. There was no space for him to reach in from above, so he pushed his hand under the cast from below, pressing hard against my stomach. I kept my stomach and chest expanded under the cast so he would not have enough room to work his hand up to the cocaine.

"FLOJESE! FLOJESE!"

I had never heard that Spanish word before, but I knew it meant something like loosen up. I told him I didn't speak Spanish, and for him to be careful because I had a badly broken shoulder. He punched me in the stomach and pushed his hand up harder. I felt his fingers working up close to the extra bag of cocaine that René had decided to send along at the last moment. I shrieked as if I were in pain—as if he had pushed on the broken bones. I turned from him and tried to show him my file of hospital papers explaining my accident.

He did not want to see them.

The harder I resisted, the more determined he was to feel under my cast. From the table next to us he grabbed a pair of pliers with tips fifteen inches long and jammed them up the bottom of the cast. I was fighting him off when he punched me in the jaw and kicked my crutch out from under me. I fell in a clutter to the floor. He climbed over me and forced the pliers up my cast. The pliers pinched my arm and I screamed for real this time. He maneuvered and pinched the pliers again and again. And then I heard it, and so did he. He had grabbed one of the polyethylene bags of cocaine and the plastic was rustling.

"TIENES COCAÍNA! TIENES COCAÍNA!"

I made one last feeble effort to resist him, but he punched me hard, several times, in the face. He shouted out the door for the other agents, and they came running in. I was panting and subdued, not believing what I saw happening to me through my own dulled eyes.

A Mexican doctor came in and opened his medical case. With

a pair of surgical scissors he cut off my cast within a minute. There was the cocaine. Valdez smiled proudly at the three bags taped to my chest and left arm. They had me *flagrante delicto*. I sat there bare-chested, too shocked to say anything, with my worst horror fantasy—*getting caught in Mexico*—coming true.

Other passengers came in and out of the body-search area and passed by, looking at me. I looked up to see the Chilean woman staring at me as I sat there half-naked with the bags of cocaine lying on my lap, my face sweating and flushed, blood on my mouth. Her face was stunned too, but in a very different way. Despite the gin and the four Valiums fogging my brain, I could still feel the heaviest of shame and embarrassment, stripped and defrocked in front of her and the others. She looked for a moment like she wanted to say something to me, to console me or help me however she might, but the customs agents were glaring at her suspiciously. She quickly walked off before they got the idea of detaining *her* for interrogation. We would not be having drinks together that night.

The agents led me into a back room and pushed me against the wall as though I were the trophy of a day's hunt. All the agents stood around, telling me how bad it was going to be for me. They were congratulating Valdez, asking him how he had ever thought I was carrying drugs. Valdez was basking in the praise, recounting his story again and again. Then he opened one of the plastic bags and examined the cocaine. He stuck his finger into it and scooped some cocaine onto his fingernail. He walked over to me and in front of everyone there, he slowly and deliberately *sniffed* the cocaine. He grinned like a shark and the whole room burst into laughter, except for me.

A photographer came in and lined me up against a wall covered with photographs. While he was putting film in his camera, I turned around and looked at the photos. All of them were pictures of people who had just been arrested at the airport for drugs. In the photos they were holding the drugs in front of themselves. Most of them appeared to be Americans carrying a pound or so of cocaine, not so different from myself. There were photos of some Latins on the wall too, several of whom were carrying large amounts. But most striking about all the photographs were the expressions on their just-arrested faces. All of them looked as if they were in a state of shock—as if they had just been at the scene of a disaster. They had. *Their own.*

Limping to My Apocalypse 11

I wondered if I looked the same.

As the photographer took his pictures, he leered at me, laughing and telling me how badly I was fucked. Already I was beginning to hate him. I began looking around the room, wondering if there would be some chance to make a break for it, to take off running through the door, out the airport, into the streets of Mexico City. Maybe I could get away.

Valdez dragged me back to the main room and handcuffed me to a locker. Then another customs agent, older and smaller than Valdez, came up to me and spoke in broken English.

"You think you can break the laws of Mexico?" He punched me several times. I said nothing back to him. He was fingering my address book, which he had found in my luggage.

"Who was on this airplane with you? Who are you working for? Tell me."

I told him nobody was with me. He punched me and told me I was lying. Several other agents began punching me over. Occasionally the photographer walked over and punched me to make his point.

The chief agent wanted to know from whom I had bought the cocaine in South America, and to whom I was taking it in the U.S.A. I told him the truth, that I was working for myself. He did not believe me. He began reading names from my address book to me, asking me if this or that name was the person. I kept answering "No" as they punched me. The man shouted that they were going to get the information from me one way or another, so I had better talk now. If I talked, they would go easy on me and have me deported in six months, maybe less—but if I didn't cooperate, he personally would make sure I got fifteen years *to serve.*

I had heard too many things about Mexican cops to believe him. But God, did I want to believe him, did I want to believe that *he himself* could arrange to have me deported.

"Sign the statement. Tell me who you work for and where you get your cocaine and we go easy on you."

I knew enough not to sign anything. I told them I wanted a lawyer. The older man turned around to the others and in an affected voice said in Spanish, "The *norteamericano wants a lawyer.*"

They laughed. Then several of them closed in on me and worked me over good this time. My head was banging against the locker behind me from the blows—no recoil.

"A lawyer will do you no good here! We got you. Now talk. Sing!"

I was freaked out. They meant business. I saw them, I heard them, I felt the blows, but still *I could not believe this was happening to me.*

"I want to see the U.S. Embassy," I stuttered.

They really began swinging.

"THE EMBASSY WILL DO YOU NO GOOD HERE! YOU ARE IN MEXICO AND YOU HAVE *NO* RIGHTS HERE! FORGET ABOUT THEM AND COOPERATE, OR ELSE! WRITE DOWN THE NAMES OF WHO YOU WORK FOR!"

But I remained silent—from a combination of shock, terror, Valium, and fear of signing anything, not out of courage.

The old man barked some commands to his staff and they quickly unhandcuffed me and led me down a narrow hallway to a bare cement room. One of the younger agents pushed me in and told me to undress. Numbly, I did as I was told.

The other agents came into the room together. One of them quickly threw a bucket of cold water over me. Valdez then came at me, holding a long, tubular, aluminum rod with two rounded points on its end and a cord attached to the rubber-coated handle. I thought he was going to start beating me over the head with it, so I covered my head and face. But instead, he poked it into my chest. In one reflex motion, I jumped and screamed.

It was an electric cattle prod.

He began poking it at my genitals. I turned away, covering myself with one hand while fighting the cattle prod away with the other. Other agents grabbed me while he jabbed me with the cattle prod. All the time I still could not believe this was happening to me. It was as if I were the victim in the worst horror movie ever made.

But the cattle prod was too much. While the electricity was going through my body to my brain, the only thing I could think of was to stop that electricity by whatever means possible, *stop the electricity. STOP THE ELECTRICITY!*

Whatever is to be said about Valium, it is not a pain killer. Just a few hours earlier I had taken Valium for the first time in my life, and now this was happening *to me.* I have never taken another since.

The older man continued shouting something to me. Only when I finally understood him to be asking me if now I were going to talk, did I answer him.

"YES. YES. YES! I'LL SIGN ANYTHING YOU WANT!"

They gave me a few extra shocks just to let me know what they would do if I did not sign, and then ordered me to get dressed. The old man again told me that if I cooperated, they would go easier on me—"Like they do in the *States*," he leered.

I got dressed and went back to the main office. There the older man was poring over my address book. He picked out a few names and asked me if they were involved. I said *yes* they were, without even bothering to see who they were. Somehow the fact that they were innocent of any involvement in my fiasco did not make any difference to me at that point. All I wanted them to do was to leave me alone and not give me any more electric shocks. I was telling myself that it was so obvious I was guilty anyway that it did not make any difference what I said, because *they had me.* They had already refused to believe the truth: that I was a small-time smuggler working for myself on my first cocaine run from South America.

I signed a lie of a confession that night at the airport. But what mattered about the signed confession was not that it was a lie or how it had been obtained, but rather that it was self-incriminating. The agents all smiled when I signed. Then they explained that, although it did not really matter, tomorrow I would have to sign the same statement in typed form, and they would be there to make sure I signed it. One of them waved the cattle prod again, smiling.

They had broken me. Later I would recall reading an article by George Orwell that stated that all men have their breaking points, and that any tyrant worth his chains and whips knows that. The weaker would break down sooner, while the stronger would take longer, but the only difference between the two was time. No one who *knew* questioned the fact that everybody would eventually break down.

I had lasted less than one hour.

The way I conducted myself that night of December 8, 1973 at Benito Juarez Airport ranks among the lowest moments in my life—totally devoid of any traces of honor, or dignity, or courage. I have never completely forgiven myself for it.

Thus began my imprisonment in Mexico.

2 The "Trial"

Late that evening, they took me to the *procuraduría* jail in the center of Mexico City. I would be held there for a few days while they processed my papers, then moved to a prison. At the *procuraduría* I briefly met Roger, another American of about my age who had also been arrested at the Mexico City airport for cocaine. Before we could talk very much, they locked us in separate solitary cells.

My clothes were wet and I had no blankets or mattress. It was impossible to sleep in the open, unheated steel and concrete cells. Already, although still in a stupor, I was looking for a way to escape. I kept pacing the cell, telling myself that if I could not escape, I would rather be dead than spend the next years of my life in a Mexican prison. There just had to be some way out.

Early the next morning, I heard Roger whispering for me. I put my head to the bars, and we talked. He too had received similar treatment until he signed a confession. We both agreed that the confession had to be worthless because of how it had been extracted from us. It just could not stand up in court. Roger remarked that we were really political prisoners. He felt that cocaine should be legal, and that they were holding us because they were just persecuting the "new culture."

I paused on that one. I asked him if he was smuggling cocaine to make it legal. He said yes—if not *de jure,* then *de facto.* Was he a coke dealer on the street? Affirmative. Was he campaigning to legalize coke? In his own sort of way, yeah. He tried to sniff it *every* day.

We laughed feebly.

I told him I had been smuggling cocaine precisely because it was illegal, so I could make a lot of money. The moment I said the phrase "a lot of money," it rang empty. Although yesterday that money had been the only thing that mattered, now it seemed so very far away. It was a different game now. Hell, I didn't even know what kind of game I would be playing.

But I did know that first I would *have to get out of here*—and then worry about money. I told Roger that whatever we considered ourselves to be did not really matter. What mattered now was what they thought we were—and they probably considered us serious criminals: *class A drug traffickers.* On that bad note, the conversation faded out.

After a sleepless night, three customs agents came to the *procuraduría* and took me to a small room. They set the cattle prod on the table but said nothing about it. Its presence was enough. They again demanded my cooperation. If I cooperated, I would soon be released, because they just wanted the *pescados grandes* (the big fish). But if I did not cooperate, they would make sure I got the maximum sentence. I swore that what I had told them last night—that I was an independent working for myself—was the whole truth. They did not believe me, but evidently they felt they had enough information because they didn't use the cattle prod again. They then ordered me to go with them to sign a copy of the same statement that I had signed last night—and no funny stuff.

I nodded. In view of everything else, my signing or not signing seemed irrelevant. I figured that I would eventually have to pay a large bribe and then wait to be deported to the U.S.A. Or something like that. I did not know what, but something would have to happen to get me out.

Blind hippy faith.

Four guards handcuffed me and drove me to the equivalent of the attorney general's office. They typed the statement that I had signed the night before and read it back to me.

I signed it.

All of the guards smiled at me victoriously.

One of them said, "And now, gringo, *your trial is over.* You are now going to spend six to fifteen years in Hotel Lecumberri, the most expensive hotel in Mexico."

They all laughed.

He was almost right. During the next two years, I would never see or enter a courtroom, or see a judge or a prosecutor, or even make a plea of guilt or innocence.

3 The Welcoming Committee

The guards escorted me from the attorney general's office to the car and drove me back to the *procuraduría*. The following evening I was locked inside a prisoner-transport van and driven through Mexico City. There was one small opening through which I could see the street. It was Mexico City as usual: dirty, crowded, noisy, and smelly, teeming with people overflowing the sidewalks.

I watched through the small peephole as the prison van approached a huge, monolithic building and passed between the high, iron gates in front of it. The van descended the short ramp through the heavy metal garage door into the building. From behind the vehicle I heard the door slam shut.

I had been hoping to make some kind of break for it when I got out of the van, but when they opened the van door, I saw that there was no chance. In front of me were a half-dozen armed prison guards. They were dressed in blue and grey uniforms with tinselly, crackerjack-quality, silver stripes pasted onto their shoulders. They had black leather jackboots up to their knees. The guards were all short and brown, with little black moustaches. I was head and shoulders above any of them. When they saw that I was a foreigner, they all smiled in surprise—like sharks—like vultures.

"*Un gringo! Tenemos un gringito!*" (We have a little *gringo!*)

Other guards gathered around to inspect me, as though I were some rare, prized species that they did not catch very often. Without my telling them anything, they already knew that I had been arrested for drugs. One of them began making the universal money sign with his hand as he talked about how much could be made selling drugs. He knew I was a rich man because I was a *gringo* drug dealer.

An old *commandante* strode forward and sized me up as his underlings moved aside. Unlike the others, he was not smiling. He had the practiced angry look that his position demanded, and he had practiced it so long that he had become it. He grabbed my belt and yanked me along into his office, followed by the other guards. He shoved me toward a mural depicting the Mexican army valiantly fighting off the *gringo* American invaders. Judging by the body count, the score looked like *Mexicanos:* 100; *Yanquis:* 0.

I was at a loss to explain what mythical battle this mural depicted, because in every battle where the Yankees attacked Mexico, we had beaten them with little resistance. But looking around me at the guards and the prison, I reckoned that I was not in the best position to dispute the historic accuracy of the mural; so I listened to the *commandante's* explanation.

He said in Spanish, "Maybe you gringos fucked us then, *but we are going to fuck you good now.*"

With that, he began punching me.

The other guards laughed and then went through my pockets. They took my remaining money, my ring, my belt and silver belt buckle, and my electronic digital wristwatch. I watched them as they ogled the watch. Their facial expressions were not unlike those of primitive natives when they see their reflections in a mirror for the first time. I had a feeling that if I had taken their picture with a Polaroid and handed it to them, they would have fainted from culture shock.

The *commandante* put my watch on as if it were his own. The underling guards looked at him as though he were the only dog with the bone. Obviously, the watch had been the big score of the search.

I happened to like that watch a lot. I had been fascinated by its technological precision. It had lost only five seconds in the last six months. Remarkable. And I still didn't have the slightest idea how much time *I* was going to lose.

In my own sort of Spanish, I asked the *commandante* to return *my* watch to *me.*

He immediately stopped smiling at the watch to glare at me. He looked like a little dog growling. The other guards imitated his expression as best they could. Then he began punching me, and the others followed suit—monkey see, monkey do—knocking me around until I was no longer concerned with getting the watch back.

The *commandante* shouted at me in broken English, "You be here a *long* time and you have bad time here. When you come here, you leave your balls outside!"

They punched me around some more, and then they pushed me into a large holding cell.

I did not realize how true the *commandante's* words were going to be.

4 Descent into Lecumberri

Later that evening I was led off to dormitory "H," the temporary holding dormitory at Lecumberri for new prisoners. In "H" we were lined up and counted over and over. Apparently they were having trouble getting the count straight. More prisoners than fingers and toes.

Looking around at the ninety other new prisoners, I noticed that I was a giant among them, even though I stand only five feet ten inches. There were several who were my height, but none were taller. It also appeared that I had more teeth than any five of them together, and my shoes put me in the definite minority. But except for their shabby clothes, the other prisoners looked just like the numerous guards walking around us. All of the other prisoners were looking at me, repeating the ubiquitous *gringo* and the more insulting *gabacho,* while they made the universal money sign with their hands.

While I was standing there in the plaza on that winter night, a newcomer to prison life, I saw something that shocked me—although from then on I would be seeing it every day. The Mexican prisoners were constantly reaching for, touching, and massaging each others' asses—while flirting and leering their semitoothless smiles at each other. Foreplay and stroking behavior among the chimps. Under the cold blue mercury vapor lights it was sickening to watch, although sunlight would not have helped any either.

And then suddenly I felt someone's hand touch *my* ass. I quickly turned around, but from the blank faces behind me, I could not tell who had done it. Throughout the remainder of the lineup, someone from behind continually *touched my ass.* I finally managed to see who it was out of the corner of my eye. When they told us to break formation and get to our cells, I quickly turned around and hit him a good one on the blind side. It felt good. Immediately there were four or five Mexicans swinging at me. The guards quickly broke it up and ran us back to our cells and locked us in. At first I figured that the other Mexicans had joined in to help him just because he was so small. But that wasn't my fault. It didn't mean he could play with my ass with impunity, even it it *was* at his face level.

But I was wrong about their group behavior. They did not attack me *en masse* because I was bigger than the little punk. No, not at all. It was because I was a *gringo norteamericano* and they were Mexicans, and, I later learned, they would inevitably gang up on any American when they fought him. The Mexicans in prison have few qualms about fighting someone in ratios of from five- to ten-against-one, and on the street it is not much different. They call it *a hacer un montañ*—to make a mountain (on him). There is no Mexican equivalent of the Marquis of Queensbury rules of fighting—no Roberto's Rules of Disorder. Anything goes, and if you are a *gringo* in a Mexican prison, then you are always a minority, and you can never forget that.

That night I was locked in a three-bunk cell with ten other Mexicans. None of us had a mattress or blanket. There was no electricity, running water, or toilet. When someone had to urinate or defecate, he did it on the floor, and (you hoped) in the far corner.

No sooner had I lain down on the top metal bunk in the darkness than someone grabbed me by the ankles and yanked me onto the floor. By the faint light coming through the barred window I saw my assailant get into the bunk he had just cleared. I jumped up and pushed him off of it. He came at me and we punched inconclusively at each other in the darkness, wrestling around, kicking an empty pop bottle in the process. As the bottle went clinking across the cement floor he lunged and grabbed it. I let go of him and quickly swung myself onto the empty top bunk as the bottle flew by my head, shattering against the wall in a shower of glass. Then silence.

It did not occur to me that I was now in an ugly fight with a stranger for something so petty as a bunk, or that if things continued to escalate, one of us could get hurt—or killed. In fact nothing occurred to me at all. Numb with disbelief at being here in the first place, I was beyond shock, beyond fright, blinded of any perspective.

Maneuvering in the darkness while lying low, I used my cuff to sweep the small glass splinters off of the nine-foot-high bunk as best I could. Glass tinkled over the floor.

A light flickered below me. The man had lit a candle in the far corner and was glaring up at me. He was slightly shorter than I, but much stockier. A thick, black moustache, irregular teeth, small, dark eyes, a deep scar on his cheek—and a bottle in each hand. *Ratface.*

The other Mexicans were huddled together in the bunks below, avoiding stray fists, kicks, or bottles. Ratface moved around in the candlelight, waving the bottles over his head, poised to throw. I covered my head with my arms, peeking through them to watch him. He faked several throws, each time coming closer. With one hand I quickly felt behind me until I grabbed a large piece of broken glass. I flung it at him, hitting him on the head. He jumped back. I felt my finger bleeding. I grabbed another piece and tossed it at the candle. Miss. My second one hit. The candle toppled, flickered, and then went out. Good. I could still see him, but he couldn't see me. He squatted over the candle again, trying to relight it.

Suddenly I heard the guards outside begin yelling "FAJINAS! FAJINAS! FAJINAS!" Everyone in the cell, including Ratface, raced outside to the small stone patio. It was about 2:00 a.m. Bewildered, I followed them. The guards shouted and pushed us into a line. Then they flung rags in our hands and proceeded to run us back and forth over the stone patio in a fast backward duckwalk, scrubbing the floor. They drove us again and again, randomly kicking anyone any place while stomping the hands of those who weren't scrubbing fast enough. Cold sweat ran down my back as I maneuvered myself as far as possible from the guards. The floor was clean but they continued driving us nonstop to the cadence of furious jackboots and violent staccato Spanish, kicking, stomping, and hitting. Whenever I got out of line with the prisoners around me, the guards whacked me with a club. This went on for two grueling hours. It was a vision of galley slaves from some dungeon hundreds of years ago.

I could not believe what I was doing. We were duckwalking backward as fast as possible, chased by guards with clubs. And yet I had to believe it, for with every whack of the club I found myself moving faster, even though my legs were screaming with pain. This, I would later learn, was *fajinas:* compulsory work detail. If I did not pay a large sum of money quickly, I would have to do this work indefinitely.

Finally, after what seemed to be forever, they let us go back to our cells. I passed out immediately on the floor, too tired to care about where I slept.

At the first light of dawn, seemingly no sooner than I had lain down, the guards came around again, screaming to get running for *lista,* the twice-daily head count. I got up quickly, but I could not find my shoes or socks. And my pants pockets were empty.

I had been robbed.

I went out to lineup barefoot while the Mexicans laughed at me. Everyone knew what had happened. I looked around for my shoes, but it was hopeless. I would now be going barefoot.

"BAÑOS! BAÑOS! BAÑOS!" The guards were screaming, swinging their clubs as they lined us up. Then they proceeded to run all of us through a series of winding corridors and narrow gates. I quickly lost all sense of location and direction, so confusing were the odd angles and passageways.

We made a sharp left and all ninety of us had to cram into a hot, humid fifteen-by-fifteen-foot room. We were chest against chest and back against back with our arms overhead to make room. I was instantly overwhelmed by the heat and the body stench. From outside a guard shouted something while swinging his club. Everyone frantically began trying to undress all at once, elbows, knees, and hands banging into everyone else. Fists were thrown and a guard waded through, whacking everyone in front of him with the now ubiquitous club. Another command was shouted and the nude bodies began forcing themselves through a narrow, rusty metal door into yet another small room. The mass of bodies carried me with it.

This room was no more than twelve by twelve feet. Motion was impossible; no one could breathe without panting laboriously. Everybody was shouting and pushing, jockeying for position. Then a sputter, followed by a roaring hiss. Hot steam.

Quickly the top of the room clouded up with a scalding heat. People began shouting even louder, pushing themselves away from the source of the steam. There were a few screams. More fists were thrown. I couldn't breathe, the hot, oxygenless steam burning my nose and lungs. Suddenly I was hit on the side of my head. I turned to see Ratface swinging at me with his one free arm. My arms were pinned against me. He struck me again and again. I tried to lower myself, finally lifting my feet and sinking into the midst of the packed, seething flesh, out of his reach.

More screams and pushing. The room temperature was unbearable. Through the mass of flesh I saw a concrete bench against the wall. I elbowed and clawed through the fighting bodies until I wormed my way under the bench. With my cheek to the floor I gasped at the remaining air, while all around me limbs flew, arms pushed, and bodies leaned. The steam had dispersed to the floor level by now, so at head level it must have been unbearable. I could barely see through the steam as the room echoed with one overwhelming scream. A few people had passed out. Visions of Nazi gas chambers.

And then, after an eternity, the roar of steam sputtered, then died. A few loud clanks along the pipes, and cold water began pouring from the two shower nozzles overhead. Everyone clamored to get under the water to cool themselves off and to drink. I remained under the bench until the room had partially cleared before I stepped under the soothing cold water. I almost expected it to burst into steam from the heat of my skin. But no sooner had I gotten under the water than it clanked off. A guard stepped in, swinging his club, shouting for everybody to clear out. I jumped through the narrow doorway, then groped to find my clothes. My T-shirt was missing.

With no towel and no time to dry, I pulled my dirty pants on and ran along with the others back to "H." First bath.

I ran into dorm "H" wet and half-naked on the near-freezing winter morning to find, of all things, *women* sitting and *children* running around all over the patio of "H." A guard whapped me across the back with a leather strap, shouting for me to cover my bare chest in the presence of "ladies." Borrowing a towel, I covered myself as fast as possible. Then I looked over the bench. A number of short, squat, expressionless women were quietly rolling fly-bespecked tacos, changing cloth diapers, and nursing filthy babies.

So women and children could visit prisoners in a Mexican prison. In Mexico they could throw you into prison for anything, but then your whole family could visit you in the relative privacy of a cell. How contradictory. I had no idea at all of what a prison was supposed to be like, but I certainly had not expected to see women and children in the prisoners' quarters.

Later that day, after another round of *fajinas,* the lawyers began arriving in the dormitory like vultures descending on a carcass. These were the first lawyers I had seen since my arrest, and all of them wanted to talk with me. I spoke with the lawyers Jorge Aviles, Enrique Ostos, Alfredo Benevendu, and Pablo Sotomayor.

"How can I get out of here?"

"I can get you out. But it will be difficult. It will cost a lot of money."

"How much?"

"Fifteen thousand dollars."

"Twenty-five thousand dollars."

"Ten thousand dollars."

"Forty thousand dollars."

"Five thousand dollars down, and ten thousand more when I get you out."

They all gave me different estimates, but they all agreed that, although it would cost a lot of money, *I could in fact get out.*

That was a major relief to me—just what I had wanted to hear.

The lawyers had all agreed independently that one thing was more important than anything else: that I pay them the money *in cash immediately*, before it was *too late*. And each lawyer, upon seeing another lawyer approach me to introduce himself and offer his counsel, would whisper to me that that particular lawyer just happened to be the very worst, cheating, robbing, swindling, no-good, scummy, incompetent, *ratero* lawyer that ever existed. Every last Mexican lawyer I ever met said that about every other Mexican lawyer I would ever meet. To hear any of them tell it, it just so happened that *every other* Mexican lawyer in the country was a total thief unfit to practice law in a dog pound; but that *he himself* was the only lawyer who could save me from fifteen years in prison and maybe death—for a large fee of course. Even Mexican lawyers working in teams told me that their partners were no good—and their partners told me the *same thing!*

At first I did not know whom to believe. But later I would discover that on this one and only point—the general integrity of the Mexican lawyers—the lawyers were all telling the truth.

5 Initiation

Lecumberri prison—officially *la Carcel Preventiva del Districto Federal*—is about four miles to the east of the center of Mexico City, in the midst of one of the city's worst slums. It is known throughout Mexico as *el Palacio Negro*—the Black Palace. Run by the Mexican military police, the prison was built in 1900 to accommodate 800 male prisoners, although in 1973 it held 4,000 male inmates, all awaiting trial. The only person ever to have escaped from Lecumberri was the legendary Pancho Villa.

The entire complex covers an area of about thirty square blocks. The front appears to be an ordinary turn-of-the-century building, except that guard towers rear up above and behind it. The other three sides are nothing but thick, high, monolithic walls regularly punctuated by numerous machine gun turrets.

The federal and state courts are attached to Lecumberri. It is here, in prison, that the prisoner receives his "trial." If he is found guilty, he stays in prison. And if innocent, he will sometimes be released. In the meantime, until his guilt or innocence is established, *the prisoner will remain in Lecumberri until his trial is over.* Bail, as it is known in the U.S., simply does not exist in Mexico, except for the most trivial of offenses. In Mexico, a man remains in prison until his innocence is proven, or until he has done his time.

I knew none of this about Lecumberri, or about Mexican prisons, when I was sent to dormitory "O" in Lecumberri. I was just a totally freaked-out new prisoner. I was more scared than I had ever been in my life. All I knew was that I wanted out *now*— and that I had absolutely no control over what was happening to me.

On the early evening of December 18, 1973, after a week in the hellhole "H," I was told by the guards that "O" was my new permanent dorm. The other Mexican prisoners told me I was lucky: in "O" the cells had beds and desks, chairs, and even hot showers. Some of these Mexican prisoners had never seen a hot shower. *Campesinos.*

· I was led through a maze of passageways, gates, and corridors that branched and wound from each other at odd angles, never allowing me a moment to get my bearings. The guards stopped at an isolated area that had double walls around it and unlocked both of the double doors. Later I would learn that "O" and "M" were maximum security, the most maximum security prison areas in all of Mexico.

As soon as I arrived, they led me off to the *"mayor's* assistant."

The *mayor's* assistant? What was this?

A gangly, wrinkle-faced man in his late thirties shook my hand and introduced himself as James Dean Brown.

An American!—the first one I had met since I'd been in Lecumberri. Now maybe I could find out what was going on here—and how I could get out.

Brown first made it very clear to me that he himself would be leaving shortly. He had been arrested with a half-gram of cocaine that the Mexican police had planted in one of his Rolls Royces. He was thoroughly innocent and was here only by mistake. He was so confident about it that I believed him without a doubt.

But I was not going anyplace, Brown said with equal finality. I would be staying here in prison for at least *seven more years*. Guilt, innocence, or bribes would change nothing in my case. I was stuck and that was final.

That hit hard. I refused to believe it.

But I could live decently in prison, Brown said, with a semi-private cell, good food, prostitutes (or young houseboys—Brown laughed through his premature wrinkles). There was only one catch: money, and lots of it.

I wasn't interested in whores or good food. I wasn't worrying about my finances either. I just wanted out.

Brown shook his head. He said that I'd better start thinking about money fast, because I would be needing it immediately for the *mayor*, Fernando Gardner-Pasqual. Brown explained that Gardner-Pasqual was a prisoner too, although you'd never know it. He had been here for five years for murdering his best friend. He was a Mexican national who had grown up in Los Angeles and consequently spoke English fluently. As *mayor* of "O," his word was law.

I wasn't interested in Gardner-Pasqual. I wanted to talk about *getting out* of here. What should I do? Who could be paid? Was escape possible? But Brown wanted to talk about one thing: money. He said that I would need it for everything. For soap, toilet paper, baths, bed, food, electricity, water, a cell, *fajinas*, rent—

"RENT?"

"Yes, rent," James Dean Brown nodded his head. "If you want to exist here, you've got to pay Gardner-Pasqual the money. He's got twenty *commandos* here who'll do anything he tells them. He even orders the guards around. And I'll tell you another thing." He breathed out a cloud of smoke through his nicotine-stained teeth. "If you don't pay it, *they don't evict you*."

Then Brown began interrogating me: What did my father do?

How much did he earn? How much did I have in the bank? Where had I worked and for how long? It was the kind of information a credit company would ask.

I stumbled around, but I answered. I have never been a good, spontaneous, stand-up liar who could keep his story straight and credible—probably because I had not been in enough situations where that was an asset. I would soon be learning the price of naïve honesty.

With no warning, a stocky, bald man in his thirties charged into the room. He came straight up to me, grabbed me by the collar, and shook me.

"I am the boss here, understand! Anything I say, you obey. Got that?" He shook my head violently. He had been listening from the outside.

I was too stunned to answer.

As abruptly as the *mayor*, Gardner-Pasqual, had charged in, he quickly waved for James Dean Brown to step outside with him. I heard the two of them talking, although I could not make out what they were saying. They both came in a moment later.

"Worker, your price is $2,000 for *fajinas* and cell. If you don't pay it, you work six months or a year, eighteen hours a day, and I bust your ass hard. But with $2,000 I set you up good. I get you women, anything. Everything."

Gardner-Pasqual abruptly waved two other American prisoners into his cell. One of them was Roger. The other one was introduced as "Cowboy." Gardner asked them in front of me if they were going to pay him the two grand. They looked at him, then at me, and nodded mutely. Like a robot, Gardner turned to me.

"See your buddies. They pay. You pay me too."

It was as if he had just proven that I, too, was going to pay. It made perfect sense to him.

Gardner then shook Roger. "Now you tell Worker what else I'm going to do for you."

Roger started to mutter something, but Gardner cut him off.

"Never mind. I tell him." Gardner-Pasqual turned to me with his face far too close to mine, speaking full-speed-full-blast. A raving maniac.

"Worker, my brother-in-law Luis is a lawyer. He has a good friend in the third court. He can get you and these two *gringos* all out of here *libre*—free—for three grand apiece. So you going to pay me five grand—two grand for your cell and three grand for your freedom. That's cheap for freedom, man. You just gotta hurry with the money, then you be free."

I didn't say anything to Gardner. Although he was pathetic as a con man, I could see he was dangerously insane.

Gardner walked out of the cell to talk to James Dean Brown again. I grabbed Roger's elbow and whispered, "Hey, you're not going to give him the money, are you?"

Roger gave me a wavering look. He didn't know for sure.

"Well, don't give it to him. *Don't*. It's just a dirty ripoff."

Roger evaded me. I told him again that I wasn't giving it to Gardner. No way.

Roger kept looking out the door to see if Gardner was listening. He wasn't, but Roger was still scared shitless. So was I, but I wasn't going to promise Gardner anything.

Gardner walked back into his cell in a hurry.

"You see, Worker, for every American that Colonel Cardenas lets me have in this dorm, I got to pay him $1,000, if I get any money or not. Cardenas runs this place. He's the boss. We got to obey him. So I run a risk getting you. I got to get this money from you, because you costing me money. You got to pay me."

He paused, his body twitching, lips moving but no sounds coming out. His bald dome glistened with sweat and his eyes were big and wet. His face was again too close to mine.

"When you going to pay me the $2,000?" He zeroed in.

"I don't have it."

"Yes, you do."

"You can get it from your parents," James Dean Brown cut in.

"I need my money for a lawyer."

"YOU PAY ME!"

"But how can I pay now?"

"Just promise you pay me now and I let you off."

I didn't promise him.

He yelled down the hall and a number of *commandos* came running up. Gardner barked some commands to them and then told me I was going to see what I thought of *fajinas*.

The *commandos* grabbed me roughly and ran me down the halls to the bottom of the dorm. There they immediately put me to work in the duckwalk position washing all the floors. A runty nineteen-year-old, semitoothless punk with a club ran me up and down the hallway shouting commands as I worked. No matter how fast I moved, he shouted, pushed, stepped on my fingers, and hit me with the club. I started to swing at the guy, but another American saw me and warned me to cool it, or they might fuck me over bad. Somehow I didn't think they'd do that to a foreigner, even though I was a prisoner. But I got back to work washing, wiping, and drying the same hall over and over again.

What was worse than the actual exhaustion of the work was the fact that once I finished the hall, I had to do it again and again and again. There was no end to it, none at all. It was not work that needed to be done. Its sole purpose was to exhaust and break me. They were going to run me like this until I collapsed.

Finally, three hours later, at 10:00 p.m., it was time to quit. Prison sleeping hours. I was drenched with sweat, exhausted to the bone. My hands, feet, and legs were aching, as were the welts across my back.

I was run to the *cuartel,* where I had to sleep with twenty others on the dirty, cold, eight-by-six-foot cement floor without a blanket or mattress. Even though the place was teeming with lice and bedbugs, I fell asleep the moment I hit the floor.

The next thing I knew, they were waking me up. It was pitch dark. They ran me along the outside of the building, but still within the double-walled perimeter. It was cold. I had to carry all the garbage from a pile to the garbage wagon. This meant that I had to plunge my hands elbow-deep into rotten, fetid slop and load it up on the wagon, while *commandos* ran me with a club. Then I had to wash the whole floor down and wipe and dry it until there was no trace of garbage. It took hours. I got no more sleep.

All that day I cleaned and recleaned and re-recleaned the floors. As I went up and down the halls cleaning, I saw lots of other American prisoners. They had apparently made their deal with Gardner, because they did not have to work. But the moment I began to talk to any of them, the *commandos* separated me from them and told the Americans to shut up. If they talked to me anymore, the *commandos* would tell Gardner. Whatever that implied was enough so that all my countrymen could give me when I asked them what was happening, what I should do, was a stony silence. They were afraid to talk to me, another American.

For breakfast that day I was given a bowl of half-cooked beans and some watery coffee, then it was back to work. Except for a brief dinner break of beans, coffee, and bread, I washed floors and did cleanup work until 10:00 p.m.

I lay thinking on the cement floor of the *cuartel* that night, packed against the others. Maybe I could physically take the bullshit makework if I had to. But I could not take the punk *commandos* screaming at me and hitting me all the time.

To have to do the *fajinas* right now, on top of my arrest and everything else—to be told that I would be working eighteen hours a day *every day* for six months—was too much to take all at once. I needed to sit down and rest, to talk with the other Americans here and find out what was happening with the courts and lawyers, to learn how to survive in prison, to figure out just what I had to do to get out of here.

I could not take it. I would have to get out of *fajinas,* and I was not planning to pay Gardner $2,000.

At 4:30 the next morning they sent me to the kitchen to work. As soon as I got there a crazy-looking, 40-year-old Mexican cook and his 5-foot-2-inch, 400-pound, obscenely ugly assistant came at me, one of them waving a knife. They were straight out of a Fellini movie. Before I knew it, the two of them and another cook were beating me, shouting at the top of their lungs that I had to give Gardner the money. While I was getting hit I glanced over to the one other American with me in *fajinas* and he motioned to me not to fight back.

I wanted to. They had no right to be treating me like this, even if I was a prisoner. They had to respect the rights of foreigners here or it could become an international incident. *I was an American,* and I didn't care what that other American was trying to tell me about not fighting back; no one could take this kind of treatment. Surely they weren't going to beat me up too badly or kill me. They were just pushing me as far as they could go to get the money out of me. If they went too far, they could get in trouble—couldn't they?

I glared back at the scummy cooks. I wanted to hit them—but I didn't. In a minute I was back to the eighteen-hour-a-day cleanup.

Later that day, I was taken into the control bunker at the entrance of "O." In it were bunk beds, a small kitchen, and an antiquated telephone terminal that connected the bunker to the rest of the prison. Several guards were sleeping; a few were eating; the remainder were intently reading comic books.

I had to clean up the whole bunker. That meant carrying the garbage, washing the floors, and cleaning out the filthy bathroom. While a *commando* shouted orders and hurried me through the bunker, I noticed two stairways and a tunnel leading from the bunker. This was obviously the central access point to all the walls, machine gun turrets, checkpoints, and the gate.

And then I was overwhelmed at what I saw. Propped against the corner no more than fifteen feet away from me were four *machine guns*. I was the man nearest to them. If I made a dash I would surely be the first to reach them. Maybe they were empty, and even if they weren't, what would I do after I had them? But *four machine guns*—all within reach! I couldn't believe the guards could be so lax. This would never happen in a U.S. prison, would it? The guards seemed to be inviting an attempt.

While I finished the floors, I continued to stare at the machine guns. The guards, who were busy with their dominoes and comic books, paid only cursory attention to the *gringo* slave scurrying over the floor. I got to within five feet of the machine guns when the guards called me out of the cell.

I was moved to the galley and forced to work like a dog. All that afternoon, while making me work in the midst of food, they refused to let me eat. I had to grab what I could off of the returning food trays and eat furtively when no one was looking—like some wretched street urchin going through the garbage. If they caught me chewing they would punch me hard, telling me no food until I paid Gardner.

I was on my knees again, working as hard as I could, feeling hungry and weak. Finally, in the late afternoon, I got up and told them I would have to eat. The *commando* in charge swung a broomstick at me and broke it over my back. I jumped up to punch him while a bunch of beaners rushed to join in. I was raging at them. I spun away and walked straight to Gardner's room, followed by several Mexicans.

Gardner was busy talking to a few of his cronies when I started shouting at him. He was surprised. I told him he would have to call off his goons. I was tired of this shit, and he was going to have to change it.

Some people gathered around the door outside. Gardner looked even more stunned. Then he hit me. He hit me again. I hit him.

Some Spanish was yelled and some people rushed and grabbed me. Gardner yelled something to them and five of them dragged me down the hallway into the kitchen. There they threw me into the large walk-in freezer, and about five Mexicans, including Gardner, charged in and slammed the door shut. Before I got a chance to do anything, they had me down on the floor and were kicking and stomping on me. I was screaming, rolling over, and getting knocked around while trying to protect myself. I was also shitting and pissing in my pants.

In a minute they stopped and dragged me out of the cooler and threw me on the floor. I got up, trembling—bruised and hurting, but not damaged. My blue prison-issue pants were torn and wet with piss and I felt shit sliding down my leg.

Gardner was screaming at me insanely, a madman telling me he would have me KILLED KILLED KILLED—DON'T FUCK WITH ME—I WANT THE MONEY OR I'LL GET YOU—YOU'LL PAY OR I'LL KILL YOU—he was worked up into a sweat, a sick little punk protected by his twenty punk *commandos*—I wanted to kill him, to kill all of them right then . . . .

Gardner ordered the *commandos* to take me to the *cuartel*, and in an instant they had me running down the hallway. When I got there the second-in-command in the dorm shoved me into the *cuartel* and hit me. I hit him and hit him again, and then I kicked him in the nuts. I was starting to get him good. I had nothing more to lose and if I was going to get beaten up anyway, I might as well fight back, so I was swinging and kicking and getting at him and it looked like a fair one-on-one fight. It felt good hitting one of them. But then a mob of Mexicans came through the door, with Gardner among them, and I was on the ground. They were jumping on me and kicking me and hitting me with clubs and I was moving and kicking and trying to squirm my way under a concrete bench, but they grabbed my feet and pulled me out and there were deep, dull, hard thuds jolting throughout my body and more crap was coming out of me and I could feel things tearing in me and I was trying to roll up into a ball to protect my face and guts when something came down hard on my head.

Vaguely, I recall being held under a shower until I came to. I couldn't walk. Something in my back and hip. They thought I was faking until I fell on the floor in front of them.

Much later I was washed off and dressed. Gardner was there. He was telling me that if anyone asked me anything, I was to say *"Yo me caye"* (I fell) and nothing more. Then they lifted me onto a stretcher.

The middle section of the canvas beneath me was almost rigid.

I lifted my head to look at it. Virtually the whole stretcher was stained with dry blood. Below my neck and stomach it was so thick that scabs of old, coagulated blood crinkled off of the canvas, telling the story of dying prisoners being carried off to the hospital. I laid my head back and faded out as they began carrying me to the hospital.

The last thing Gardner said to me was that when I came back, I would pay him the money.

A vice consul in charge of prisoner affairs at the U.S. embassy in Mexico City stated early in 1974 that the purpose of arranging for American prisoners to be transferred to maximum security dormitory "O" was to protect them from the extortion and beatings.

When asked by the parents of a U.S. prisoner about the extortion in Mexican prisons, he replied that all new prisoners, Mexican and American alike, went through a "hazing period. This period was to be likened to hell week in a fraternity, nothing more than an initiation."

6 Hospital

Four prisoners carried my stretcher by a circuitous route to the hospital. In the darkest passageway they abruptly dropped me on the ground. Some hands quickly went through my pockets while others worked on my feet. My hands and wrists were also checked. In a minute my pockets were empty and the shoes that I had just acquired that day were gone. Then the prisoners proceeded to carry me onward. It was December 21, the winter solstice. Christmas was coming.

At the hospital the doctors examined me. I was in a daze. I couldn't move my lower back and when I tried standing up, my legs fell out from under me. Sharp stabbing pains in my side. They checked my eyes and head. I heard them say *contusion*.

The doctors would not be able to X-ray me until tomorrow morning, so they gave me some pain pills and carried me off to the intensive-care section. The moment they laid me on that bed—the first bed I had been on in two weeks—I was asleep. They would be checking my blood pressure, temperature, and pulse every four hours. Being able to sleep comfortably without being harassed felt almost like being free.

Much later that night the lights were turned on. There was a commotion around the bed next to mine. I turned my head and watched as the orderlies laid a prisoner-patient on the bed while two doctors stood above him. The patient was gasping at irregular intervals. When the orderlies stepped aside I saw that the shirt covering the patient's torso was sticking to him like a wet second skin, completely soaked through with fresh blood. The doctors pulled the shirt from him and looked at what was spilling out of his stomach. Blood ran from his side onto the bedsheets. He gasped convulsively and his midsection lifted up involuntarily, almost as if it were a separate entity presenting itself to the doctors for closer observation. And then he lay still, except for an occasional distant gasp.

The doctors examined the wounds closely, and then looked at each other as if to compare their conclusions. Neither of them did anything. Some more people walked in and out, and shortly afterwards, the doctors were gone and the lights were off.

I woke up late next morning. They had let me sleep. I looked over to the bed next to me. It was made with clean, fresh covers and there was no one in it. There was not a trace of blood.

Torn ligaments in the back, dislocated hip, brain contusion, and various welts and bruises, but nothing broken. I would be all right, although I could not walk. I asked the doctor if I could have crutches. He did not have any, but maybe the orderlies did. An orderly brought me a pair of new crutches. I adjusted them to their full length and tried them. I could hobble around. I thanked the orderly for them, but he continued standing there, looking alternately at me and then the crutches.

They would cost 500 pesos.

I told him I would pay him when I got my money.

No credit.

I asked him if I could borrow them until I could walk—but no, they had had a problem with stolen crutches.

He took the crutches away.

I thought about that crutch I had used in my disguise as the injured mountain climber. Maybe I could get that crutch. I really needed it now. But that crutch was in the court with all my other belongings and there was no way I could get it from them since they were going to use it as evidence *against* me. It seemed ironic to me that two weeks ago I had been using a crutch for the first time in my life for a fake leg injury; but now when I needed that crutch for a real leg injury, I could not have it. I wondered what the relationship was between the two—my contrived illusion becoming a grim reality.

Somewhat later that morning an old Mexican man who was in my room limped up to my bedside on his crutches, laying them on the foot of my bed. He told me I could use his crutches whenever I needed them. His offer surprised me. A glance at the crutches told me that he had laboriously constructed them himself from scraps of wood. Although they were too short for me, they would still serve to get me to the toilet, shower, or mess hall. I put my hand on his and squeezed it. This old man, who had been in prison for five years, with five more to go, who had not had a visit in years, who did not know me at all and possessed absolutely nothing except his sentence, his disability, and his crutches—this old man was willing to risk getting his crutches stolen by loaning them to me.

I did not have the words in me to know how to thank him.

He hopped on one leg over to his bed as I hobbled on his crutches to the bathroom.

I had several visitors while in the hospital. All of them were lawyers who opportunely visited me on different days. Every last one of them told me he was going to get me out of prison—for a lot of money, of course. And when they saw that I was laid up on my back in the hospital, these lawyers went a step further—they were going to arrange for my "protection" while I temporarily remained in prison, for just two or three thousand dollars more.

I borrowed money, stamps, and envelopes from all of them, telling each one individually that he personally would be my lawyer. I collected 600 pesos, which I planned to put to good use. I was learning their game.

It was a week before I began walking, and just barely, with a lame, one-foot-at-a-time shuffle. I limped up to the patio on the second floor of the hospital. From here I had the best view of Lecumberri that a prisoner could get: tall, massive walls, continuous pillboxes and machine-gun turrets, and countless power lines haphazardly strung amid barbed wire and screen to impede any attempts to scale the walls.

I remembered reading about Joel David Kaplan's helicopter escape from Santa Marta prison. Kaplan had tried to break out of Lecumberri for five years before he had been transferred to Santa Marta. There he spent five more years attempting to escape before he finally pulled off his helicopter breakout. The helicopter had been painted identically to that of the Mexican attorney general. The prison guards, seeing the helicopter land *inside* Santa Marta, did not know whether to "shoot or salute." Thus Kaplan escaped, after ten years of frustration and millions of dollars spent on futile attempts.

The guards now had orders to shoot any helicopters hovering near any prison. It would not work again. But, I thought, looking down into the courtyard through a tangle of power lines, maybe an airplane would: a slow-flying airplane pulling a dragline that would hook onto a catch line. I could wear a special harness that would be attached to that catch line. The plane would snag the line and literally lift me out of the prison. I had seen films of such an operation—the U.S. Army had used it for evacuation in Vietnam when no landing strips were available. It could be done here too.

There were innumerable high power lines to get tangled in, steep walls to get smashed against, machine-gun turrets to fly by, and buildings to crash into. I would have to work on smuggling a military-issue harness into Lecumberri. I would have to figure out how to set up the line for the hook to catch onto, and what to do to insure that the plane connected on the first pass. There would be no second chance.

But what plane? What pilot? Who would ever be insane enough to try it? Where could I ever get enough money to finance such an outrageous plan? I didn't bother with the mundane logistics. Somehow, some way, and soon, a great white bird would be sweeping out of the sky to carry me away.

I wrote a long, detailed letter to my brother explaining what he had to do to help me arrange my escape.

In the hospital I met a prisoner named Genaro whose nose was all bandaged up. With a stammering tongue and through dull, listless eyes, Genaro explained that he had sniffed too many drugs in his dorm. His nose had bled profusely and then scarred up so badly that he could not breathe through it. After months of waiting, the doctors had finally performed adequate surgery. Now Genaro was breathing properly again and would soon return to dorm "G."

Genaro said he had learned his lesson. He would no longer be sniffing or using drugs. No. Now he would just buy drugs cheap and sell them high. That old business axiom. He was very much in debt in "G" for having used so many drugs on credit, so he would have to pay off his debts. Then he would get rich—a familiar story. I didn't have anything to say, so our conversation faded off into oblivion, as do most mismatched communications. Genaro excused himself, explaining that he would have to pack his things to return to "G."

The next afternoon, as I was hobbling around in the open patio of the hospital, I saw the orderlies hurriedly carry a stretcher into the emergency room. I did not pay it much attention at first, having by now seen enough stretchers come and go.

A little later another patient told me that they had just carried Genaro back to the hospital from "G." He had been hurt. I hobbled through the restricted area to the emergency room and looked around the door. The doctor was washing his hands in the sink. It was the same doctor who had rebuilt Genaro's nose. When he saw me, he told me to hurry back to my bed. I asked him about Genaro.

"Genaro es muerte," he said in a simple, matter-of-fact voice. "They killed him. Now go back to bed."

To one side of the room I could see the legs of someone covered with sheets. I did not look any further. I believed him.

Over the next week two more dead prisoners were brought to the hospital. The second body was officially declared to have been a suicide by hanging. But later that day I heard the doctor confiding to one of the patients that the body also had numerous mortal stab wounds. I was the only one in the ward who was surprised at that information.

They weren't playing games here. The stakes were as high as they got. Everything was up for grabs. I hobbled back to my bed to lie down and think about my situation. Except for a limp and some soreness, I was getting along decently now, and I would soon be sent back to "O." As I eased myself onto the bed, I heard and felt something dully crinkling below me. I felt the blanket. Something was below it. I reached beneath the blanket and pulled out a large piece of thick, roughly torn paper. Printed on it in a large, primitive scrawl was, "WORKER YOUR GOING TO PAY ME *NOW*."

A chill went across my chest to my stomach. I felt nauseous. How had Gardner gotten into the hospital? I hadn't seen him. He wasn't supposed to be here. No, he had sent someone else to plant the note. Who? I looked around. Any of the Mexicans here might have done it. I was learning that I could never, never trust any of them. Behind whatever they said, or did, I was not one of them, and Gardner-Pasqual was. There was no changing that dividing line.

I was more than afraid. What would I do next? Then I had what I thought was a good idea. I wrote a letter to the U.S. Embassy detailing what had happened to me in prison, including Gardner's threat on my life. I asked for their protection in any way possible, because shortly I would be sent back to "O" and into Gardner's hands once again.

I had just found a visitor who was willing to smuggle out the letter and mail it when two guards came up to me and told me to get my things together. *I was going back to "O."*

Fourteen months later, in March 1975, Ms. Katherine Mullins, vice consul at the U.S. Embassy, called me to the central prison office for a personal interview. At the end of the interview she mentioned that the embassy had received a letter from me in January 1974, asking them for their "protection."

Speaking pure officialese, she asked, "And what kind of help were you referring to?"

7 Ripped Off!

I was sent back to dormitory "O" on December 31, 1973. New Year's Eve had lost all its significance to me, just as Christmas had meant nothing, since I had been immobilized on my back.

Fernando Gardner-Pasqual ordered me into his cell. His forehead and bald dome were covered with sweat.

"*I want the money,*" shouting. "But I tell you what. I make you a deal," pointing at me. "You pay just $1,500 for *fajinas* and cell." Gardner was even more worked up than usual.

"I don't have it."

"You'll get it. Already I pay Colonel Cardenas $1,000 for you, so I got to get the money back."

I stood silent in front of Gardner-Pasqual. I knew he couldn't throw me into *fajinas* right now because of my injuries. But as soon as I had healed up sufficiently, he would get me. Gardner waited impatiently, then sent me off to a cell to live with three other Americans, warning me that I would have to pay him soon.

For the first time since I had been in Lecumberri, I was permitted to wander around and talk to the forty other Americans in dorm "O." The Americans I met did not fit my stereotype of prisoners, but then, I didn't fit my stereotype either. Most of them were in their early twenties and looked more like college students than prisoners. They played guitars and poker, read books, fixed up their cell "rooms," played such sports as handball and soccer, and smoked pot when they could get it. Some of them were taking courses by mail, while others did craft work and made trinkets. Many of them seemed to sleep a lot. They talked often of the United States and of what they would be doing back in their home town, or at school, or at work. In some strange ways, this place did not seem too different from a college dormitory or fraternity.

I walked into a cell and saw Roger, the American who had been arrested at about the same time as I had. What had *he* finally done with Gardner?

Roger shook his head listlessly, explaining that he had given Gardner the five grand: two for his cell and three for the lawyer. I asked Roger why he had done it. He shrugged his shoulders and evaded the question. He didn't appear angry.

"What's wrong with you, Roger? Why did you give him the money?"

". . . Well, look at what happened to you."

Roger wanted to avoid violence—with $5,000 as an installment. He said he figured Gardner would eventually get his—karmically, of course.

I couldn't believe Roger could be so philosophical, so emotionally lobotomized, so *ball-less* about getting so cheaply conned for so much money. Here was a peace-and-love hippy who was the perfect prey for some two-bit punk extortionist like Gardner. Put him in a cage with someone like that and it was no contest. Roger just did not have the psychological self-defense necessary to survive against a predator like that. He was too spaced-out to function at the physical, violent level of this prison; and unless he changed himself drastically, he would pay heavily.

I looked Roger in the eyes. I wanted to shake his shoulders and tell him he was fucked up. I wanted him to see things as I did—but then I saw it in his eyes. Roger was stoned out of his head, just like he had probably been every other day here, including the day he had given Gardner the five grand.

I was more enraged than Roger that Gardner had ripped him off. I walked out of Roger's cell, loathing his feeble passivity as much as Gardner's ruthless extortion.

The other Americans said that Gardner always had Americans beaten up for money, although I was one of the first to go to the hospital. I asked what Gardner had done to them. He had beaten them, worked them, and broken them until almost all of them had paid the money.

How much? It ranged from $500 to $5,000—whatever Gardner-Pasqual could get from them. He would take whatever he could. There was no ceiling.

The American prisoners told me that Gardner, along with ten other *mayors* of the different dormitories, had a complete monopoly on all the dorm and prison business. They could do anything they wanted to for money. The *mayors* did all this with the permission and under the direction of Colonel Edilberto Gil-Cardenas, the military man who ran the prison with an iron hand. The *mayors* had to first buy their positions for thousands of dollars, and then pay high rent to maintain them. Colonel Cardenas had to pay off Those Above in PRI *(Partido Revolu-cionario Institucional)*, the one ruling party of Mexico, to keep his position and get rich. To run Lecumberri was considered a political plum, with all the potential income from extortion, heroin dealing, and the free labor of 4,000 slaves. The Colonel had the *mayors* and *commandos*—all prisoners—do most of the dirty work. That way Cardenas and his guards could avoid blame.

The *mayors* of Lecumberri didn't live like prisoners at all. Many of them lived far better in prison than they ever could on the street. Some of them *avoided* leaving prison so that they could stay and continue their high prison incomes. They had three- and four-room cells, many servants, women visiting them at all hours, good clothes, televisions and stereos, free movement within the prison, and virtually unlimited power within their dormitories—their private fiefdoms in which they ruled as absolute monarchs. The *mayors* would never defy or expose Colonel Cardenas. On the take themselves, their lives were on the line. Cardenas could have them killed. He had done it before. The prime difference between the *mayors* and the prison guards was simply that the *mayors* didn't go home at night—but they made far more money.

Fajinas payment usually ran from $150 to $600 for a Mexican. But for an American in a Mexican prison, the payment ranged from $1,000 to $10,000 depending on your "assessed value." One only needed to watch the *mayors* of the various dormitories arguing and fighting over whose dorm was going to receive the new American prisoner to realize how much Americans were prized as captives—as hostages. Americans in Mexican prisons were big business.

And paying *fajinas* did not mean that I would receive the "luxuries" that Gardner and James Dean Brown had. If I got into trouble, I would be sent back to *fajinas* and have to start all over, which was a prison euphemism for "pay again." It happened all the time to the Americans.

I heard the American prisoners using a word I had never heard before, *re-extortion:* what you have to pay the second and subsequent times you are extorted from. They used this word without a trace of irony. They had learned by hard experience that just as the prison system had the right to extort money from the prisoner, so did it have the right to *re-*extort. The only point worth learning about re-extortion was how to avoid it. But no one questioned its existence.

Then I began to hear the first of *the rumors:* all of the American prisoners thought we would all be going back to the U.S. soon. Some said we would be deported, while others favored extradition, but whatever the *modus operandi,* the end result was always the same: soon we would all be free. Americans constantly exchanged rumors concerning the "hows" and "whens" of our release. No one questioned the "ifs." I did not meet one American who believed he would be staying in prison for very long. He was leaving because of a prisoner exchange, parole, Amnesty International, deportation, new lenient drug laws in Mexico, extradition, bribery, U.S. congressional pressure, a proposed tourist boycott, or violations of rights in his case—*anything*—but he was going home.

But in the meantime, some of the Americans advised me to make a deal with Gardner-Pasqual—maybe for less money—just to get him off my back. If I didn't, Gardner would be after me as soon as I had recuperated until he had gotten the money. So far no one had managed to avoid paying. I understood their logic, but I didn't want to give Gardner-Pasqual the pleasure of getting my money, not after what that bastard had done to me. I was certain that there had to be a way out. After questioning a few American prisoners with no results, I remembered my letter to the U.S. Embassy. I announced that the embassy would be bringing help soon.

That brought a laugh from Hank, a tall American from the South who had been awaiting trial for eighteen months for ten grams of coke. He explained that the U.S. embassy had had all the Americans moved to dorm "O" for our "protection." Pointing at me, Hank said "And you must have shot your mouth off an awful lot to James Dean Brown, because he figured you were worth five G."

"WHAT? You mean that Brown was working with Gardner-Pasqual to get my money?"

"Yes, asshole. What do you think—that everyone here is nice hippies? Do you know why Brown will be going free soon? Because he made the woman who was carrying all his coke at the airport take the blame—even though she was just his burro. And get this: she thinks she and James Dean will be getting married soon, although James Dean now denies that he ever even *knew* her. He's going to leave his fiancée in prison for seven years to save his ass." Hank paused for a moment. And then, still pointing his intimidating finger at me, he added, "There's scum all over the world, especially in prison."

An American working for a Mexican to help extort from other Americans? For some reason I thought of American POWs during World War II who had cooperated with the Japanese.

Why, he ought to be—KILLED! Every American in the dormitory repeated the same thing: Gardner-Pasqual and James Dean Brown ought to be killed. It was the first consensus among the Americans.

Suddenly this did not seem like a college dormitory anym

"Well, who's going to kill him, then?"

"NO ONE!" Hank shouted. "I been here a year and a half an
I've heard talk about killing him *every day*. And the more you talk
about it, the less chance you'll do it. What you're gonna do is lie
down and take it up the ass like you been takin' it. A murderer
doesn't talk about killin' someone. He just kills him. It's the quiet
one that'll get you every time."

Everyone sat there silently for once. If anyone had wanted to
kill Gardner-Pasqual, they could easily get a knife, walk down to
his cell, and *kill him*. It wouldn't be difficult. But no one moved.

I watched the new Americans coming to dorm "O." They all
arrived as I had, knowing nothing and forbidden to talk to any
other American. Gardner beat them up until they came across
with the money.

All the chips were on Gardner's side. He had the law and the
Mexican military backing him, and he was a master at extortion.
He had the experience of having extorted money from hundreds
of prisoners, whereas none of the new Americans had ever been
extorted from, and so lacked the "street wisdom" or whatever
would have helped them resist. How could they stand a chance
against such odds?

Not many of them did. I watched Gardner extort another
$100,000 from the new Americans arriving at "O." I saw
nonviolent skiers, ex-college students—ex-*everythings*—sit around
in cells after only one month in prison and matter-of-factly agree
that Gardner *must be killed*—if not now, then later, when they were
free. Such were the transformations of prison: there we were,
sitting around coolly talking of first-degree murder. What
sounded sick from the outside could make perfect sense on the
inside.

I was jolted from my cell one afternoon by six *commandos* who
came in and yanked away my blankets and few other pitiful
possessions. One of them snarled that Gardner-Pasqual had
ordered them to confiscate everything I had except the clothes on
my back until I paid him the $1,500. And if I didn't come up with
the money within a week, bellowed Gardner's chief goon *commando*, beating his fist into his open palm, it was back to the
fajinas.

"O l'hospital otra vez," another *commando* shouted, punching me hard on the shoulder. They laughed as they carried away my few belongings. *"Regressaremos!"* (We'll be back) they shouted.

Gardner was closing in.

Now, out of both hatred and self-defense, I wanted to kill Gardner-Pasqual like never before. Along with the other Americans, I complained, raged, threatened (privately), and finally vowed to get him. But although Hank wasn't very popular, he knew the score. None of us killed Gardner, or even tried to. We were extorted and re-extorted, and put up with it as best we could.

What kind of commentary was this on young, stoned America? Were we that deeply nonviolent—or just stoned, passive vegetables who would take anything rather than resist?

One, at least, was not. Rob, a Vietnam veteran, came up to me after I had returned from the hospital and slapped me on the back. At least I had fought back before I went down. He respected that. Rob began talking to me confidentially. He had no illusions about getting released early. He said no one was leaving unless they did it themselves. I nodded, mentioning that when I had cleaned up the bunker house while on *fajinas*, I was amazed to have seen several machine guns leaning against the wall, unguarded.

"You mean those Browning 9mms!" Rob's face lit up. "I couldn't believe it either when I saw them. I almost grabbed one right then."

Rob took my elbow and led me off to a cell. He introduced me to two of his buddies, also Vietnam vets. After I had promised absolute secrecy, he cautiously told me their plan.

The plan was simple. Get a few pistols smuggled into the prison. At the right moment, charge into the bunker and get the draw on the guards. If any of them resist, *shoot them dead.* Strip the other guards, tie them up, put on their uniforms, add false moustaches, black hair spray, and other appropriate disguises.

The other Vietnam vets liked the plan. They had already written letters to former Nam buddies in the States who could arrange the smuggling of weapons and the other escape logistics. They wanted to know if I was in on it.

I didn't commit myself. I wanted to check it out in detail first. I had to know what the odds were, what unforeseen circumstances might arise, and what contingency plans could be made. I told them that I would need some more time to decide, but not to count me out.

A week passed and I still hadn't committed myself to the bunkerhouse raid. I was being pressured into it without enough time and thought. I told Rob that I thought it was too dangerous. A stone wall of silence descended around them. Whispered conversations ended in icy silence the moment I entered the room. I was intruding. You were either in on it, or you weren't.

The first of the Vietnam veteran visitors from the U.S. arrived. They were casing the place out. Were they bringing the weapons in? Were their guns *already* in? Would it be happening any day? Or would it take more time and precision planning? Was it too late now to join them? Would I regret it later, one way or the other? I had visions of dead guards and prisoners, of forty years more in sentences, of spending my entire life in a Mexican prison—of dying here.

Was I ready to use guns to get out of here? No. There must be another way out. But what if there wasn't? I had no intention of staying here for seven to fifteen years. If it looked as if they had a good chance to get out, did I want to go with them?

I plied Rob with more questions.

Deep, dark, offended eyes. Stonewall silence. Don't mention it again.

The visits from their Nam buddies abruptly stopped. It must be getting close.

But time was going by and my leg and back had recuperated enough so that Gardner would throw me back into the *fajinas* any day. That would mean ninety hours of work a week, no rest, more fights, and who knew what else. So against every principle I had ever felt, I decided to make a deal with Gardner-Pasqual. I would give him a minimum of money to get him off my back. I despised myself for selling out to the man I most hated on this earth, but I rationalized that it was expedient to buy him off. Gardner called me to his cell and we verbally agreed on $500 total. That was $500 more than I wanted to give him, but I was learning to deal with the system. I hated myself for compromising with him. I was no better than the others.

I got permission to make a phone call to arrange to have the money sent to me. My parents had sent the money to a mutual friend, Susan Corley. Susan had originally planned to visit me and bring the money personally, but for various reasons she would not come. I would call Susan and have her send me $500, and Gardner $350. I would pay Gardner the other $150 later.

Gardner and several *commandos* escorted me to a small military communications center within dorm "O" to make the call. This was not normal procedure. Usually all international phone calls were made from the main office section.

Gardner had his head next to the phone when the call finally got through. I had barely begun talking to Susan when Gardner yanked the receiver from my hands. He began yelling into it in his staccato English.

"Worker must pay the prison right now or it will be very hard on him. Don't you care for your friend? Don't you know he's down here getting hurt and beat up because you don't send money? What's a matter with you?"

I tried to grab the receiver from Gardner, but the *commandos* held me aside while Gardner continued shouting at Susan. As I was fighting to get loose from the *commandos*, Gardner barked orders to them in slang Spanish. They twisted my arm behind my back so Susan could hear me screaming in pain. All this time Gardner kept demanding that she send him the money. I tried to shout to Susan to send the money to *me*—not to Gardner, but he would not let me say that into the receiver. Finally, he allowed me to tell Susan to send the $850 to me, but *in care of Gardner*. For some lame reason, I said that would be okay.

Gardner did not let me say anything else to her. I heard her crying on the other end, saying she would send the money today. Gardner pulled the receiver from me and told her again to send the money or it was going to be tough on me. Then he hung up.

I was crying. I had never been more enraged in my life. If I had had a gun with me, I would have shot them all through their heads, smiling through it all. If. . . . Sometimes "if" doesn't mean anything at all.

I stormed back to my cell, trying to figure out a way to get a message to Susan to tell her *not* to send the money in care of Gardner—but there was no way. There were no more dorm visits that day, and no other prisoners had phone calls to make to the United States either.

I paced back and forth, knowing that right now Susan was preparing to send the $850 and that I could not stop her.

I was powerless.

Gardner got the $850 and I never saw a cent of it.

8 Ties to the Outside

I kept expecting the bunkerhouse shootout to happen any day. The three vets still conspired silently, so it must be "go."

But I had learned more about the prison in the intervening weeks. It was illegal for the guards to wear their uniforms on the street. They could only put them on after they entered the prison and they had to remove them before leaving. To do otherwise would be to invite arrest on the spot. Prison officials had already guessed that prisoners might try to escape dressed as prison guards. This way such escapees could be quickly detected—and shot. To walk away from the high, turreted prison walls in a guard's uniform would be an invitation—an order—to get a clip sprayed into your back. The Americans might succeed in taking over the bunker and killing the guards, but that would be all. The rest would be suicide.

But I still expected to hear a burst of gunfire any day. I was ready at the first shot to run and hide in my cell. *Any day.*

But it never happened.

Rumor had it that a tunnel was being dug—not from the inside out, but from the *outside in.* Their buddies were going to tunnel us all out!

It was either go *over, through,* or *under* the wall—or stay within it.

The beatings hurt and the *fajinas* were hell, but the worst part was still the shock of finding myself in a Mexican prison for up to fifteen years with no apparent way out. Nevertheless, I had not yet broken down throughout the first two months of *la prueba*—the test.

I had heard about another American prisoner, Frank L., who had supposedly acted crazy when he was arrested (or maybe he had not acted at all) to get out of prison. They sent him to the psychiatric ward a year ago, and no one had heard from him since. Everyone thought he was "lost." No, it was very important to keep all my panic and fear and pain wrapped up and safely stored away inside me, because if these emotions did get out of control, I could really get hurt. Already my anger had landed me in the hospital, so I should know.

I maintained my stoicism pretty well until I first spoke with my parents over the phone. In the central prison office there were about ten Mexican military officials talking loudly when, over the crackling of a distant international phone connection, I heard my mother.

"Yes. I'll accept charges."

Sometimes I don't understand the telephone at all. So far away, and vaguely connected, each person sharing a bit of his here-now with the other, linked only by precariously connected wires. Here I was with my voice suddenly in my parents' home, as if I were coming through the wires—while around me all I could see were bars, wires, machine gun towers, and armed guards. I could hear all those uniformed monkeys chattering in their loud, boastful, *macho* Spanish, like petty little cock roosters waving their spurs and braided tailfeathers. They were proud to be fighting to get on top of this shitpile. And suddenly here was my mother's voice in this room, just barely competing with all the prison noise. Telephone conversations could be so strange.

I could just barely hear her. How was I? I was fine, I lied. *(Don't mention the hospital; it's still too near Christmas.)*

"What can we do for you?"

"Please speak louder, I can just barely hear you. Mom, listen. Don't send any more money to *anyone*. Don't get a lawyer; he can't do anything. He'll just rob us. Don't do *anything* with money at all right now, hold on to it or we'll just get robbed like everyone else here."

Silence, then—

"Dwight, Dad was thinking of coming down and visiting you."

That terrorized me. My father, who had never been outside the United States except to go fishing once in Canada; who didn't speak a word of anything except midwestern English; who had already had one heart attack—for him to visit and see me here in this hole; for him to go through the harassment and insults and bribery, with every possible Mexican trying to rip him off; and then to see me now in the shape I was in and to realize that *there was nothing he could do to get me out*—

Oh, God, it would kill him. It would kill him on the spot.

"OH GOD NO Mom. Please don't have Dad come. Not now. Please don't. There'd be nothing he could do now anyhow. It would be a waste of . . ."

"But I'll come if you want, Son . . ."

It was my father on the extension. He had been listening the whole time, but in the confusion of the call had not said a thing. My mother was the more articulate and functional under stress of the two. My father had been listening to us and he was willing to come to Mexico City—a place he would never have normally dreamed of going—to help me out. He wanted to come. But worse than that, my father was crying.

I had seen my father cry twice—when my younger brother died and when my older brother Wayne was paralyzed from the neck down in a car accident. Wayne's accident had almost broken my father. Now I heard him crying again, telling me through his sobs that anything, *anything* he could do to help me, to get me out—he would do. Don't be afraid to ask. . . .

And I had feared that my parents would disown me because of why I had been arrested.

Now both my parents were crying. It was hard for me to talk. I repeated to them *not* to send any money to anyone yet, and not to come and visit me. I repeated it again, telling them that I would send a letter explaining.

I couldn't hear what my parents were saying because of the bad connection and the loud talking in the room. In my imperfect Spanish I asked the officials if they could talk more softly so that I could hear my parents. One diminutive, grey-haired, moustached man glared at me. His chest was covered with so many medals that it looked like he had won World Wars I and II by himself. He angrily shouted something to his assistant, who quickly came over, grabbed the receiver from my hand, and hung up.

I would not hear my parents' voices again for two years.

I was crying full force. My face felt contorted and ugly. Having to break the news to my parents of just how grim my situation was, in front of these runts in their organ-grinder's monkey suits, was too bizarre. Now they saw me as the crybaby, sissy, un-*macho gringo* because I was crying *in front of them.*

"*Mande ese pinche chillón gringo a su dormitorio!*" (Send this damned crybaby *gringo* to his dormitory!) shouted Colonel Cardenas, looking like a Mexican version of Joe Stalin. He hated me from the start. In the future, I would be running into this man all too often. At his command, they grabbed me and ran me back to the dorm.

•

That night I lay in bed and thought of my parents. Thinking about them hurt more than being in the prison.

My parents did not deserve this. They had brought me up well and had always taken care of my needs. In their own way, they had helped me whenever and however they could. They had supported me through college and had refused my proposal of paying them back. My father has never broken the law in his life and he had taught me likewise. In his own way (the way my friends and I had thought so quaint) he had warned me about drugs, and of course, I had ignored him.

I was now in prison for doing exactly what my father had warned me never to do: traffic in drugs. And here I was at age twenty-seven, calling on my parents to *help me*. I had betrayed them and yet my father was willing to spend his life savings to get me out of prison—even though I was guilty.

I would almost have felt better if my parents *had* abandoned me.

Somehow I knew my mother would make it. She had that essential feminine quality of endurance and continuance; survival was so much a part of her that she would carry on. But for my father to continue going through this just might kill him. Not "it" might kill him, but *I* might kill him. It had always been difficult for him to release his feelings and to express himself. With all the pain and anxiety and fear that this was now putting on his shoulders—that *I* was putting on his shoulders . . . Then it hit me like a lightning bolt.

I might never see my father again.

That thought was the hardest to take. My father might die while I was here. It looked as if I were going to be here long enough for that to be a real possibility. If my father died while I was here, then his last thoughts of me would be of me in prison with my fate unresolved. I could not let my father die knowing that. It would be too much a final betrayal of blood.

Later I was to witness two American prisoners receiving the news that their fathers had died. Strangely, neither of the men appeared very grief-stricken. They were stoic compared to what I imagined I would have felt in their place. Maybe prison had just numbed them to all feeling; but something was missing in their response—or lack of it—to such a primal grief.

Letters from home were slow in coming. It was difficult enough to mail a letter from a Mexican prison, but tougher still to receive one. The Mexican post has never been noted for its reliability, speed, or efficiency. Somehow those three words and Mexico are just not used in conjunction.

When letters finally did arrive, a low-ranking guard would walk the hallways with the letters until a crowd of Americans had gathered around him. Then the guard would try to pronounce the names on the envelopes. None of us could ever understand him.

But suddenly you might see an envelope in his hands with your name on it. You want that letter—*you must have that letter*—but the guard wants two pesos first. What? If you don't come across with the *propina* (tip), he holds your letter back. Either pay or—and with his hands he goes through the motions of tearing up paper. Now, you do not know if he will in fact destroy your next letters if you do not tip him, but do you want to test him on it? So you give him the pesos and he smiles with cheap bravado, like a victorious mutt who has just bluffed away a bone from another dog. Only then does he give you your letter. The daily shakedown.

You open the letter. In the beginning, friends are shocked. They write, promising to take care of your affairs and work on getting you out. Then months roll by, and they realize that getting you out of prison is going to be difficult, if not impossible. Your friends care for you and miss you, but what can they do? For them, you have temporarily checked out of existence.

Looking around me, I noticed that other Americans had to some extent been abandoned in prison. Business partners were always the first to go. Some prisoners fantasized and plotted revenge. Cheap talk behind bars.

I also noticed that the majority of the American prisoners were single. That had something to do with the fact that marriage and lots of drugs don't mix very well, or for very long. The prisoners' lovers quickly deserted them. The slick jet setters of the coke scene were about as casual and ephemeral as the coke high they pursued. Even if they could arrange for a "conjugal visit"—an expensive and frustratingly brief meeting—they had little interest in coming back. Furtive, hurried, daytime fucking—if they could still do it—in a foul, dirty, noisy prison was enough to end any relationship right there.

Visitors were even more scarce than letters. I waited for weeks to greet Stephan, my first visitor. He should have been my third or fourth visitor, except that the others had all found convenient reasons to cancel out at the last moment. I began to wonder if anyone was ever going to visit me. I knew that Stephan had been in Mexico City for a week already, even though he had not yet shown up. I had waited every day at the window to get a glimpse of him.

I couldn't wait to tell Stephan my plan. He had been my best buddy and I knew he would help. I had some vague ideas about escape. For two weeks I had been braiding string together into a rope, late at night when everyone else was asleep. I already had thirty feet. A few more weeks and I should have a good rope ladder. I only needed something to serve as a grappling hook. With Stephan's presence for a few months and his help in carrying out the escape, I could be free. I was sure that if anyone could pull it off, it would be him.

Finally, late one visiting day, Stephan came staggering in. Fernando Gardner-Pasqual was following him. Stephan was pale and shaking. He quickly gestured at Gardner and whispered to me that he had had to give "that bald-headed bastard" $200 just to get in to visit me.

WHAT?—Oh, no—the score was now Gardner $1,050, me zero. I couldn't believe that even Gardner would pull off such a scummy thing—much less get away with it. I must kill that bastard—KILL HIM—slowly. More fantasies of revenge.

Stephan had been trying to visit me for ten days, but the guards had refused to let him in. This was not unusual. Many parents have waited in Mexico City for weeks to visit their sons and daughters in prison, and then returned to the U.S. without ever having seen them.

Stephan had finally gotten through all of the checkpoints when Gardner had stopped him and told him that he could not come in and see me unless he had money. The prison guards went along with Gardner for a small cut, so Stephan had to go back out and get the money. Only then did they let him enter.

Stephan was too nervous to talk coherently. I kept telling him to calm down, but to no avail. He was shaken. I sat down with him alone in the small, dirty concrete plaza and I told him about the rope ladder I was making. If he could help me get a grappling hook and street clothes into the prison, and then be ready to pick me up in a getaway car at the precise moment, I could go over the wall and be free.

Stephan was too dazed to respond. I explained it to him again, this time pointing out exactly what I would need from him. It would entail some calculated risk on his part, but not too much. He was, after all, on the outside.

"Are you really serious?" he said, shaking his head, trembling. "If you did make it over the wall, what are you going to do about the twenty armed guards standing out front? It would be suicide." He pointed at the four machine gun turrets visible from where we were sitting.

Stephan refused to talk anymore about escape. His primary concern at the moment was how to get himself, as a visitor, out of this prison *today.*

And then, Stephan *got up to leave.* A rush of terror. *Stephan please don't leave me here.* He had come to see me as I had asked. He had gone two weeks and 5,000 miles and $1,000 out of his way, and now he wanted to go home. With his face disjointed, he stood there looking at me as though I were a leper. His eyes were pleading with me to understand.

Please don't DON'T leave me here Stephan . . .

"I'll send you books, money—whatever you need, but forgive me—I've got to get out of here *now.*" He stuck a roll of money in my hand.

I watched Stephan as he hurriedly walked out of the dorm, barely two hours after he had arrived, carrying all of my ill-founded fantasies of escape with him. I felt myself sinking into the prison, suffocating, the walls closing in on me. I was going down. I went back to my bunk bed, shaken and trembling beyond tears.

The most painful visits to witness were those of parents seeing their children in prison for the first time. To do that they had to fly thousands of miles, wait days in Mexico, and then pay exorbitant bribes to sleazy guards, enduring their insults and body searches—all for the privilege of *seeing their son alive.* Having journeyed all the way to Mexico City, what parents would let several hundred—or even a thousand—dollars keep them from their son?

I heard too many mothers sobbing and saw too many re-strained tears running down fathers' cheeks. It was too much for me to witness, and these were not even *my* parents. Oh, God, I did not want my parents to see me in here like this. I would not be able to bear it, and neither would they. Please, *please* let me go through this by myself.

But the hardest task of all was greeting my oldest brother, Ken, when he arrived for a visit. He tried to force a smile when he saw me, but he could not hide his feelings. The first thing he said to me after we hugged was "I want to kill those bastards." He had arrived at the opinion independently, after two days of dealing with Mexicans. Mexican harassment of Americans in Mexico is the true "Montezuma's revenge."

We sat down and talked. I told Ken I had to escape from here. Could he help? He looked at me skeptically. Jailbreaks were things from movies and newsreels. He had never had a thing to do with anything resembling that in his life. He wouldn't know where to start. After all, I was the first prisoner-convict he had ever known. He was not used to dealing with such people.

"Ken, *I have to get out of here!*" The despair showed through.

He flinched as I said it, helpless to change the situation, his face pained. I could see that he thought I was going crazy.

He sat silently for a long time, and then said that he would have to think about escape. That was serious business. He would be returning to the U.S. in a few days. Obligations of job and family. I told him how sorry I was to put the family through all of this.

"You should have thought of that earlier."

Nevertheless, he knew I was now sincere. He told me how incredibly hard it had been on Mom and Dad. I already knew that. Then, in these bizarre surroundings, Ken used his sharp humor to try to relax us both.

Ken had gotten me a lawyer, Francisco Lopez-Portillo. Francisco's first cousin, Jose, was later to become the President of Mexico. I was very wary of any Mexican lawyer, but Kenny insisted that Francisco was the best Mexican lawyer that could be found, and an honest one at that. I was very skeptical. But Francisco Lopez-Portillo had at least told my brother the truth. There was no way I could get out. The very best he could do was to get me a six-year sentence. With a work commission—and luck—I could be out in five years. Francisco promised to do all of this for a relatively modest fee.

Then Kenny changed his tone. It was hard for him to speak, but he told me to look at it this way. I was twenty-seven years old, still a young man. I would be just thirty-two when I went free, with plenty of life to look forward to. Five years was not too long. I could make it. Remember, I was guilty; I had done it to myself.

Ken's tone became more intense. He told me that I might not like what he was going to say, but he had to say it. He was not trying to hurt my feelings. I could tell that he was almost afraid to say this to me. Then the words came out.

"Dwight, do you know what I would have said about your getting arrested for smuggling cocaine if you were not my brother? Do you?" His voice was weak and unsure. "I would have said, 'Fuck you. You got what you deserved. Now rot in prison.'"

It was harder for Ken to tell me that than for me to hear it, because, in a way, I agreed with him. I think Ken was speaking a gut sentiment from middle America.

For the rest of the visit we talked about family, Ken's work, and the U.S. in general. And then it was time for him to go. At the gate, we gripped hands. Ken told me to be strong and tough, and to carry myself with dignity. He was crying. We hugged each other, and he left.

It was the first time in my adult life that I had ever seen Ken cry. I realized then and many times afterwards that after all the friends and lovers, and even some husbands and wives, had abandoned the prisoners to tough it out on their own, on whom could the prisoners depend? By far and away it was their parents, and their brothers and sisters. Direct relatives. *Blood.* Parents were always there to help their imprisoned sons or daughters however they could. These were the same parents who had totally disapproved of drugs and of what their sons or daughters had been doing with their lives. These parents often had had no contact with their sons or daughters for years before, yet now they would help their children until they were free and on their feet again.

Many young Americans of the "stoned generation"—including myself—had previously ignored or avoided our parents, preferring "our generation." We quickly learned that despite sociological rhetoric about the "disintegration of the family" and "ascendance of peer groups," the hard, hard lesson is that blood is still much, much thicker than water.

9 Castigado!

I was lying in the sun on the small concrete patio during the early afternoon of March 2, 1974 when I heard someone scream in English. I ran to the stairway to see what was going on. A new American who was in the *fajinas,* Ted Shafer, lay on his stomach crying in pain, surrounded by six or seven Mexicans kicking and stomping on him. Another American, Judd, and I ran down to him and pushed the Mexicans away. Ted was shouting that they had jumped on his back and hurt his spine. Through his moans he said that he had once injured his back while skiing and they had just reinjured it. He said that he couldn't move his legs. I believed him.

Judd and I stood guard against the Mexicans while a crowd of Americans gathered around. The Mexicans tried to drag Ted by his legs to the *cuartel,* but the Americans prevented it. A few blows were thrown and just when it looked like a major fight might erupt, twenty guards arrived and broke it up. Ted was thrown on a stretcher and carried off to the hospital.

I was standing in the midst of a clump of Americans when Gardner walked up to us with ten guards and pointed at me, shouting in Spanish, "That's the other one!"

The guards waded through the Americans and dragged me away from them. None of the other Americans offered any resistance or help. Another group of guards grabbed Judd and began punching him hard. I felt a deep, cold terror in my back and stomach, like I had felt when they had thrown me into cold storage and beaten me.

The guards ran Judd and me outside the dormitory. There stood Colonel Cardenas. He told the guards *"darlos la madre"* (to give them the mother), Mexican Spanish for "beat the shit out of them."

Sixteen guards—eight on each of us—pulled us to opposite sides of the garage. I heard Judd screaming.

They pushed me against a prison van. Four guards held my limbs while the others proceeded to take turns kicking and beating me in the guts. I was screaming and squirming, trying to keep my unprotected stomach as tensed as I could for the blows.

The first punches weren't that hard because the guards were all pushing at each other to get into position to kick and hit me.

Then the blows came raining down. I could not avoid them or protect myself. And pushed solidly against the van, I had no recoil. I could only scream in pain. Over my own shouts I could still hear Judd gasping and grunting as he got the wind knocked out of him.

I was getting hit in the face too, but they were after my torso. One kick caught me in the balls and I screamed and flinched and let my stomach go loose for a moment. Then the blows really hurt. They surrounded me like a pack of little snarling, snapping dogs, pummeling me against the van. I was pissing in my pants again. Then they spread me open and a big Mexican stepped in front of me and really began punching. He knew how to swing and he worked me over until I couldn't breathe. My guts went into a spasm and I vomited over his uniformed arms and was hit in the jaw and my head turned and I vomited over the neck and shoulder of the man holding my left arm. They all dropped me into an oil slick on the cement.

I tried to squirm under the van. I grabbed the drive shaft and across the floor I saw a circle of grey legs kicking something that was screaming loudly. *Judd.* They broke my grip on the drive shaft and kicked me while I squirmed, pleading for mercy, trying to keep my face and guts covered. They went on and on and on and I was thinking *they're killing me* when finally they left me lying on the floor. To the side I could still hear them beating up Judd. They went on and on with him while he shrieked like a man in his death throes.

Then they had Judd and me on our feet and were running us to the *polígano*, the large control tower in the center of the prison. They pushed us in and left us.

Judd and I both buckled over, holding our guts. Our backs and chests were covered with red welts and the swellings of incipient bruises; but my guts hurt the most. My clothes had been torn and frayed and I felt a big cold spot in my pants from the piss. I hurt worse than from the first beating but, unless something in my guts was ruptured, nothing felt broken enough to warrant the hospital. That was too bad, for at this point the hospital would have been my only sanctuary.

Judd had pissed in his pants too. He was a big, muscular man who could do straight-arm pullovers with 110 pounds and had trained for the U.S. Olympic Swim Team in 1968. But no one man could resist ten men jumping on him—Bruce Lee fantasies aside.

That night Judd and I had to sleep on the cold cement floor. I had only a torn pair of pants, my sandals, and a vomit-covered vest that I had made from a blue prison shirt. Within this vest I had sewn three $50 bills that Kenny had given me: all the money I had in Mexico. I always kept my money in this vest because I wore it constantly; that way my money was with me at all times, safe from the ubiquitous thieves. I felt some security in having it with me now. I might be needing it soon. And I was right.

By morning I was so sore and stiff that it was a major effort to stand up. My whole body was screaming with deep, bruised pain. My ribs and back were beginning to discolor into deep purple blotches with sickly greenish edges. My chest was literally checkered with bruises, and Judd's was even worse. We sat there that morning shivering, sore, and weary.

Later that day, boxes of Judd's and my belongings from dormitory "O" arrived at the *polígano,* followed by Fernando Gardner-Pasqual. He looked even more sick and insane than usual, his motions spastic and his dark, beady eyes glistening. He bore a pathetic resemblance to *il Duce.*

Gardner pointed to me and said that he was going to fuck me over bad this time. I was to be permanently transferred from "O" to the worst dormitory in the interior, dormitory "A." And I would be *castigado* for my entire stay there. Then Gardner left abruptly.

Castigado—punished.

Castigado. I knew what it meant in Spanish, but I did not know what it meant in prison. I would soon learn.

I did have sense enough to figure out that they would search me upon entering the new dormitory. They might find the $150, so I had better hide it. Where?

I searched around. Surely all the external stashes would be vulnerable. I thought of the traditional jailhouse stash: up the ass. But that struck me as repugnant, and it would be impossible to do it here in front of the *polígano* guards anyway. I also knew that when one American had been sent to solitary confinement for two weeks, they had searched his rectum.

That left one other choice. I would swallow the bills. Furtively, I took the three $50 bills out and folded them as tightly as I could.

Then I took a dangling thread from a ripped seam in my pants and bound the bills together. I tried to swallow the tiny packet. I couldn't. The dry paper scratched my throat, forcing me to gag.

I saw a puddle of dirty water left over from the morning's floor washing. I stuck the bills in the water, put my foot over them, and waited for them to soak. Then I examined them. I didn't know a guard was standing over my shoulder. He reached for the bills, but I saw him and quickly stuffed them into my mouth. With one tremendous gulp they went down. The guard angrily ordered me to start cleaning the *poligano*.

A short while later, a guard told Judd and me to gather up our stuff; we were going. They took Judd to dorm "G" and me to "A." I knew nothing of the interior dormitories, but I was shortly to learn.

"A" was the dormitory of the *reincidentes*—recidivisits—who had already been in prison at least once. At the dorm gate I saw Gardner talking to someone in "A" who was dressed and acted as though he were important. Gardner pointed to me.

"You going to like it here, Worker."

I walked through the gate and immediately a crowd of prisoners gathered around. I was the only *gringo* in the dorm of 400; only one other prisoner of those 400 spoke any English at all.

They led me to the office. I set my box of belongings down and they began asking me questions. Name, age, crime—the basics. While the clerk-prisoner was getting my data, the *commandos* went through my belongings. They were trying on clothes, looking through books and papers for money—taking anything and everything they wanted. They bickered and fought among themselves as to *who* would get *what* shirt. The box was emptying fast.

I looked around at my new "home." Behind me was the gate through which I had entered, set into a wall of bars forty feet high. These bars faced the *rondin,* the circular passageway that enclosed the *poligano*—the hub—and from which radiated all the dormitories of the interior. Through the bars I could see the machine-gun nest crowning the *poligano*.

I turned back toward the interior of the dorm. Every surface was painted a dark, dingy grey. The dorm patio measured approximately 200 by 30 feet and was open to a narrow patch of sky. There were two cell tiers, the bottom one opening directly onto the patio and the upper one opening onto a tight catwalk. Stairways at the four corners of the dorm joined the upper and lower tiers. Spanning the patio overhead were a few sparse clotheslines strung between the catwalks. At the far end of the patio I could see the cement cubes that were the urinal and *baño*—shower room. Next to them were two *pilas*—deep Mexican sinks with built-in washboards—the sole clothes-washing facilities for however many people existed here. But from the looks of the creatures peering out of dark doorways toward the rear of the dorm, few, if any, of them washed their clothes anyway.

I looked around at the prisoners of "A." They were older than the Mexican prisoners of "O." They were squat and fat and virtually every last one of them was covered with big, crudely-done prison tattoos. Some were completely toothless and none of them appeared to have more than half of his teeth. One of them sported an immense scar that ran across his jaw to the corner of his mouth—a remnant of a previous knife fight.

The one who was ordering me around called himself "Marciano." The inside of his left forearm caught my eye. From the hollow of his elbow to the palm of his hand, his forearm was corrugated with thirty or forty scars from slashes. The hollow of his left elbow was bruised a morbid black. Marciano was a junkie who was right-handed whenever he hit up or tried to kill himself.

I looked at the other *commandos.* The three who had short-sleeved shirts on all had tracks. They were all junkies. And then I saw him, wearing a *commando* arm badge. He recognized me at the same moment, and smiled broadly. *Ratface.*

"*MI PUTA GRINGA!*" reaching over, pinching my cheek. Then he turned and spoke softly to Marciano.

Marciano ordered me to follow him. Escorted by six other *commandos,* I was led into the *baño* and told to undress. I did. Seeing my body covered with bruises and welts, they laughed. They felt through my clothes, checking the seams of my pants and vest. Good thing I had swallowed the money. They checked my sandals, belt—everything. They knew all the prison stashes. Then Marciano motioned for me to bend over. So they knew that one too. But the thought of that sick excuse for humanity checking my rectum for money was too much for me. I just couldn't let him. Ratface and the other *commandos* quickly grabbed my arms, legs, and body and bent me over. I began to resist, expecting to feel Marciano trying to force his fingers up my ass. (Mexican folklore probably had it that *gringos* shit thousand-dollar bills. God! what they would do for a buck.) But as they braced me down over a concrete bench, nothing happened. I looked over my shoulder and saw Marciano drop his pants.

Marciano was going to try to fuck me in the ass—to rape me—

I went insane—screaming, bellowing, kicking, fighting, pushing them off, shouting that I was a Catholic, that this was against the laws of God. They tightened their grips and punched me. I got a leg loose and kicked into Marciano's gut before someone grabbed it again. I had never in my life felt such panic, and from that panic came the insane energy to fight them off, to keep moving. They would have to knock me out cold, they would have to *kill* me before—

Keep fighting keep fighting keep fighting—

I could feel Marciano's thighs pushing against me like some wretched boar pig against his mount. But he couldn't get close to my anus; I was moving too much. I didn't feel any fatigue at all, or any of the soreness from the beating the day before, or even from their blows. I only felt the worst, most terrorizing panic of my life.

Some of the *commandos* were yelling at Marciano. He backed off for a moment and, still screaming insanely, I managed a look over my shoulder. Marciano did not have a hard-on. Ratface, who had been holding my leg, was arguing with him. Then the two of them switched positions.

Now Ratface was getting his chance.

"Coje el culo de ese pinche gringo! Cojelo! Dalo la madre!" (Fuck that gringo's ass! Fuck him good!)

That explained it. *To fuck a gringo in the ass.* The ultimate Mexican revenge against the *yanqui* who stole Texas and California and who had beaten them in war. To fuck that white, blonde asshole of that *gringo. The ultimate humiliation.*

Ratface tried harder than Marciano. He was stronger. They all clenched me as tightly as they could, but I kept squirming and shaking and kicking and screaming. From the outside it must have sounded as though they were killing me. The struggle went on and on. He tried and tried, but he could not get close to me. They would have to kill me first.

They pushed again, arguing among themselves. I looked around and saw that Ratface didn't have a hard-on either.

Good thing they were all junkies.

Then Ratface picked up a heavy black hose, the kind with

cable inside it that remains in whatever shape you twist it. He lifted it with two arms and brought it down as hard as he could across my ass. I screamed like never before. He brought it down across my buttocks again and again, and across my lower back and thighs. I screamed and screamed and screamed—deep, primal, reflex-reaction bellows of agony. They took turns beating me. Finally, after what seemed like forever, they stopped and dropped me to the floor.

I leaned against the bench, shivering, drenched in cold sweat. Although I could feel the blood beginning to trickle down the backs of my thighs, my body was too shocked to sense the pain I was in. I felt only the deepest relief in realizing that they had settled for whipping my ass bloody raw and were finished trying to rape me.

I was immediately thrown into *chochos*. Doing *chochos* means that you must rub a rock across the cement floor of the urinal nonstop for as long as they tell you. They gave me the heaviest stone—a fifty-pound piece of black basalt that had one side worn completely smooth from millions of *chocho* rubbings. This rock was identical in type to the stones used in the construction of the pyramids of ancient Teotihuacan nearby, except that then—600 years ago—the Aztecs used more modern technology to shape stone.

Along with twenty other prisoners doing *chocos*, I had to rub my rock on the floor of the urinal. The moment anyone lagged in the slightest, the *commando* in charge beat him with that same hose until he got moving again. By now I was in deep pain. My body was becoming one purple bruise; the slightest movement was excruciating. The stench of urine and feces was so overwhelming that I was sure I would pass out; but the moment the *commando* hit me with the hose, I screamed and pushed and pulled the boulder faster. This continued nonstop for four hours, until the 10:00 p.m. horn signaled sleeping hours.

I quickly pissed in the urinal in which I was standing. I noticed that my urine was a dark translucent orange in color. It worried me.

I was run into the *cuartel* where I would live with fifty other *fajineros*. This *cuartel* was fifteen by twenty feet. There were six wide cement bunks where the six *cabos de fajina* (work gang leaders) slept. The remaining forty-five had to sleep on the floor, which was so packed that everyone had to lie on his side. I would have to do that anyway since my buttocks were too sore for me to lie on my back.

All of us were packed in on the floor when Marciano entered. He unfolded some rolled newspaper and he and the other five *cabos* proceeded to hit up, one at a time, on heroin. They got so stoned that they literally walked on the bodies of the *fajineros* below them. The *fajineros* knew better than to ever complain or even groan in pain.

The head *commando* of the *cuartel* was known as "La Maria." La Maria was an old, skinny, toothless, homosexual junkie whose face resembled what Popeye might look like with terminal skin cancer at the age of 110.

Stoned on junk, La Maria commanded me to stand up. I did. Then he told me to strip. I refused. The other *commandos* punched me around and pulled off my clothes. They all laughed at my bruises and especially at my *"nalga de mono"*—my purple monkey's ass. The other *fajineros* remained silent. Then Maria commanded me to walk around naked *over* and *on top of* the other *fajineros* while the *commandos* all whistled at me. They whooped and shouted and jeered.

There is no possible way for me to describe the bizarre perversity, the sick, leering, wretched faces of those *commandos.* Never will I forget them.

Maria told me to get in bed with him/her. I refused. He hit me, but it was like an old lady swinging a fly swatter. I put my clothes back on and lay on the floor. I slept with my clothes on. There were no blankets, but plenty of thieves. Also, my pants kept my wounds covered.

We could not sleep until after the junkies had finished hitting up. Only then did the lights go out. I slept packed like a sardine next to the others, with my body halfway under a bunk.

La Maria made a *fajinero* boy get on the bunk next to him. Sounds came from the bed. I would later find that La Maria was an oral homosexual. All he did was suck cock. Every day in the *cuartel* I could walk in and catch him sucking off one of his current young favorites. The deal was that if you would let him suck you off, he would go easier on you. Eventually La Maria sent over one of his punks to explain that to me. I looked at La Maria's horribly wrinkled and scarred, toothless face and got even sicker to my stomach.

Castigado! 63

I would not have shit on him from fifty stories up.

On the bunk above me sat two *commandos*. After much loud talk and laughter, they ordered a young *fajinero* to get up on the bed between them. The kid hesitated. They punched him and then dragged him onto the bunk and stripped him down. Then they took turns fucking him in the ass. I heard him whimpering and crying, and later that night, gagging and coughing as they made him suck their cocks.

Within a few weeks the conversion would be complete. That misplaced Mexican kid who should never have been in "A" in the first place would be a jailhouse woman, plucking her eyebrows and using makeup and getting it up the ass and down the throat and all. And I had to listen to and watch her forced conversion every night.

Somehow I would have to learn to sleep with all this going on just a few feet away from me.

Late that night I had to make a bowel movement. When I got up, a *commando* yelled at me. He wanted to know where I was going. I told him and he insisted on going with me, followed by a few others. As our procession walked to the toilet, we startled dozens of rats.

It had been just twelve hours since I had swallowed the money, so I figured that it would not be coming through yet. I pulled at my underpants but they would not come down. They were stuck to the coagulated blood on my buttocks. I had to sit in a trough of cold water and soak the scabs until they softened. Then I pulled my underpants hard, ripping off the scabs. Oh, did it hurt!

As I squatted over the open hole in the floor, the *commando* moved his head to one side to get a better view. Several other Mexicans came in and did the same. They were all staring at me—total cretins—*watching me shit*. Did they know about the money? I was afraid the guard had told them.

They watched every detail closely. Then I figured out why. They did not know anything about the money at all. No. They were there because they wanted to *watch a gringo shit*. They had never seen a *gringo* shit before and they just wanted to see if I did it like they did.

They had me up and running at 4:00 a.m. to carry garbage. But my sandals were gone! They had been stolen again. When would I ever learn?

The first day I had to work two hours carrying garbage, ten hours washing the floors, and four hours in *chochos.* Never had time gone so slowly. Every minute during the floor-washing there was someone standing above me with a club or a whip, whacking me no matter how hard I worked. I had to carry two five-gallon cans of water while running full speed barefoot over the rough stone floor to the front of the dorm. Then I had to turn around and run two more cans of water back. I would have to do this twenty or thirty times while a goon chased me with a club, making me run faster, while the whole dorm watched.

Once, someone tripped me as I was running. I fell headlong and water flew everywhere. I was drenched. The whole dorm laughed. It was humiliate-the-*gringo* all day. They were out to fuck me over and debase me as much as they could.

This was what *"castigado"* meant. I was bottom man of the 400 in dormitory "A." I was last in everything. Anyone could do most anything he wanted to me and I could do nothing back. It was open season on *gringos.* I was the target, and Ratface was their ringleader.

It was from this position that I began to see the relationship between U.S. and Mexican prisoners in Mexico. The Mexican prisoners heaped every possible bit of abuse on me. They blamed me personally for stealing Texas and California from Mexico. I was the capitalist robber, the *gringo* invader who stole their land and exploited their people. It was me. I had done it.

In my position on the bottom rung of the ladder, the Mexican prisoners could freely dump on me every bit of national hostility and resentment. Through me and the other American prisoners they could finally get back at the *gringo* they were jealous of and hated. They could say all those things that were brewing deep within their dark *animas,* but which they had never been able to say while playing lackey to U.S. tourists in hope of a tip.

Although later I would learn how to deal with their insults to me and my homeland, at this point I stayed silent. For now, I would serve as their catharsis of hatred.

My next day was as unbearable as the first. I was so sore that I never thought I would make it. With every kick, punch, and clubbing, the *commandos* screamed for more money. Every last instant was hell.

I had to eat *rancho,* a fetid mixture of rice and boiled cow entrails. Whenever the *commandos* dipped the ladle into the foul-smelling cauldron, I never knew what might come up: half a kidney, a long strip of stomach, a piece of chopped bovine intestine with the partially digested rumen still inside it, or other bizarre unidentifiable entrails. But when I saw the *commando* pull out part of a cow's tail with boiled, sopping-wet fur still intact upon it, I gagged. It was then that I began to believe that they tossed whole live *mooing* cows into gigantic Osterizers and boiled the chopped-up pieces to create *rancho.*

I offered my dirty tin of *rancho* to the other *fajineros.* They all jumped at the chance and quickly swept my tin clean with their hands. As hungry and weak as I was, I couldn't believe they could eat this foul shit and not even complain about it.

In dorm "O" I had avoided *rancho* by eating with other prisoners, but here, it was inevitable. Either that or nothing. To my horror, disgust, and revulsion, I found myself picking through my next tin of *rancho* for the most edible parts. Hunger.

Late that afternoon I felt a bowel movement coming on. It must be the money. I got permission to go to the hole. When no one was looking I quickly defecated into my hand. I squeezed through it and found the money. Washing it off as best I could, I peeled off one $50 bill, then rebundled the other two. I heard the *commandos* yelling for me, saying that I was taking too much time. I was afraid that they might find the money on me, so I quickly washed it off again and stuffed the horribly fetid folded bills into my mouth and reswallowed them, gagging horrendously as I did so. I could not believe I could actually be doing this. The *commandos* charged in and ran me out of the urinal to rejoin *fajinas.*

That evening, after a bowl of cold beans, they sent me to *chochos.* I grabbed Marciano and told him I could get him some money if he would let me off *chochos.* When I said "money," his dark, beady, reptilian eyes registered. The magical litany of Mexico: money, money, money. I told him that I could get fifty dollars from a *gringo* to pay out of doing *chochos.*

He had no idea in the world how many pesos that was.

I lied that it was around 800, more or less, and he quickly nodded. "Give me the money and no more *chochos.*"

"But if you throw me back into *chochos* after I pay you, I'll never give you anything again."

"GIVE ME THE MONEY!"

I gave it to him and he took me out of *chochos.* Now I would be working fourteen hours a day instead of eighteen—a big difference. I went immediately to sleep.

But that fourteen hours was still unbearable. I had gotten a staph infection that had spread all over me. The welts on my back were abscessing. It felt as though they were seething underneath, just getting ready to erupt. My bare feet were raw wounds from running across cement all day. The bruised areas of my body looked more dead than alive.

Marciano had shot up the fifty dollars within a few days. Now he wanted more money, so he ran me harder than ever in *fajinas*. I couldn't go on like this, so I made a deal with Marciano. I told him that I received 2,000 pesos a month, at the beginning of each month. I would give him 1,500 of that every month if he would go easy on me. Going easy on me just meant that they would not beat me. Fourteen hours of work, yes, but no clubs or kicks.

"Okay. Give me the money now."

"No. I just said I wouldn't have it until April first."

Marciano looked at me with dark serpentine suspicion. He didn't believe in anything that was not right in his hand, and he knew that all Americans were millionaires.

I asked him if I had given him that fifty dollars or not. Reluctantly, his vacant eyes nodded. I told him that I would pay him this time too. He called the *commandos* over and told them to take it a little bit easier on me. Then Marciano reached into his dirty pocket and handed me a small tinfoil packet. Without opening it, I knew what was in it. Dark brown Mexican heroin. I had seen all the other Mexicans here hitting up on it whenever they could. No, I told him, I didn't use the stuff. He shook his head. That didn't matter. Since I now had money, I would have to buy heroin from him—a minimum of four dollars' worth a week.

"But I don't use it."

"'NO IMPORTA!'"

I had to buy it. And I couldn't dare try to resell it, because they would find out and then really beat me.

I held the tinfoil in my hand. Marciano held out his hand for four dollars. I told him I would pay him later. He walked out, knowing I would.

Heroin. I wouldn't use it and couldn't resell it. So that meant that I could give it to some junkie for his pleasure, or throw it away. I flipped it into the sewer.

My strategy was to buy time. I could not take the regular

beatings anymore. I was not going to receive any money on April 1. Even if I were, I would never give it to that bastard. But it served my temporary interests that Marciano believe that this money was coming. In the meantime, I would keep my $100 in the only safe place I knew: my stomach. I would have to repeat the ritual of reswallowing it every few days. Somehow, someway, I would get out of this dorm and my *castigado* status soon, before the month was up. It was March 8, 1974.

Another week went by—the longest week of my life. Every day they ran me to the breaking point; every day Marciano asked for his money; every day I had to remind him that it would not be here until April 1.

I saw Judd for a moment at the gate, carrying a fifty-kilo bag of flour. He was filthy, pale, and haggard. I scarcely recognized him. I yelled to him and he stopped and looked around. A *commando* pushed him. Not seeing me, he started moving.

Did I look like him?

One day I saw a stretcher leave for the hospital carrying a blood-covered Mexican, moaning in his death throes from knife wounds. This Mexican had been insulting me earlier that day, along with Ratface and a few others, and now he was dying. I felt no pity at all.

I had to clean up the trail of blood across the floor.

I had to get out of this fucking dorm.

Probably the closest thing to hell in the Americas was the far end of dormitory "A" in Lecumberri in Mexico City. I had to walk into these cells daily and carry out the garbage. The *mayor* of dorm "A" kept his most frightful specimens of subhumanity in the rear of the dorm, where there was the least chance that any visitors might see them. Some of them were specifically forbidden to leave their cells whenever there were visitors. One look at them would explain why.

There were thirty to forty men, middle-aged and older, who had lived most of their lives in this prison, much of it in this very cell. Up to eight of them were packed into each bare eight-by-twelve-foot cell. The walls were oily black from years of candle and kerosene fire. There was no electricity. The cement had been turned brownish black from decades of organic debris, and polished smooth by years of walking and by the rubbing, rolling, and perspiration of sleeping bodies. There was a pervasive fetid stench from too many humans enclosed for too long a time; it had soaked into the very pores of the metal and could never be aired out.

These prisoners had been forgotten long ago by whomever might have survived them on the street; and in turn, they had forgotten. They had never had a lawyer or bothered with their cases in court. They did not know or care.

Their bodies were covered with interlacing massive tattoos, and knife and suicide scars. Their mouths had no teeth and their faces were prematurely aged. Some of them had the frosted corneas of blindness while others were missing their eyes entirely, strange red flesh filling their empty eyesockets. Some had clubfeet, deformed limbs, twisted backbones. Some had growths on their ears and necks that would have been removed as a matter of course in the United States. I saw my first cases of dry leprosy. Collectively, these men looked like birth defectives that had lived. Rejects from a freak show.

Most of them could not read, write, or do anything. They just lay around on the floors of their filthy, vermin-infested cells, doing nothing, thinking nothing, feeling nothing. They were even deader than they looked.

I was ordered into their cells to carry out their garbage. Occasionally one of them might groan *"gringo,"* but apart from that, I was met with pure apathy. But was it apathy? Is a hibernating reptile lethargic?

When I walked into one cell a very short, fat specimen was standing next to the sink. Holding a small mirror between his legs, *he was looking at his asshole* while he masturbated. He turned to me, surprised at first, and then smiled and continued masturbating with his pathetic little hard-on pointed at me.

"Gringo," he leered, a sick mouth revealing a few snaggle teeth, and he waved his cock at me. A few creatures in his cell saw what was going on and managed to laugh from their death trances. He stood there with his subhuman grin, jerking off.

I wished that I had a sharp meat cleaver. I walked out of this tenth circle.

I had to get out of this place.

One morning I was called out of *fajinas* and told to go to the gate. There stood Hank, wearing his electrician's tool belt and carrying a large roll of wire. Hank knew more about electricity than anyone else in Lecumberri, so he ran the whole electronics shop. Because of this the guards left him alone. He also talked a mean, dirty Spanish that all the Mexicans respected and he dealt a lot of heroin to the Mexicans. Hank always had money. I stood at the gate filthy and in rags. He saw the bruises on my arms and showing through my unbuttoned shirt.

"You're lookin' good," he said loudly.

"How long am I going to be in here?"

"I don't know. What about that U.S. Embassy of yours that you sent the letter to?" He started to smile.

"I'm serious. What can I do to get out of here?"

"Time—or escape. Now what do you think of your little brown brothers?" Now he was smiling broadly.

"Can you help me?"

"Nope." His expression was colder than his voice. "But why *don't* you try to escape, *hero?* You know no one's escaped from here since Pancho Villa sixty years ago."

"Hey, stop fucking around with me. What can I do . . ."

"Look, Jack. You're doin' *fajinas.* Boot camp. I had to do the same thing. No one helped me. I lived. You'll make it or you'll sink. It's that simple. Next time don't play hero in the dorm, *champ.*"

I wanted to grab his long neck through the bars and bang his smiling head against the steel. He was actually *enjoying* seeing me where I was.

I turned and started walking away.

"Hey, asshole, get back here. I've got something for you."

I turned, then came back. He furtively handed me a roll of paper. I stuffed it in my underpants.

"Don't tell anyone I ever did anything for you."

He walked off.

I went to the toilet to see what he'd given me. It was thirty dollars.

10 Reprieve

I met a Mexican, Raul, in *fajinas* who was in for murder. In our own sort of way, we got along with each other. I talked to him one night, and we arrived at a deal. If I got him a good knife and paid him 300 pesos ($24), he would stab me. Not too badly, but enough to get me out of the dorm and into the hospital. Then I could refuse to come back to dorm "A" by saying that my life was in danger there. And if I ever *did* finger Raul, the he *would* kill me. I believed him. He had killed others.

Very surreptitiously, I managed to buy a knife made from a broken hacksaw blade. Although it was very dull, I figured it would do the job. I gave Raul the knife and the money. It was all set.

I met him that night on the stairway and quickly lifted my shirt. He put the blade up to my stomach and pushed. It did not go in; it was too dull. He pushed again, harder. It cut skin but still did not penetrate. He didn't want to take a full roundhouse knife swing because then it might go in too far. He pushed again and again, still unsuccessfully. Just then footsteps sounded on the stairs and Raul split.

I would not get stabbed tonight. I had some surface cuts, but not enough to warrant the hospital. They would figure that I had done it myself.

In the *fajinas* the next day, I talked to my would-be stabber. He said that I would have to get him a better knife. But the next day, for whatever reason, they moved Raul to another dormitory. Goodbye to 300 pesos and relief via the hospital.

Then Marciano really began pushing me for the money. The beatings got worse. Finally, one day while I was scurrying across the floor doing *fajinas,* something popped on my knee. Pulling up my cuff, I saw that the large, festering wound there had finally broken up. A combination of pus, blood, and lymph was running down to my ankle. Surprisingly, the *commando* let me out of *fajinas* when he saw it. I talked to the dorm officials and for fifty pesos they let me go to the doctor.

The doctor said that I had a lymphatic staph infection. I was to get penicillin injections for three days. He also wrote a work-release slip stating that I was not to work for one week. I thanked the doctor profusely. He understood. A decent man.

I clutched that work-release slip to my side like a high denomination bill. It was. I had already lost fifteen pounds in three weeks, was infected, sick, bruised, beaten, and sore all over. This release would buy me time to recuperate.

When I returned to the dorm, Marciano called me into the *cuartel*. What had happened at the doctor's? I handed him the work release.

Marciano could not read.

Another Mexican read it to him. Marciano looked at me and then at the release slip.

He tore it up and shouted for the *commandos* to take me down to *fajinas*.

I was running out of time. The whole dorm knew that I was supposed to be getting money on April first and everyone was waiting. Whenever I got mail the *commandos* crowded around while I opened it, looking for bills. Not finding money, they punched me around, telling me that it had better be in the next letter—as though it were up to me. I had had it.

No matter what, I was not going to participate in their stupid weekly ritual of saluting the Mexican flag. For the first two weeks I did it, strictly out of fear. But after realizing that they were going to fuck me over no matter what I did, I decided not to salute their flag.

After formation, I was dragged to the side and punched around. I shouted at the *commandos* that we (Americans) weren't supposed to salute any foreign flags. They punched me some more. Then Marciano warned that he personally would break my arm if I didn't salute next time.

For the next flag formation, I put my left arm on my heart. That seemed to satisfy them. They did not notice my middle finger protruding conspicuously from my fist. I waited for a feeling of small triumph. It did not come.

In the last week of March 1974, I was called to the *polígano* from *fajina* work. I walked in and saw a well-dressed American man in his late forties. It was Dan Root, vice-consul in charge of prisoner affairs from the U.S. Embassy in Mexico City. I was relieved to see him. If anyone could protect me from the beatings, here was the man.

Root told me this would be a brief, routine visit. Did I have anything to say before he left? I told Root that I was refusing to salute the Mexican flag, and they were beating me, trying to force me to salute it.

"Go ahead and salute their flag, damn it," he said, irritated.

I unbuttoned my shirt and showed Root the wounds and bruises from the beatings and my infected leg. I told him that I was being extorted from and beaten up every day. If I did not come up with a lot of money by April 1, they were going to maul me, and who knew what else. They were mauling me every day already. I asked Root to help me now before it was too late.

Root looked bored. He said there was nothing he could do. He did not run the prison. It was not his fault that I was being punished. He was busy today, and now, if I would excuse him . . .

"But wait—I need your help." My voice got louder. "I'm not asking you to get me out of prison or anything like that. I'm just asking for your protection."

He stood up impatiently and said that I was exaggerating. I told him that if he did not help, I would have to write my congressman and senators and point out his negligence. But from the depths of a Mexican prison that must have been the most ridiculous thing I could ever have said. It even sounded stupid to me as I said it, with all its presumptuousness, petty bravado, and false self-importance—as if *I* would tattle on *him*. Me, a hard-drug smuggler.

Root stopped in his tracks, his expression changing from impatience to anger. Then he turned and walked directly into Cardenas's office. He emerged about five minutes later and left the central prison area.

I was sent back to dorm "A." At the gate, a group of *commandos* met me and escorted me to the *baño*—the shower room. They told me that I had spoken very badly of "A" to the American. I had threatened to make trouble for the prison, for dorm "A," and for the "embassy man" as they called him. That was very serious. I should not talk about this prison or the "embassy man" like that.

In the *baño* they held me still and whipped me with the hose until I could no longer stand.

They hated me and I loathed them. They wanted my money and they were determined to get it one way or another. That situation I could live with. The other situation, the one I found simply intolerable, was that every day I bore incredible insults because I was an American. It no longer mattered that I had smuggled cocaine. Nothing mattered. They were doing this to me because I was an American.

That was my crime. And they hated the other Americans with the same nationalistic vengeance. What was happening to me in "A" was just a concentrated example of what Mexicans do to American prisoners throughout Mexico.

I had been spit on, beaten, kicked, whipped, and thrown in urinals to be pissed on, continuously having to listen to the lowest vermin of Mexico cursing the United States. No matter what I did or did not say, they insulted and beat me, so I began to speak my mind. My Spanish was improving. I would not deny anything. I would speak from the gut.

I formulated answers to the standard charges made against me as an American by the run-of-the-mill scum in the dormitory:

Accusation: Why do you capitalist Americans exploit Mexico?

Answer: Because Mexico is *so easy* to exploit. You cannot resist our power. You are too weak and puny. The strong *naturally* dominate the weak.

Accusation: Why did the *gringo* armies attack the Mexican armies?

Answer: For practice. You were so easy to beat. And watch your mouth or we'll do it again. We like Baja California, you know.

Accusation: Why does the U.S. control over seventy per cent of big business in Mexico?

Answer: Because your government is always looking for foreign investment. We'll get the other thirty per cent too because you Mexicans can't even run your own country. Without us, it would completely fall apart and you would starve. You need *gringo* technology and food and investment and know-how far more than we need your trinkets.

Accusation: The U.S. imperialists stole Texas and California.

Answer: Damned right, and a good thing we did too, because if Texas and California were in Mexican hands right now, they'd be overpopulated, underfed, and as backward as Mexico. We should have taken more. We will, too.

Accusation: You *gringos* treat Mexicans badly in the U.S.A.

Answer: Right. You treat us badly here, too. We don't want any more *mojadas* (wetbacks). If you Mexicans don't like the U.S., then why are millions of you trying to get in? You don't

see any *gringo* wetbacks trying to get into Mexico, do you?
Accusation: Gringos are all racists.
Answer: Mexicans are all jealous.
Accusation: Gringa women are racist too because they don't like Mexican men.
Answer: Gringa women have good taste. They don't like Mexican men because they act so *macho* and don't treat any women, including their own, like humans. Mexican *machos* have the manners, charm, and technique of billy goats. But *gringa* women also don't like Mexican men because they are such *enanos* (dwarfs) and because they have such little *pititos* (little boys' penises).
They particularly did not appreciate that last comment.

And finally, when they began insulting my white skin, calling me *gabacho* and *cara pallida,* I coined a phrase for them. I called them *"un nación de enanos de color y estatura de mierde"*—"a nation of dwarfs who are the color and height of shit."

They quickly stopped insulting me and accusing me of past American misdeeds. They had never before heard themselves described in such a way. They did not want to hear any more of my answers, so they stopped asking their leading questions.

But in dorm "A," as I began kicking their national *macho* in the nuts, they became even angrier with me. I knew it and I felt better seeing them offended like that. If they had talked sensibly, I would not have denied that problems exist in the U.S. But I just could not stand silently and let such low people attack my homeland in such a vulgar manner. I felt that I was defending the United States by showing them that *gringos* would not just sit and let their country be insulted. Insulting them back became an act of patriotism for me.

So they were enraged and beat me more; that was *fine* with me. I just didn't care anymore. Fuck them fuck them fuck them. They hated me and I hated them. I had cut that last rope. At least I could be free with my mind.

On March 30 Marciano informed me that he had just upped my *fajina* payment, from $160 on April 1 to $1,000 total. A modest increase. I was not going to pay him the $160 on April 1; now I wouldn't be paying him $1,000 either.

On the evening of March 31 I received three letters. None of them contained the 2,000-peso check I was not expecting.

Everyone else was expecting it, though, and many of them thought the check would be for them. Marciano personally went through the letters, to see if the check was hidden inside. He did not know what a check was, but if there was one, he would find it.

But there was no check. Poor Marciano. No junk tonight. Marciano punched me around a little bit to remind me that I had to pay him the money tomorrow. And then the *commandos* punched me around for not getting a check. No junk for them either. At least I was upsetting their plans.

I stuffed the letters into my pockets and got back to my work for the evening: sweeping up the top cell tier and the stairways.

In the stairway, three regular, scummy Mexican prisoners gathered around me and told me that *they wanted the letters. They knew* that I had money in them.

I told them that I did not have any money.

They called me a *"pinche puto Americano"* (fucking American queer).

Returning the compliment, I told them they could all go fuck their stinking Mexican whore mothers in the ass.

One of them swung at me. I jabbed him in the face with the broom. From behind, another one hit me hard over the head with something. I went down. He hit me again with it. Another one was jabbing his hand into my guts. I felt each jab go in distinctly. *He was stabbing me.* They hit me over the head again and hands were going through my pockets when I faded out.

I came to, lying on the dark stairway. My head hurt. Blood was running down my neck. My shirt and pants were soaked with blood, and I felt deep pains in my stomach. Someone was stepping over me. I asked for help. He saw the blood and quickly scurried away. He did not want to be blamed. Others did the same. I grabbed the banister and stumbled downstairs.

When the *commandos* saw the blood, they dragged me back to the *cuartel* and checked the wounds. Abdominal wounds, but they had seen worse. I was not dying. They wanted to know who did it. One of them slapped me, telling me that I did not have to fear retaliation. They just wanted to get the person who did it. They slapped me some more and then, deciding that I really did not know who did it, they sent me to the hospital.

It was April Fool's Day, 1974. I was sewn up and left to heal in the hospital. Fernando Gardner-Pasqual was standing above my bed.

"Worker, tell me who did it. We going to get them!"

"You did it, Gardner. You paid someone to do it."

"I DID NOT! Don't you ever say that again!" Gardner was defensive and afraid. He was bluffing.

I paused.

"Look, Fernando. The food's not too good here, plus I need shoes and clothes . . ."

He gave me 300 pesos. I told him it was not enough. He gave me 300 more and said they were going to find out who did it. Gardner then walked out in a burst of mania.

Later that day, the Doctor and I talked about Ted Shafer. Ted was the American in *fajinas* whom I had rushed to defend, the one who lay on the floor screaming and crying in pain, claiming that his back was seriously injured. The Doctor told me that the X-rays and examinations had shown nothing wrong with him. He had been faking it. After a few days observations, the Doctor had sent Ted back to dorm "O."

That was what had started this whole nightmare. I lay in bed reflecting. Ted Shafer had faked an injury, and because of it, *I* got one. Two weeks ago I had paid someone 300 pesos to stab me, and with no results. But now someone had done the job for free. I felt the same cold irony that I had felt when I needed the crutch the last time I was here in the hospital. The injured leg that I had faked at the airport had become my reality; now the faked knife wounds had done the same.

I would have to be more careful about fantasizing my illusions into reality.

While I had been *castigado*, Ted Shafer had never made one effort to help me. I was to see him many times after that but he never said so much as thanks to Judd or me for our futile efforts to help him. His eyes were as stoned as Roger's.

I never forgot that.

After I had healed up sufficiently in the hospital they again sent me back to dormitory "O."

11 **Hunger Strike!**

On July 6, 1974, a minister from *Gobernación* (the all-purpose and all-powerful governmental control agency in Mexico) came to dorm "O" to talk with the Americans. He was escorted by Colonel Cardenas, the bastard who had had me beaten up by his goon prison guards. But today Cardenas was smiling and cordial, a rare posture indeed for him. I was suspicious.

The minister told the Americans that the U.S. Embassy had filed an official letter of protest over abuses of American prisoners in Lecumberri, and that he was here to investigate. We were all to submit truthful, signed depositions about our treatment in Mexico. From the way this man talked and Cardenas kept his mouth shut, it was clear that he was Cardenas's superior. And from the way Cardenas smiled and nodded, it was obvious that he was worried. The minister told us not to fear any repercussions. We were to write our depositions.

Good, I thought. I would write it all down and maybe fuck Gardner around in the process.

In the middle of writing our statements, Gardner summoned all the Americans to the dining room. He said that he had just talked to Colonel Cardenas and he had this information for us. The Colonel had said that *regardless* of whatever *Gobernación* found out about the prison, we would not be released. They might bust some prison officials and throw them behind bars, but they would not release us, because we had committed crimes. (Gardner avoided mentioning that he himself might be re-arrested with additional charges against him.)

But, Gardner said, he and the Colonel had come up with a "good idea." If the Americans would criticize *only* the courts, the arresting officers, and the U.S. Embassy for its neglect of our situation, and *avoid* criticizing the prison in *any* way, the prison officials would allow the Americans to go on a hunger strike. It would bring so much publicity to our case that we would all either get deported from Mexico as undesirable aliens or get extradited to the U.S. on phony conspiracy charges that we could easily beat in the States. Gardner said that Mexico would never let us starve to death in their prisons, and swore that frankly, Mexico no longer wanted us here.

Later that day the minister from *Gobernación* would tell us the same thing: Mexico did not want to keep us here in their prisons, but was under pressure from the U.S. Embassy to do so. We were becoming a big problem for Mexico because the bad publicity resulting from our continued presence could threaten tourism.

There was excitement in the air. The Americans had a closed meeting and talked it all over. The consensus was general agreement with Gardner. A vote was taken. The Americans agreed not to criticize the prison in any way and to immediately begin a hunger strike "until freedom or death." We would all be in it until the end. This was the first real show of unity among the Americans in Lecumberri.

We wrote our depositions against the courts, legal system, arresting officers, and the U.S. Embassy. I talked with my roommate and closest friend, Brian, about not criticizing Gardner or the prison. Brian thought that was bullshit. He was going to write everything down. That was what I wanted to hear. In my deposition I mentioned everything I could about Gardner and the prison.

Brian Harrison Fitzpatrick had been arrested on January 16, 1974, in Chapultepec Park in Mexico City. He had been sitting by himself in the park when two English-speaking Mexicans who were smoking marijuana sat next to him and asked if he wanted to smoke. Brian would later learn that the two were Chicanos. Together they strolled deeper into the park to find a secluded place. While they were walking, six plainclothes Mexicans claiming to be cops surrounded the three of them. These men found five grams of grass on the two Chicanos and began arguing with them. Brian could tell that they were insulting Americans in general and that they wanted money—something that he did not have.

While the Chicanos and the Mexicans argued, Brian walked off. With no warning, they shot at him. He ran for over a mile, trying to flag cars, catch a bus—anything to get away. Brian didn't think they were police at all, until they cornered and arrested him.

They had their *gringo*.

Brian could not pay the bribes that the cops wanted for the five grams of grass that the two Chicanos had, so all three of them went to jail. The first three Mexican lawyers that Brian's family hired all robbed him; he had thus far been waiting six months for his trial.

Brian is a six-foot-four-inch Nebraska country boy. He is the kind of person who could not tell a lie. He just does not have that in him. He was a twenty-five-year-old military veteran with no police record when he was arrested in Mexico City, and he was no candidate at all for future crime. He felt with absolute conviction that he had been totally wronged by the Mexicans. He could prove that at least four articles of the Mexican Constitution had been violated in his case, and yet they were keeping him in prison, because they wanted him to buy out. They wanted his money.

Brian was more determined than any other American on the hunger strike, and with good reason. He figured that smugglers were a different breed of cat from him—that our cases were more serious—and he was right. He did not know about drug smuggling. He had never done it and never would. Brian had no intention of remaining in prison while they tried to extort from him. He wanted out with the passion of a truly innocent man.

Later that day, Gardner looked over all the depositions. He told Brian and me to change ours. We refused. He was angry, but since he was not in a position to intimidate us right now, he let it go for the moment.

Gardner then took the depositions to the Colonel, who turned them over to *Gobernación*. The prison now had signed, documentary proof that the U.S. prisoners had virtually no complaints with the prison and that the problem lay basically with the courts, the arresting officers, and *Gobernación*. So the hot potato was now in the hands of *Gobernación* and the U.S. Embassy.

Seventy Americans were not eating. We barricaded ourselves in the south wing of "O" with a feeling of camaraderie and brotherhood unprecedented among us. Finally, we were doing something together to help ourselves. It was the first time in a long while that we felt we had any control over our lives.

Late that afternoon Gardner came along with a big bag of oranges. He said that we could have as many oranges as we wanted, and any other food too. He said it did not matter whether we ate or not, but only that *they* (meaning the outside) *thought* we were not eating.

That sounded suspicious. I had once previously fasted for a week and I knew that there was no real danger in going several weeks without eating. But only a few other Americans in the dorm had ever fasted, so a number of them were apprehensive.

The Americans got together for a meeting. We decided that we could have the juice of a couple of oranges a day for vitamins, but no food. Brian objected to the oranges. I mentioned that even Ghandi drank orange juice on his fasts. Still Brian wouldn't concede to it. The general consensus was that orange juice was okay, but anyone eating food would have to pack up and move to the north side of the dormitory. This would be a test, and we would have to be strong.

It was three days into the strike and we were all hungry. The hallway was covered with signs like "FREEDOM OR DEATH" and "DO NOT EAT." One drawing depicted a drooling mouth and tongue. It said "DON'T EAT NOW SO YOU CAN EAT PUSSY LATER." There was a well-drawn picture of a Trojan horse depicting a bunch of businessmen jumping out of its belly. On their briefcases was written "U.S. EMBASSY." The picture was labeled "BEWARE OF THE RUMOR-MONGERS. DO NOT ACCEPT ANY WOODEN NICKELS."

Rumors. There were still hundreds of them going around. Someone always had a new, hot rumor dealing with one topic: the impending release of U.S. prisoners on drug charges in Mexico. Now that I had been in Lecumberri for seven months, the complexity of the rumors seemed to have become more sophisticated. First it had simply been a matter of deporting us as undesirable aliens. Then I heard we would be extradited to the U.S. on conspiracy charges. Then came the first of the prisoner-exchange rumors: we would be swapped with Mexican nationals in U.S. prisons. Other rumors followed: Mexico was going to grant parole for drug offenders, and our sentences would be reduced forty per cent. Amnesty International was investigating how Mexico had violated our rights and *they* would arrange our release. Some parents of American prisoners were going to have the U.N. pressure Mexico to release us. The Mexican drug laws were all going to be changed to allow the U.S. prisoners to pay large fines and then be released. (That made sense. Mexico wanted money. They did not want to pay the upkeep on U.S. prisoners.) All foreign prisoners in Mexico would be sent to their respective countries. Mexico did not want them. There would be a massive boycott of U.S. tourism to Mexico until Mexico released the prisoners. Acts of terrorism were beginning against Mexico to force the release of U.S. prisoners. Some Mexican official would be kidnapped and then we would all go free. When

Mexico nominates their next president, he will release all foreign prisoners. When Nixon gets thrown out of office, we will be released. When Mexico *changes* president, we will be released. Congress will force the U.S. president to take the action necessary to release us. The latest revelations of DEA (Drug Enforcement Agency) corruption will force the U.S. government to reexamine its whole drug policy and have us released. There is a new judge in the first court; he'll do deals—just pay. This lawyer here says he can get us out. Congressman so-and-so says "this situation cannot continue." "My mother sent me a letter and she says right here that she is not going to let me stay in a Mexican jail for five years." "But I'm going to win my appeal." "Sloan's mother says they are going to 'hang the DEA'." We will be released for Christmas of '74—Fourth of July '75—Christmas of '75—Fourth of July '76. Any Democratic president in the U.S. will release us. . . .

And inevitably, I would hear U.S. prisoners say "Something's got to give. They're not going to keep *me* behind bars for six more years. If nothing else, I'll escape."

Hope springs eternal.

In my first year in prison, I was to hear perhaps one hundred *bona fide* rumors that we were "all going home." Only once did I believe that we were, and the other ninety-nine times I was right. Throughout all the rumors, there remained one consistent reality: *Not one of the 150 Americans arrested at the airport for drugs went free.* Just by that track record alone, you would expect that the prisoners would be suspicious of any new rumors, right?

Wrong. We were always eager for a new one. Blinded by the hole we were in, we had lost all perspective. We couldn't see the wall for the bars.

Peter Petersen, consul general of the U.S. Embassy, came into dormitory "O" for a special meeting with the striking American prisoners. Dan Root would not be coming.

I had discovered a lot more about Dan Root since my meeting with him when I had been *castigado*. At another group meeting I had heard him say to the U.S. prisoners, "If I were a prisoner here, I would use Jorge Avilés as my attorney. If there's anyone who can get you out, it's Avilés." Root gave this same advice to other prisoners and their relatives. Subsequently, over a four-month period, relatives of U.S. prisoners collectively paid Jorge Avilés over $100,000 in attorney's fees. They never received any legal services, or saw Avilés or their money again.

U.S. consular officials are specifically prohibited from recommending individual lawyers to U.S. prisoners beyond our borders. The most they are permitted to do is furnish a list of lawyers from which to choose. Root knew that. He knew what he was doing.

At the front of the room Petersen asked us to end the hunger strike, because to continue it would only offend the embassy and "the people who could make a difference." He was clearly upset about its prospects.

The Americans had many questions for Petersen, and more statements to make. A large number of U.S. prisoners in Lecumberri were Vietnam veterans. Almost all of them had honorable discharges, and some of them had Purple Hearts. There was even one POW escapee from North Vietnam.

The escapee spoke first. He was nearly shouting.

"I spent four years in U.S. Army Special Services in Vietnam. I was a POW in North Vietnam for four months before I escaped. I've never done drugs in my life and never will. The man I was traveling with was carrying cocaine, but I didn't have a thing. The torture they put me through at that airport during the first twelve hours was far worse than anything that ever happened to me in North Vietnam. It was so bad that I signed a confession written in Spanish that I didn't understand just to end the electric shocks. Since then I've sent the embassy a number of letters asking—pleading—for help, but they haven't even answered one of them. And now," he shouted, "will you just answer me this one thing, Petersen? Why in the hell was I fighting for you in Vietnam?"

Loud cheers. Petersen was at a loss for words.

Someone shouted out about how Dan Root had told him and his parents to use Jorge Avilés, who later defrauded his parents of their life savings. He claimed that Root and Avilés were splitting the ripoff. More angry shouts of agreement. Other Americans yelled out their grievances, until finally another Vietnam veteran got the floor.

"They stuck a cattle prod up my ass at the airport *in front of a DEA agent* who was speaking English and wearing a badge. His name was Arthur Sedillo. And you want to know what I think? I think I should have been shooting at you instead!"

A loud burst of approval filled the room. Petersen had no tactful response to this threat. It was beyond the rhetoric of diplomatese. Petersen looked around at his captive audience. They were openly hostile to everything he had said. He looked toward the exit door and saw that it was open. Just making sure.

The lines were drawn. The interests of the prisoners and those of the embassy were diametrically opposed, and any further talk would be useless. But if nothing else, the meeting had provided some good drama. As Petersen left, the Americans charged upstairs waving their fists, shouting, "STRIKE! STRIKE! STRIKE!"

Some of the U.S. prisoners were getting very hungry. After a week the first two Americans officially dropped out of the hunger strike. One of them "couldn't take it any more." The other one, John H., said that he was quitting on his "Mexican lawyer's advice." John did not want to "offend Mexico and jeopardize my case."

I could not restrain myself. I called them cowards and traitors. Their petty immediate needs of food mattered more than the next six years of their lives.

Later that day Lee pulled me off to the side. Lee didn't speak very loudly or very often. He was educated and literate, arrogant and aloof, avoiding most of the daily prison talk because he felt it was nowhere. The aristocrat among the smugglers, he held a slight condescending disdain for everyone and everything around him. Looking around me, I could understand why. Lee told me that I shouldn't have gotten so down on those two other Americans, because a lot—maybe half—of the other Americans were eating on the sly. The other two were just honest enough to admit it.

"Who else is eating?"

"Well, for one, I am."

That surprised me, but then again, it didn't. Lee had always been bone skinny, looking like he hadn't eaten in two weeks. As he walked away, I wondered if that many Americans really were eating. Didn't they realize that the strike might possibly gain us our freedom? *What was wrong with them?* What was the purpose of having a hunger strike if we did not have the negative leverage of our hospitalization—and maybe even threat of death?

I began watching the other Americans more closely. I would walk quickly into cells unexpectedly late at night, checking for remnants of food in their ash trays and garbage cans. I spied on Americans passing money through the bars of the locked gate to Mexicans to buy them food. If one Mexican knew that an

American was buying food, then *all* the Mexicans knew. And their conclusion would be that all the Americans were eating.

Lee was right. Many Americans were eating on the sly. Too many of them. I realized that if these Americans were eating now, *before* any pressure was put on them, then they would yield immediately the moment the prison administration tried to break up the hunger strike. And again the question came up: *What kind of people were these anyhow?*

Later that day, while lying in bed, I heard shouts and cheers coming from the hallway. Someone must have some good news, so I got up to check it out. Hank was standing in the middle of a circle of Americans with his electrician's belt on, shouting.

"JAMES DEAN BROWN GOT SEVEN!"

Cheers.

"JAMES DEAN BROWN GOT *SEVEN!*"

More cheers. Some Americans were dancing and jumping.

"THE TURNCOAT EXTORTIONIST'S HELPER, THE PRE-CIOUS, HOLIER-THAN-THOU, 'I'M-INNOCENT-AND-GOING FREE-SHORTLY' JAMES DEAN BROWN, WHO PUT THE BLAME ON HIS FIANCÉE, WAS SENTENCED IN COURT TODAY TO *SERVE SEVEN* YEARS!"

I cheered with them.

That night, feeling particularly obnoxious and self-righteous about the strike, I yelled at Phil Nullard when I found him eating a steak.

"So what?" He dangled it in my face. "It tastes *good.* Want a bite?"

I wanted to hit him, but I didn't. I was skinny and weak; he was energetic and well fed. He would have beaten me badly.

"I'm going to eat as much as I want to. I know that my own eating or not eating is not going to make the difference, just as long as there are some of us striking. You can starve yourself, but not me."

"But we're in this together."

"You know where you can stick it. Don't preach morals to me, coke smuggler."

I walked out.

To me, the Americans who were eating were like my one-time friends on the street who had abandoned me the moment they heard I was in prison. I had misjudged what they would do when put to the test. I had failed in some of my tests in prison too, to my own surprise and disgust, but many of these Americans did not even see it as a test of will or integrity at all. They just did what was easiest to do at the time, given the circumstances—just as they had done on the street.

Drugs are a pleasure trip. Good dope, good women, good travels, good times, and—*good food* go together. The epicurean-hedonistic matrix. And if they were smoking pot on the fifth day of the hunger strike and got a case of the uncontrollable mad eaties, they *would eat some food*. It made sense—hedonistically.

Looking around at the other Americans and myself, I got my gravest doubts about the drug "culture"—or lack of it. I felt that if I had taken an ordinary, nondrug-using group of Americans and put them in a similar situation, with the potential stakes of six to fifteen years of their lives, there would have been far more unity and guts among them. Drugs and self-discipline don't mix.

I did think about "eating by myself." It was similar to my feelings about smuggling cocaine "by myself" before I had been caught. At that time, I had figured that only I would know what I was doing. And if no one else knew, then it would be as though I had done nothing wrong, right? So why don't I just eat by myself too? No one would know. What difference would it make?

But I did not eat. I would have been breaking a vow to myself. And if I could not control and trust myself now, then when would I? Surely not later. Maybe that was why I was here to begin with: because I had no self-discipline. It was at this time that I began to think seriously about the moral implications of my actions.

July 22, 1974. The hunger strike was two weeks along and there were still a number of Americans holding to it—perhaps thirty. We were getting skinny and weak. One look would now tell you who was fasting. Bones were showing through the gauntness. Early concentration-camp stage.

Whenever I stood up from my bed, I had blackouts. I would have to hold on to the bed and wait for my equilibrium to return. Most of the day all I wanted to do was lie in bed. I did not have enough energy to walk around and talk much, and my mind was even too dulled to want to read a book for long. I had long since lost my appetite and food fantasies. I was minus twenty-five pounds and had lost every trace of fat. My muscles were going and my cheeks were sunken. Strangely, though, in the mornings, after a long night's sleep, I felt good and clear. Throughout the two weeks I had eaten in total a handful of peanuts, a cracker, and a *bolillo* (Mexican hard roll). And I had drunk the juice of perhaps thirty oranges.

Brian and several other Americans were fasting completely—only drinking water. I respected them. Fifteen of the weakest Americans had already been sent to the hospital to receive intravenous feedings. They had all pulled the needles out of their arms. The hospital director ordered them back to "O." He was not going to waste the bed space.

There had been a fair amount of publicity in the press. Now, with our generally declining physical condition, something had to be done. I was hoping. The prison officials and *Gobernación* had gone to the U.S. Embassy to resolve our situation this morning, July 22. We had been told that an answer would be coming shortly.

Once again, the *rumors*. Right now there was a big military bus waiting in front of "O" to take us to the airport to fly us home. The U.S. Embassy IRS limousine was also parked in front of "O" with phony tax charges on all of us so that we could be extradited to the United States. There we would be arraigned, get out on bail, then beat our cases and be free. (I wondered what the hell IRS was doing with a limousine in Mexico City.) The rumors assured us that we were all going home to the United States shortly, and that *we would be free.* Virtually every American believed these rumors as fact, and so did I. And then I saw the Americans do something I had never seen before.

They began packing up.

Some were exchanging addresses, making plans on rendezvousing with their jailhouse friends later to have a beer blast and get high. A real celebration. It sounded as if it were the end of the semester, and everyone had just barely passed and was now going home. "Whewww! What final exams!" Americans were walking around shaking hands, slapping me on the back, congratulating me—absolutely convinced that we were going home. There was no longer any doubt. We *knew.*

The Americans were summoned to the cafeteria. The Colonel of the prison and the minister from *Gobernación* were back from the U.S. Embassy with some important information.

This was it! The announcement! It was only a question of whether we would be deported as undesirable aliens, or extradited on phony conspiracy charges. We filed into the cafeteria to hear the music.

In the corner of the cafeteria sat a short, bespectacled lady draped in heavy silver and turquoise jewelry. She held a note pad and puffed deeply on a cigarette. Not bad looking. I sat next to her, wondering who she was.

"Hi, there," she greeted me loudly, offering me a cigarette. I declined. "My name's Mame Levinson. I live here in Mexico City. What's your name?"

I introduced myself. Mame's accent was straight out of New York City, and her voice was gravelly and rough. Who was she? What was she doing here?

"Dwight, you guys had better watch out. The first police *guardia* has brought in fifty extra billyclubbed guards for a second shift. They're out front of the dorm right now."

That sounded ominous to me. A few other Americans sitting near me had heard what Mame said too. They conjectured that the guards were there merely to escort us to the bus and make sure we did not escape into the streets of Mexico City.

"Ms. Levinson, how did you get in here?" I had to know.

"Call me Mame. I was visiting a friend of mine in another dorm—he's here for a traffic accident—and I heard of your hunger strike so I walked on over to "O.""

"But how did you get in *here? Only* prisoners are supposed to be in this section!"

Her eyes sparkled. "I can do anything I want." Brash and confident.

In the front of the room Gardner announced that he would translate for Cardenas. As Cardenas walked to the front of the room flanked by two bodyguards, Mame muttered, "This guy Cardenas is the worst old crock of shit I've ever seen."

Startled, I turned toward her. Encased in a billowing cloud of grey smoke, Mame sat smiling. Some other Americans had heard her and were laughing.

"*Gobernación* has met with the U.S. Embassy this morning to discuss the U.S. prisoner problem," Gardner translated. The embassy said that the hunger strike must end. The complaints, whatever they are, can be settled by some other means. But the hunger strike must end."

"That's your fucking embassy for you," Mame spoke up again.

Then Cardenas told us to take a vote on whether to end the strike.

"Like you do in the States," added Gardner.

"First, all those who want to end the strike."

Perhaps a quarter of the Americans raised their hands. I was shocked that anyone would vote to end it.

Gardner reminded them that our own U.S. Embassy had told us to end the strike, in addition to *Gobernación* and, finally, the colonel himself.

A few more Americans raised their hands, perhaps a third of the total.

"Now all those who want to continue the strike."

Brian Fitzpatrick, Lee Tyler, and I raised our hands. Three total. I started talking to the people around me, telling them that it was the only real weapon we had, and that without it, we could only beg to them. We *already* knew how that would result.

Then James Dean Brown told us that the prison had *ordered* us to eat, so now we would have to obey.

Obey? Obey and EAT? *You slimy bastard Brown you ate every fucking day of this strike anyhow you goddamned shrivel-faced turncoat faggot cocksucker! And just because they tell you so? What if they tell you to stay here fifteen more years and to keep your mouth shut—or open? What if they tell you to bend over more so they can stick it further up your ass, James Dean Brown, you wretched excuse for a human. Obey?*

Gardner: "Is that all the people voting against ending the hunger strike?"

There were just us three. No more. In soft Spanish I heard the colonel tell Gardner something.

I turned to Mame Levinson. "Did you understand what he said?"

"Yeah. The bastard told Gardner to write down the names of those who voted to continue the strike."

Gardner then told us to go back to our cells and eat. The meeting was over. I got up and stopped in front of Mame's chair.

"I'll see you."

She took my hand and squeezed it. "I'll come back and visit you some time."

"Please do." Whoever she was, this eccentric, tough-talking, chain-smoking lady with her thick Manhattan accent, I liked her and wanted to see her again.

The Americans all walked glumly back to our cells. Visions of beer blasts and orgies were fading fast, back into fantasyland. The other Americans were complaining but there was little hard substance to their feelings. If Gardner had ordered them to eat beans right now, they would have yelled up a storm, and then done it.

I went back to my cell, feeling very weary.

A short while later a number of guards came down the hallway. They called the names of three Americans: Brian Fitzpatrick, Lee Tyler, and Dwight Worker.

Me. I slid out of my bunk. The guards wanted us now, immediately.

"Where to?" I asked a guard, while the other guards were searching for Brian and Lee. The guard did not answer. One of the guards standing next to me was reading a piece of paper, trying to pronounce "Lee Tyler." I looked at it and in ink were written our three names. Below them was written *"A psiquiatría"*—to the psychiatric ward.

A number of Americans had gathered in the hall to see what all the commotion was about. I immediately began shouting to them.

"Hey, they're taking us to the interior—to the psychiatric ward!"

No one did a thing. But what could they do anyhow? They were just as powerless as I was.

I realized that I had no money with me and I would surely be needing some immediately. I asked Roger to loan me some money. He didn't answer. I asked him again. Glazed, vacant eyes. I asked all of the Americans around me if *any* of them could loan me some money for a little while. I would be needing it where I was going.

Blank faces.

I promised to pay them back—but I needed it *right now,* because the guards were ready to take us.

Blank faces.

These were the same Americans who a few hours ago had been slapping me on the back and shaking my hand and making plans to reunite with me—and all I got from them were uniformly *blank faces.*

The guards pushed me along and as I left, the last thing I saw in dormitory "O," besides the bars and gates and locks, was a hall full of people I had once considered my friends.

I would never forget those vacant, blank faces.

12 Psychiatric Ward

They led Lee, Brian, and me through the patio of the main hospital. We saw the remaining Americans who had been hospitalized for not eating lying in the grass in front of the hospital. Brian and I assumed that they were still hunger striking.

The guard let us stop and talk with them for a moment. They told us they had all started eating today. That meant that Brian and I were the last two Americans not eating.

Lee, although naturally bone skinny, had been eating regularly throughout the strike. He always looked as if he hadn't eaten in two weeks. His crime, along with Brian's and mine, had been that he had *voted* to continue to hunger strike. So much for American-style elections in Mexican prisons.

The other Americans felt the hunger strike was hopeless. They told me that those fifty extra guards with billyclubs were there to break the strike if the Americans continued refusing to eat. Brian said that maybe the guards could beat us up, but they couldn't make us chew and swallow. We could still resist. I wanted to persuade them to continue the hunger strike, but the guard led us off to the psychiatric ward.

The guards led Lee, Brian, and me down the stairs to the bottom level of the ward. The blank, grey halls stretched ahead, lined with single isolation cells. I was overwhelmed by the nauseating, acrid stench of vomit, urine, and feces. This had to be the worst hole in the prison. They locked Lee and Brian together in a bottom-tier dungeon cell and put me in a separate but adjacent cell.

I checked out my new quarters. No light, toilet, water, or bed. There was just a hole in the corner to defecate and urinate in. Later that evening I would discover that rats also entered through that hole. There was a small slot where food was slid under the door, and that was that. The cell was totally bare.

It was eight paces long and three paces wide. The only light came through the bars in the otherwise solid door, at an angle from the hallway. We were too deep within the building to see any sunlight whatsoever. It occurred to me that if we were left alone here for very long, we might lose track of the days.

This had to be the *worst* place in the prison. Peering across the hall, I could see into another, larger cell containing a number of Mexicans in various states of unconsciousness. Their one common denominator was that they were all obviously *crazy;* no doubt about that. Eyes askew, catatonic stiffness, incoherent speech, aimless motion—yes, all the people in that cell over there were gone. I just wondered if they were like that before they arrived here, or became like that after . . .

A little while later the orderlies led some patients down the hall, past our cells. One look at their faces told me that they were not operating on the physical plane either. But if this place was a veritable zoo, then we were the newest captured exotic specimens. I had no idea what they planned to do with us.

I could not see Brian or Lee, but we could easily talk to each other. So what did we do now that we had been locked up in the bottom dungeon of the psych ward at Lecumberri prison in Mexico City—in the pushead of the pimple on the asshole of the world?

We laughed and laughed and laughed.

It was gallows humor time. We attacked everything. We laughed at our fate; we complimented Mexico on its hospitality; and we planned our next vacations. We bet each other on who could kill the most rats; we disputed over whose cell was more repugnant; we argued over which of us would receive the first lobotomy. This was the last straw. The whole thing was just too surreal, too extreme, too *extravagant* to react in any other way. Laughing was the only possible sane response to this ultimate example of Mexican justice.

We were making so much noise that some guards warned us to keep it down. One of them pointed to the large tank where all the "real crazies" were kept, indicating we might be (or were) going there. He walked off, angry and threatening.

I wondered if we sounded like the others had. Did they come here like us, only to go insane later? Was this the end of my line? What were we laughing about?

I shut up.

I couldn't sleep at all that night, and it wasn't because of the rats or the cold floor or the human howler monkeys across the hall. Something had snapped inside me. At this point all I could feel was pure, clear hatred—of Mexicans, of Mexico, of Spanish, of anything and everything associated with Mexico. I felt I could subsist on hatred alone—and its essential corollary, revenge. They might be able to take everything else away from me, but they could never, never, *never* even graze the immensity of my loathing and hatred for them.

I was running on the raw nervous energy of hate. I paced the dungeon all night.

Early the next afternoon some guards and orderlies escorted us to the psychiatrist's office. He sat at his desk, hiding behind his pseudo-omniscient crocodile smile: *the beaner shrink.* He wore small, wire-framed glasses and a mouthful of gold teeth. There was so much metal in his mouth that I was surprised he could hold his jaw shut. Surely he would have to speak very slowly. Light-complected, balding, and in his late forties, he reminded me of a short Adolf Eichmann. With that in mind, I figured the gold in his mouth to be worth hundreds of dollars.

I had found myself comparing a number of prison officials to members of the Russian, German, and Italian armies in World War II. Granted that I saw them from less than unbiased eyes; but it was still the case that Colonel Cardenas looked like a fourth-rate Joe Stalin, that Gardner moved and looked like Mussolini. And now, *Señor Doktor Eichmann del Taco.*

He could not stop smiling when he talked, so I knew something was seriously wrong with him. He told me that he was the psychiatrist.

He would start at basics. Just to call his bid, I told him that I too had a degree in psychology. He thought that was "very interesting."

Then Lee asked him in Spanish, "So, Doctor, and what is your problem? What can we do for you?"

He stopped smiling.

"*You* are my problem, the three of you. You have shown antisocial behavior. You have refused to cooperate. We are going to keep you here for observation and perhaps treatment."

Lee interrupted him, still smiling, as he told *Eichmann del Taco* the truth: that he had been eating throughout the hunger strike; that he was just naturally skinny.

The shrink took one look at Lee's bone-thin body and figured Lee was a psychopathic liar—and a bad one at that.

I asked him what he meant by "treatment." *El doktor* explained that it meant staying here on a more-or-less permanent basis and beginning electroshock therapy.

My brain quickly translated that phrase into English, and then—in neural self-defense—into panic.

I knew several people who had had extensive electroshock

treatment. Every last one of them had a somewhat dazed, confused, indecisive air, and could not recall the past at all clearly. One girl I knew, whose parents had forced her into electroshock treatment, remembered nothing prior to age seventeen, when the treatments had ended. She had lost something forever. Truly permanent damage.

Every day we are supposedly losing 100,000 nerve cells. We're all getting dumber and dumber. Biological fatalism. The devolution theory. But no sense to speeding up the process. I got up, walked across the room, picked up a stale, trashy, nutritionally X-rated Mexican cookie and stuck it in my mouth. Lee did the same.

But Brian still refused. I admired him for it, even though it was hopeless. If there had been fifty Americans as steadfast as Brian in the psych ward, perhaps it would have made a difference. But not one person. Six months alone in this place would leave Brian as crazy as the rest of them, and then the prison would swallow him up.

Lee and I talked slowly to Brian. I talked about electroshock, explaining what it might do to him. Brian knew that the threat was serious. He had seen the Mexicans in action too many times already. We told him it was over.

Later that evening, seventeen days after he had begun fasting, Brian ate.

They won.

13 Adjustment

After I began eating in the psychiatric ward, I was sent to the hospital to recuperate. There, with access to decent food, I ate gluttonously—six meals a day. I was ravenously hungry.

After a week I was told to pack my things to move. I thought I was going back to "O," but instead they took me to "F," the dorm in the interior for drug offenders. I panicked. I wanted to be back in "O" with the other Americans, even if Gardner was *mayor* there. We prefer familiar catastrophes to unknown ones.

In front of the gate of "F," I stopped and refused to enter. I told the guard that the last time I was sent to a different dorm, I was stabbed. I was not entering this dorm until I knew I had protection.

The guard went to get his chief, *Siete Cabezas* (Seven Heads), a very short *commandante* who had gotten his name from allegedly killing seven people. He was the chief henchman of Cardenas's prison guards, the same man who had directed the guards the day they had beaten me up in the mechanics' garage. But this time he was all smiles and humor. Somehow I got a strange feeling that since he had once already had me beaten up badly, we would now be friends. I had passed the initiation. He also knew I was afraid. He liked that. He assured me nothing would happen to me. The guards would not touch me.

But my fear was not of the guards; it was of the *mayor* and *commandos*. I told *Siete Cabezas* that if anything happened to me, I would hold him *personally* responsible.

His face turned serious. He then called the *mayor* of "F," Jorge Granados, to the gate.

Granados had already served five years on a ten-year sentence for fraud and embezzlement. He was a large, immensely fat man with powerfully-built shoulders, biceps, and forearms. Later I would learn that he had traveled with the Mexican wrestling team to the Tokyo Olympics in 1964. He and *Siete* talked, and I heard *Siete* tell that I was not *castigado*, but rather *protejido* (protected).

With that, I entered the dorm. I didn't have much other choice.

I was still afraid. I was expecting beatings, *fajinas*, *chochos*, extortion—the whole works. After I was registered in the dorm, I was called to Granados's cell. In clear, loud Spanish, Granados told me that if I didn't make problems, he wouldn't bother me. But if I did, he would fuck me over royally. I was sure he could. He then put me in a cell with three others and told me I would have to do only one week's light *fajinas*.

"Okay, *jefe*," I said, and he dismissed me.

A tall, European-looking man came up to me and introduced himself in impeccable English as Jaime Valdez. He was an Ecuadorian who had lived in New York City for five years and was also doing time for drugs. His wife and three-year-old son were in Santa Marta women's prison in Mexico City. He hadn't seen them in a year. Jaime told me this dorm was not so bad compared to others. Granados, although greedy like all *mayors,* was not as ruthless. The important thing was to play the game with him: don't resist or fight him, pay the rent and other bills, and don't get into trouble. With that, he and everyone else here would leave me alone.

Leave me alone—I hadn't been left alone since I'd arrived here. Gardner, the *commandos,* and the guards had continually been after me, always singling me out from the rest. But then, maybe I had provoked it by fighting back. But for right now, I just wanted to be left alone, so I listened to Jaime.

I did the week's *fajinas* without a problem, keeping a low profile. I was surprised when no one insulted or tried to extort me. For the rest of my time I talked with Jaime and met the other prisoners. Virtually all of them were young Mexicans serving four- to five-year sentences for small marijuana arrests. They weren't heavy criminal types. There were a few South Americans in "F" for cocaine, but no other Americans. I found the prisoners essentially friendly, decent people. I could leave my cell door open all day and seldom would anything be stolen—which was really a surprise.

Then I learned something important. Jaime told me I was "lucky" to be an American, because even though the guards hated Americans, I *looked* like a Canadian.

"But why?"

"The next time they start to beat you up, just tell them you're a Canadian," said Jaime. "You'll see."

I didn't have to wait long. One day an unfamiliar guard "decided" I had stolen a blanket and raised his arm to beat me into confession. "YO SOY CANADIAN!" I yelled, holding my arm up to ward off the blow. But he stopped, looked at me quickly, and walked away. "I don't believe it," I said to Jaime later, "are they afraid of Canadians?"

"Afraid of the Canadian *Embassy,*" said Jaime. "Canadians, Australians, and the British are never beaten or tortured because their governments can bring pressure to bear and just won't allow it."

"Won't *allow* it?" I had to laugh. The great, strong, omnipotent U.S. Embassy was "powerless" to intervene, but tiny (in terms of power) Australia had stopped the torture long ago. I would have to remember that the next time Dan Root came by to "visit."

And Jaime was right about Granados. Although out for money like all *mayors*, he had more class and honor than Gardner. That wasn't saying much, since Gardner was *pura lacra* (pure scum). But at least if you made a deal with Granados and lived up to your end of it, he would most likely do the same. For his part, Granados left me alone, and in his own manner of *patron*, he took a liking to me.

Granados was, among everything else, a buffoon, especially when accompanied by his twenty-four-hour-a-day servant "Gasolino." But in Gasolino's case, "servant" meant that he was actually Granados's slave, punching bag, and sacrificial lamb. Each and every one of Granados's slightest whims was automatically obeyed by the subservient Gasolino. Every day, for some semireal or contrived reason, Granados would publicly punish Gasolino. Sometimes Granados would hook Gasolino by the seat of his pants to a meathook that dangled ominously at shoulder level from the second cell tier. Then Granados and the *commandos* would surround the suspended Gasolino and use him as a *living* punching bag, hitting him hard. Despite Gasolino's screams—or *because* of them—they continued giving the bag a long, hard workout.

As another punishment, Gasolino would be ordered to be someone's *esclavo* and carry him around the dorm to wherever he wanted to go. Gasolino would then spend hours obediently lugging someone around in his arms, attending to all his needs.

Dorm "F," under Granados's supervision, had its own "horse races." The *commandos* would hop on their selected *fajinero* mounts and race each other. The riders carried improvised riding crops and spurred the *fajineros* on with their heels, and other *commandos* bet on who would win. The winning horse might receive a Coca-Cola and, if he was lucky, a decent dinner. Granados might even take a liking to the winning "horse" and patronize him by taking him out of *fajinas* or *chochos* for a few hours.

But all of the losers got the *pura verga* (the pure cock). They were punched around and then forced to pile themselves into a ball of squirming human flesh on the floor. The *commandos* then ran through and jumped on any exposed or unprotected part of the *fajineros*. This was what they got for losing the race, and consequently, their riders' money. It also greatly added to the *fajinero's* incentive to win. So the races, although a joke to

Granados and the *commandos*, were serious business for the *fajineros*, because they surely did not need more punishment.

The 275-pound Granados would often ride too, and who was his chosen mount? Why, it was the 135-pound Gasolino, of course. Gasolino's legs nearly buckled as Granados first jumped on him and then beat on his head to make him run faster. Poor Gasolino was lucky just to complete the laps at a slow stagger while the *fajineros* with lighter riders galloped off far in front of him.

Gasolino had lost again! Poor Granados could never win a race. He has lost five more pesos! That called for punishment, and of the worst sort. Gasolino pleaded with Granados for mercy, but Granados, ever the strict disciplinarian, would have none of it.

"DROP YOUR PANTS!" bellowed Granados.

Gasolino begged and pleaded for mercy, trying to explain that it was not normal for a rider to weigh over twice as much as his mount—that this was not the ideal strategy for winning races. But Granados refused to listen to Gasolino's excuses.

Gasolino dropped his pants.

Granados then sat on the concrete bench and grabbed Gasolino's head. He stuffed it between his legs, under his immense, overhanging belly, leaving Gasolino's naked rear end protruding upward and highly vulnerable to the whole dorm. By prison standards, Gasolino was in a *very* compromising position. Then Granados summoned any and all takers. Quickly a line of dumb-looking, goofy Mexican *peones* queued up behind Gasolino's ass.

The first of the line, while fully clothed, quickly mounted Gasolino's naked buttocks and pretended to fuck him. *Uhh uhh uhh, ohh ohh ohh, ugh ugh ugh.* While the *fuckee*, Gasolino, emitted muffled moans for mercy from between Granados's thighs, the *fucker* continued ooohing and aaahing away as if he were in the midst of orgasm. Eyes rolled deliriously, tongues waggled dementedly, mouths leered, and everybody cheered and heckled as the fucker pumped away. *Dogfucking.*

Then it was the next man's turn at simulated butt fucking; and on and on until they had all finished with Gasolino. Then the *commandos* carried him over to the small, filthy fountain *cum* fish pool and dipped his bare ass in the water.

"TO CLEAN IT UP FOR THE NEXT TIME!" Granados bellowed.

Such were the cultural activities of Lecumberri. The first time I saw this spectacle, I couldn't believe it. But in time I got used to it, since it happened every night. Got used to it? How could anyone?

Granados also decreed that every Sunday night in the dorm there would be a drag revue. All of the dormitory "women" would dress in improvised skirts, padded bras, makeup, and shoddy improvised wigs, and then parade around the dorm. Some of them were done up so well that a casual observer would be fooled. I was shocked the first time I saw two women walking in the dorm late at night, eight hours after visiting hours, and then I realized that their sweeping arm gestures and exaggerated hip movements could only belong to female impersonators.

In dorms such as "A" and "G" there were over twenty full-fledged "women" strutting their stuff and doing their thing. One "woman," *La Cuca*, deliberately transferred from "F" to "G" to live with her "boyfriend." Everyone called him *El Cuco*. *La Cuca* eventually set up a beauty parlor: *La Salon de La Cuca*, of course.

And Lord, could it get outrageous! As the "women" promenaded about, they were universally whistled at and courted by their audience. Prisoners danced with the ladies to radio music in an obscene parody of a fifties sockhop. *Mexican Graffiti*. Dick Clark would have croaked. Some of the men would hold their crotches while leering at the "women" and soliciting them to enter their cells. It was the most grotesque travesty of man-woman courtship ever committed on the face of the planet. Each "woman" would then mince and coo and hesitate coyly among her ladies-in-waiting, like a slut feigning to be selective, and then "accept" her suitor's offer.

Thirty minutes later, she was out on the cruise again, looking for a new "beau." This procession, with all its sleazy mimicry, was a regular event.

Then one evening, one of the "girls" walked up to me and shook her ass. Her "sisters" giggled as she waited for my response to her invitation.

"No, *gracias*." I walked away. Observing was enough.

Every day I ate dinner with Jaime in his cell. We spoke in American English so rapidly that I found myself thinking of him as an American. He shared his food, clothing, and English magazines and books with me, along with some interesting stories. A true *caballero*. Just when we had almost forgotten we were prisoners, he would begin talking about his wife and son. Then tears would come to his eyes.

As I got along better with Granados, he let me have privileges. "F" was not maximum security like dorm "O," and consequently it was easier to move about within the prison. Food, clothing, and most importantly, visitors, could pass the inspection points without much harassment.

Money was still essential in "F," but if I budgeted well, I wouldn't need a whole lot. My parents had been sending $100 a month to representatives at the U.S. Embassy, who were supposed to bring it in to me periodically. But sometimes the embassy messenger wouldn't come for months, and the lack of money in the dorm made things very difficult for me.

Then, "WORK-ER, WORK-ER. *VEN A LA PUERTA! TEINE VISITA.*" The intercom rang throughout the dorm.

I had a visitor! Who? I ran to the front gate and there, in a peasant dress, draped in necklaces and hippy beads, her arms laden with full bags, stood Mame Levinson, smiling broadly.

"Mame!" I hugged her, "Am I happy to see you!"

"Told you I'd visit," she wheezed, the ever-present cigarette dangling from her lips.

I grabbed her bags and escorted her into Jaime's cell. She had brought me cheeses, fresh fruit and vegetables, books, a stack of *Newsweek, Scientific American,* and *New Yorker* magazines, and yesterday's *New York Times:* incredible gems at Lecumberri. At the bottom of the pile of food she pulled out a plastic container and handed it to me. I opened it. It was packed with CRUNCHY PEANUT BUTTER!

"How did you know? I haven't had that in over a year!" I felt suddenly childlike, squealing with delight. I could hold back no longer. I quickly made peanut-butter-and-jelly sandwiches for Jaime and myself. Mame, looking almost like a madonna, puffed on her cigarette while Jaime and I indulged in ecstasy, sweet reminders of America overwhelming our taste buds.

"So what did the bastards do to you in the psych ward?"

"Cured me of hunger striking." I told Mame of the electroshock threat, and she swore at them a barrage that would make a zoo monkey blush.

Mame and I sat and talked the rest of the day and I finally learned the history of this redoubtable prison consort. She had been a social worker in New York City, but had moved to Mexico City fifteen years ago, deciding to retire "very early." She used to love Mexico City, but after watching it quadruple in population in fifteen years, becoming a massive slum, she loathed it now. She planned to sell her house one day and move back to the United States.

Mame spoke a fluent, although Manhattanized, Spanish that could be as eloquent or foul as the situation demanded. She could cajole the highest Mexican official into giving her any privilege, and she could insult the lowest molesting street vermin with a string of obscenities that would turn all eyes accusingly against him as he shrank into the distance. She could get things moving with Mexican bureaucracies that were normally impossible for anyone else to accomplish. Such was her chutzpah. She told me of her friends in the international business and diplomatic community here, and of the outlandish parties she attended. Inevitably Mame ended up drunk and rowdy. She was well read and articulate, and had hundreds of extra books lying around her home. Would I want them? Of course. Was there anything else she could do for me on the outside?

"Yes. Could you please pick up my money and mail at the U.S. embassy and bring it to me? I need it to pay off my bills here."

"Sure, I'll do it. I'm planning on visiting you at least once a week from now on. Anything else I can bring you?"

"Yes." I jumped up and hugged her. "More crunchy peanut butter."

She laughed. Jaime and I escorted her to the gate and I kissed her goodbye.

Mame visited me regularly after that. She obtained a *defensor's* pass in my name so that she could visit me any day of the week. My diet improved with the added protein and vitamins that she brought, and I began receiving such basic articles as writing paper, pencils, and toothbrushes. I eventually told my parents to send the monthly $100 to Mame, thus bypassing the embassy's inertia.

The few visits a week from Mame, accompanied by her intelligent conversation, care packages, and bawdy humor, became the high point of my days in "F." I soon wondered how I could ever have lived here before Mame began visiting me.

Of course, being the only *gringo* in dorm "F" had not been as bad as I had expected. For one thing, I was forced to learn Spanish fluently. Jaime and I often spoke only in Spanish, so there were times in "F" when I didn't speak English for weeks.

But then one day *Mayor* Granados summoned me to his office. He pointed to a new prisoner: tattered, exhausted, and freaked out. A new American. By some arbitrary change in prison policy, all new Americans arriving in Lecumberri would now be sent to "F." The old ones would stay in "O."

Granados ordered me to translate. It was an unpleasant duty to explain to the American prisoner about *fajinas* and the policy of "work or pay." But Granados didn't speak English and the new American didn't speak Spanish, so they both needed my services as translator. Inadvertently I found myself getting involved as arbitrator in other people's problems, and I didn't like it. In the back of my mind, I remembered how James Dean Brown had helped *Mayor* Gardner. I didn't want to be pushed into anything resembling that role.

I personally warned the new American to avoid fights while in the *fajinas* or he would get beaten like I had been. Then I cracked the important news. If he had been arrested at the airport, then he would not be going anywhere. I told him the blunt, raw, dirty truth right now, before his parents blew ten or twenty thousand on Mexican lawyers and corrupt judges to find out the same thing. It would hurt to hear the bad news, but they might as well get it over with. It would be less costly in the long run. He should save his money to live decently in prison.

In the coming months, the new American prisoners reacted in a variety of ways, but their one common denominator was shock. They just *could not believe* that *they* might be in prison that long. I didn't blame them, because neither had I.

When one new American asked me how long I had been here, and when I told him "nine months," he looked horror-stricken.

"NINE MONTHS! YOU'VE BEEN IN THIS HOLE NINE MONTHS!"

"Yep."

"WELL, I'M NOT GOING TO STAY HERE THAT LONG!"

I didn't argue with the prima donna. I just told him the track record on the other arrested Americans. Those were grim statistics. We were batting .000 in 150 tries at the plate.

So I had been in prison nine months. I had had time to see how things did and did not work in Mexico. I had been around more than the new Americans in prison and I had seniority.

Seniority—the one thing you hoped never to attain in prison, but if you did, you had might as well put it to use. Seniority and age were the only things you were assured of getting from prison. So, based on my short experience, I told the Americans why I thought we would not be getting released.

But still the rumors came. The new American prisoners believed every one of them. Ten rumors later they were still believers, despite the fact that they had been wrong on their last ten predictions. That did not make any difference to them, for as one American said to me, "I just have to be right once"—as if his mental attitude alone would change the outcome.

Several new Americans came regularly into my cell to debate why they *knew* that we were going home, as if in convincing me, they would sway the scales of reality. Jake, who was pot-stoned in prison all the time, told me that if we would all *think positively* about getting sent home, we would get sent home. We had to "believe in our dreams."

I asked Jake if he also believed in the Big Pumpkin.

"Look. They can't keep me here that long. I'm a *college graduate.*"

That broke me up. Poor, *precious,* privileged Jake. I dared him to tell that to the Mexican judge. I suggested that he had better put his degree to use by working on a Ph.D. here, because he had a wonderful opportunity to take a seven-year course in "Beaner Studies."

Jake walked out. Good. At least I wouldn't have to listen to him anymore.

Jake's problem was that he treated freedom and heaven alike: if you don't believe, then you don't get there. And the same applies to *deus ex machinas.* If there isn't one to sweep him away from his problems, then he'll create one to do it for him.

I had not heard such blasphemous hippy illogic since Haight-Ashbury. And how do you talk with or convince someone who clings to such mad premises? You don't at all. You just leave them alone to believe what they will, and pay attention to your own survival.

14 Fighting

I saw Brian Harrison Fitzpatrick walking by the dorm gate, escorted by several guards. His head was all taped up and his left arm was wrapped and hung in a sling.

"Brian, what happened?" I shouted.

He turned and looked at me. "Six of them jumped me in dorm "E," where they'd sent me for punishment. I got a lot of stitches, but nothing's broken. But I got to fuck a few of them over before they got me."

"WAY TO GO," I yelled to him as the guards pushed him along, away from the "F" gate.

Fighting. In prison it happens all the time.

Prison is a pressure cooker. You must live with many people with whom you would never associate normally. And not only live with them—some of whom you will come to loathe and hate—but see their faces, hear their voices, and be around them all the time. It is not like out on the street where you can just walk away from someone you do not want to be around. I had been flirting with crime for a while, and now—like it or not—I was finally getting my chance to meet real criminals—the karma of having gotten into crime myself.

After a month of being in prison, I wanted to "get" people for hundreds of reasons. What could I do when I caught someone stealing something out of my cell, or when someone insulted me, or hit me?

Could I go to the guards? No, never never never. Prisoner law does not allow it. I could either yield—or fight. So I fought. *I had to be my own law and my own enforcer*—and if I couldn't enforce my law, then it wasn't worth a damn. In the end fighting was the *only* way to protect my mental and physical territory and rights within prison.

In dorm "O," Gardner had prevented all *gringos* from getting into fights. When fights did occur, the Americans were inevitably blamed and punished *regardless* of who was at fault. This was the policy to keep the *gringos* in line and to squelch any hopes of staging an uprising. It worked very well.

But in "F," prisoners were permitted to fight. I had been moved around enough dorms to know by now that it was very important to let other prisoners know right from the start that they were not going to fuck with me. In my first nine months in Lecumberri, I had been in more fights than in my last ten years. Most of them were quick, short punchouts.

One day I caught Maru, a scummy Mexican thief, in my cell, stealing my wristwatch. In a minute I had knocked him around and made him bleed. Then the *commandos* charged in and broke it up. Maru's last words were that he would kill me.

I learned that it was essential to fuck over badly whomever you were fighting. Mark him, cut his face or mouth, blacken his eye, or chip a tooth—ideally, send him to the hospital for stitches. But do *something* to him so that when he walks around the dormitory afterwards, everyone who sees him will know that *you got him and got him good.* Imprint that message on his face so that he would now be a walking advertisement saying, "Don't fuck around with —— ——." One or two of these and you would be established in the dormitory and, consequently, left alone.

I also learned not to boast after a fight. It was enough to beat a man, too much to rub it in. So I treated my former opponent with silence and respect. I already had enough problems without having to look over my shoulder all of the time.

In "F," when a prisoner wanted to settle it with someone, he would just tell the *commandos.* Then, barring any special circumstances, he would be locked in the *baños* with his opponent to fight it out. One *commando* would remain inside as referee to make sure that the fight remained fair (no weapons) and to break it up when necessary. A fight was broken up when either of the fighters wanted to quit, or when one of them was hurt and bleeding badly. It was a very fair and useful prison setup, in that it served to reduce long-term tension.

Along with skill, endurance, and strength, raw, raging anger is probably the best weapon in fighting a man. The adrenalin rush. You must want to *get that bastard* so much that the act of doing it will be a pleasure. You must be willing to risk getting fucked over yourself in order to get him, and you must be willing to *get down* with him to the end of the fight with that in mind. Raw anger can make fighting a necessary act—a welcome and almost pleasurable relief.

If you lost a fight, it was still essential to mess that guy up badly enough so that everyone else knew it and could *see* it. You also had to make it clear that if the man wanted to fight you again, you would be completely willing to fight him *again* and *again* and *again, con gusto,* until he stopped bothering you.

One day Granados brought a pair of sixteen-ounce boxing gloves into the dorm. Now, instead of watching the fights on television, we would watch our own.

Mexicans are fanatics about boxing. It is their national sport, and they produce many good lightweight boxers. Mexican boxing champs are national heroes and all young Mexican men dream of emulating them. So that night, all 250 prisoners gathered in the patio under the lights to root and box. Some of the prisoners chose their opponents, and Granados paired off the remaining ones. The dorm was in an uproar of excitement, laughter, cheers, and hisses. It was impossible not to get involved, and besides, it was a lot of fun.

An American, John, was called to fight. He was paired against San Chirico, a large, muscular Mexican who weighed 100 kilos. But San Chirico was a totally gentle, kind, and friendly man who would never normally get into a fight. John quickly went in and out at him, hitting the stationary San Chirico at will. Within a minute he had knocked San Chirico on his ass. All the Mexicans were stunned into silence. But I was cheering madly for John. All by myself.

Now it was my turn to fight. I did not want to fight someone with whom I was not angry, so I told Granados that I wanted to fight Ponce, a particularly obnoxious Mexican who was universally hated in the dorm and had just been demoted from the rank of *commando*. Ponce accepted the challenge.

We went at it with no style at all. It was just a raw, brawling slugout until somebody went down. I kept attacking until I cornered him against a wall, hitting his head as hard as I could. He fell.

The whole dorm was screaming. Everyone *did* hate Ponce.

Ponce got up and we went at it again. His guard was down and I hit his head as fast and as hard as I could. It felt good. He kept moving backward until his back was against the gate. Then I hit him again and again until he went down. With that, the fight was over and I was declared winner by TKO. The whole dorm was in an uproar.

Although the fight had lasted just a few minutes, I was totally exhausted. But I felt great. Fighting is like that.

Jake, the new American in the dorm, knew nothing of the prison at all. He was young, skinny, gentle, and innocent. He had never been in a fight in his life. He was a *nice* hippy boy.

Jake was *terrorized* at what he saw. He feared he would have to get down there and fight someone, and he *just did not do* such things. As I walked past him, Jake got my attention.

"Hey," he whispered nervously. "Do you have to do this very often?"

"Every night."

He gulped.

The sixteen-ounce gloves prevented anyone's face from getting badly messed up. A man could not be mauled with those gloves, but he could be beaten up in front of the whole dorm, fair and square. He could not, of course, *refuse* to fight. In Mexico, it is noble and honorable to lose, as long as one loses while fighting. I could dig that. But to refuse a challenge in Mexico is totally unacceptable.

The next American to fight after me won by a knockout too, so we Americans were batting three KOs, zero defeats. I was rooting for the Americans like the worst jingoist ever. I couldn't help it. I wanted *us* (U.S.) to win and that was that.

But finally, in the fourth fight, the American tired quickly. They ended the fight and gave the decision to his opponent. So we had won three by knockout, and lost one by decision. Not bad. The Americans had done respectably well that night. We could hold up our heads. The Mexicans acknowledged this and respected us for it, and we would get along better with them afterward because of it. It was good camaraderie.

I am sure that no one at the U.S. Embassy would ever have seen it this way, but that night down there in front of that shouting crowd of 250, the Americans were, in our own way, defending the honor of our country.

15 Long Distance

There was one group of prisoners within Lecumberri that was totally different from all the rest: the *politicos*. Hundreds of political prisoners were isolated in Lecumberri, and I spoke with them whenever I had the opportunity. Without exception they were honest, polite, informed, and always eager to debate some issue. Generally they had excellent sports teams and were the very best of chess players. They didn't use drugs or participate in any of the prison rackets. Unlike the other prisoners, they seemed to have a sense of ethics.

Some *politicos* were dedicated to the armed revolution of Mexico. They had sentences of up to fifty years, so it made no difference what they said. I was awestruck at how they could reconcile themselves to such long sentences with such equanimity. They saw their personal misfortune as part of a greater struggle.

Other *politicos* were serving long sentences for unauthorized demonstrations, pamphleteering, union organizing, and strike leading. They had not been violent, but had been imprisoned for their *thoughts*. I was even more stunned. True political prisoners.

All the *politicos* were isolated in dorms "M" and the top tier of "O," living under the most security of anyone in Lecumberri, or in Mexico for that matter. By Mexican prison standards, the *politicos* were at the very bottom of the scale, even lower than the *gringo drugeros* and the child rapists. They were regarded as social cancer—these, the very best of the prisoners.

I compared myself to them. What had I done? I had tried to smuggle drugs. I was imprisoned solely because of my greed. In my own eyes, I was no more than a common criminal. For a while I carried my own cross, but in time, I came to forgive myself under the condition that I would conduct myself more positively in the future. I decided that if I were ever to go to prison again (if one could have a choice in such matters), it would only be for something I believed in.

I realized that I needed self-discipline to gain control over my life as much as possible; I did not want to emerge from prison a warped, violent ex-con or a hopeless drug addict. I decided to use my time as best I could for my personal growth, like the *politicos*. I was thinking about how to do this when an incident shocked me into action.

It happened while Jaime and I—along with about seventy-five other Mexican prisoners who were in various states of illness and injury from beatings—were waiting in the courtyard to see the prison doctor. The 50-by-100-foot patio was surrounded on three sides by the hospital, and on the fourth by a gate where guards monitored all access to the hospital. Along the edge of the patio were several concrete benches shaded by the trees which kept the area cool and comfortable and made it the only aesthetically pleasing place in the entire prison.

A tall Mexican walked by me carrying the day's *Prensa*, a Mexico City tabloid. As he passed by me I asked him if I could borrow it, but he ignored me. A moment later I heard a loud slapping sound. I turned, and ten feet to my side I saw him repeatedly jabbing a smaller Mexican with the newspaper. The small man quickly pulled out a long knife and swung it several times at the tall man, missing each time. As the other prisoners rapidly scattered, the tall one moved in again, reaching in under the little man's arms and poking him hard with the newspaper. It made no sense to me that he was attacking an armed man with a newspaper—until I saw the blood on the man's chest.

While the two stood facing each other off, the other prisoners scurried en masse to the far side of the patio. I was too stunned to move. The small man took a step backward, wavered, and then fell back, banging his head hard against the wall and then much harder with a deep, dull thud on the cement floor. There was a finality about that fall.

The tall man immediately dropped his newspaper and took off running. Out of the newspaper bounced a long, handmade knife. In that same instant I noticed that the entire abdomen of the fallen man was covered with blood that was gushing into a puddle on the cement. Blood had splattered everywhere.

Jaime kept repeating, "Oh my God, oh my God, oh my God," as we watched the man's abdomen rising and falling with less and less frequency.

My emergency medical technician training ran through my mind and I thought I should do something *right now*. I started toward the man, but Jaime grabbed my arm.

"Get away or they'll blame it on you," he whispered. I looked around. Every single Mexican prisoner was against the wall on the opposite side, as far away as possible from the dying man. I was closer to him than anyone else. Jaime steered me to the far wall.

I stared at the wall. More blood flowed. Just when I thought that he surely must now be dead, his midsection lifted for a long moment, then dropped down again.

To my amazement, no stretcher arrived. There was not a guard in sight, although I had never previously seen the hospital patio without at least two or three of them.

Ten minutes passed. No one moved. The man lay still. For that man to die alone amongst so many people in such a horror show of a prison had no more meaning than a rat getting clubbed to death in a garbage pile. Alive, and then dead—and then nothing.

Life suddenly seemed so cheap and fleeting, so easy to lose. It did not make one iota of difference to the dead man what they did to the murderer. And if someone had wanted it, that life could have been mine. That thought overwhelmed me. I suddenly felt more vulnerable than ever before.

Jaime was still staring at the corpse, chanting "Oh my God, oh my God, oh my God," when the stretcher finally arrived.

They made all the prisoners stay in the patio for the remainder of the afternoon. Photographers took pictures of the blood, and then the detectives arrived—six hours after the murder. They body searched all of us, looking for knives, wounds, blood—evidence. Perhaps they thought that the murderer had an accomplice among us. I was convinced that they had caught the murderer within minutes after the act, because after he fled the hospital patio he would have had to run down a passageway that was always patrolled by five to eight guards. Any one of them would have caught the murderer immediately. But as the detectives searched us for knives, it became obvious that they were still looking for the murderer.

I knew who the murderer was, and so did everyone else. There was no way that seventy-five Mexicans were going to keep a secret. One of them would eventually squeal. Not publicly, or by signing a *declaración*, for any witness would know that the murderer would then kill him. But privately, one of the witnesses would talk. He would do so to gain some special favor from Colonel Cardenas. And if the Colonel thought he knew who the murderer was, he would have no trouble creating a case against him.

Days passed and still the murderer was not found. I couldn't understand it. Why had the police suddenly been absent from the patio at the time of the murder? Why had the stretcher taken fifteen minutes to arrive from only fifty feet away? How had the murderer run past three or four checkpoints without being apprehended immediately? Why had the police not broken one of the seventy-five witnesses? There could only be one answer. It had been a prison-arranged murder, paid off at the top, with Colonel Cardenas getting most of the money.

Later I learned the full story. The man whose murder I witnessed had been involved with a group of Latin American cocaine smugglers who had been arrested in Mexico with *150 kilos* of coke. Two Costa Ricans were allegedly to take the blame, while the other six would pay large bribes and go free. These six, led by a Nicaraguan, Juan Nuñoz, promised to get the two fall guys out of prison at some future date. But the two Costa Ricans backed out, feeling they were being set up. They decided to go it on their own in the courts, in hopes of getting a better sentence. And maybe they would have; but in the dorm, the law was different. They were both killed in dormitory "G" one day in late March 1974. I was in *castigado* in dorm "A" at the time and I had seen their flimsy coffins being loaded onto an open-bed truck that was also carrying refuse.

The man whom I had seen die in the courtyard had helped murder the Costa Ricans. Later he too had apparently threatened to talk. And now, he was dead. He didn't understand that Juan Nuñoz and Colonel Cardenas were good friends—as long as Juan had continued paying Cardenas the thousands of dollars that he had promised.

In the coming months, there would be two more murders revolving around Juan Nuñoz, both of them unsolved. Nuñoz told me that he had paid over half a million dollars to his lawyers to go free. Four months after the murder, Juan Nuñoz and the four remaining loyal members of the original band *did* get released. Their reassembled gang is bringing cocaine into the U.S. right now.

One hundred fifty kilos of cocaine. That was more than the total amount that all the Americans in Lecumberri put together had been caught with. And Nuñoz's gang is now free and carrying on its business. The drug program in Mexico might have been putting a lot of small independents away behind bars, but it was not stopping drug trafficking at all. In fact it was contributing to it.

That lone body in the patio kept haunting me. It could have

been me. I told myself to be careful. This journey was about survival. I had to live through this thing and get myself out of here.

First, I swore that as long as I was here, I would as much as possible stay away from such sordid affairs and try to live a life of my own choosing. I would get a private cell—really private: no roommates or unexpected visitations by other prisoners. I would refuse to fit myself into the mold of prison life. In a cash deal with Granados, I was "allowed" to rent cell 39. It was filthy and bare and measured ten by seven feet. Three of its walls were of thick metal and the fourth of brick. The brick wall had a barred window about nine feet up, through which I could see a tree growing in the patio. By prison standards, this cell had a view. The door to the cell was solid metal with no barred window in it. An inside lock could be improvised so that I could, surprisingly, be assured some privacy. A sink provided cold running water at odd hours during the day, its waste water draining into a metal bowl that served as a toilet. The only means of flushing the toilet was to fill a large container with water and dump it down the bowl. I was lucky in that my cell had both a working sink and toilet—a rarity in prison. Cell 39.

But other than this, the cell was bare. No chairs, tables, shelves, or beds. If I wanted any of these, I would have to buy or rent them from the *mayor*. The dorm was his concession.

I slept on the floor my first night and was trampled by mice. There were ten of them running around at any one time, but at least they weren't the rats that flourished at ground level. Cell 39 was also swarming with bedbugs, lice, and other bizarre human bloodsuckers that I had never seen before. It was a case study in parasitology.

I would never be able to read or study or do anything until the vermin were wiped out, so after one sleepless night, I declared war. Normally I would never use DDT, but after squashing fifty blood-filled bedbugs, I quickly changed my mind and bought some from the prison store. With a bandana tied over my face, I hyperventilated and then stepped into the cell with the spray gun. I sprayed DDT into every crack, crevice, and corner of the nearly empty cell. Total biochemical warfare. Then I left the cell closed off all day.

That evening I opened the door to let the cell air out for a while, then swept and washed out the whole place, leaving a pile of hundreds of parasites in front of my cell. I knew I hadn't killed all of them.

Now the mice. Closing up all the mouseholes with cement was relatively simple, but there was no way of stopping them from coming through the barred window to maul the food on my shelf. I soon realized that the only way the mice would get to the shelf was by walking up a 220-volt wire that I had strung up for lighting. Since I didn't have any mousetraps, I decided to use this wire to my advantage by stripping the insulation from a small section of the wire that ran to the food shelf. Then I propped another bare wire that had been grounded to the metal wall directly over the bare hot wire. Any mouse walking along the hot wire would have to reach up and touch the ground wire, thus creating a short with its body.

That night, I eagerly turned off the light and lay down. A short while later I heard the loudest squeak ever uttered in the history of mousedom. I flipped on the light switch and there was the mouse lying on his back in the middle of the floor, six feet to one side of the electrical trap.

Boy, had he jumped!

His tail was lashing back and forth and his toes were trembling. Dead, I figured. It was just his nerves. I started to pick him up with an old rag, but when I touched him, he rolled over, ran around in a short circle, and then took off across the floor to freedom.

Some nerves.

Either I would have to club the mice as soon as they landed on the floor, or they would get away. Then I had an idea. I filled a five-gallon empty lard can half full with water and propped it on the sink directly below the electric trap. I turned off the light and got back in bed.

A little while later I was awakened by another monstrous squeak, followed by a splash. I jumped up excitedly and flipped on the light. Sure enough, there was the little dumbo-earred varmint swimming in the water. Probably the same one. Flushing him down the toilet, I got an idea. I turned to the wall and scraped on it: Dwight: I; Mice: 0. I felt much better when I went back to sleep.

When I woke up for the headcount the next morning, there were three more drowned mice in the can. I marked "IIII" on the wall and ran downstairs for the 6:00 a.m. lineup.

Long Distance 113

The next night I got five more, but still the cell was loaded with mice. Wow, if this kept up, I would kill 1,500 my first year! That might make *Guinness*. There were thousands and thousands of mice and rats in the prison, and I must be the only one killing them. The other prisoners seemed to get along just fine with them. Sometimes I thought that the rats and the Mexicans were allies; and in my worst moments, they even began to look alike. I must just be liquidating the overflow from other cells and dorms. The mice were multiplying much faster than I could kill them. It looked like a hopeless battle, but strangely enough, I was enjoying it.

Mame finally brought me three solid metal mousetraps from the street. When each trap was set, the trigger was so insensitive that the only way a mouse would ever spring it would be by jumping from a twenty-foot ledge and landing directly on the trigger. In any other event, these traps would only serve for mouse feeding. But if the trap did go off, the spring was so strong that the mouse would be instantly beheaded. I had to be careful walking around the cell lest I lose some toes.

I bent, filed, adjusted, and jerry-rigged the traps until they were finally sensitive enough to spring. Then I positioned them around my cell. It looked like an armed camp during a state of seige.

As soon as it got dark, a trap went off. Five minutes later another trap zapped, and then the other. It sounded like castanets. Every ten minutes I had to put down my book and empty a trap. I was killing them faster than I could reset the traps.

This went on for the next few weeks. The score on the wall went into the hundreds. And then, suddenly, the attack ended. The traps fell silent. The food in my cell went unmolested and the cell was at last free of little scurrying and munching noises. No longer would I be interrupted by the insidious creeping of parasites and rodents over my body.

I painted the cell a cheerful yellow and beige, in contrast to the drab prison gloom throughout Lecumberri. Then I acquired a large bed, a table, chairs, and some bookshelves, and built a functional kitchen counter next to the sink, but very close to the toilet. Too close—I made a lid for the toilet, being careful not to forsake all vestiges of civilization. My cell was finally becoming clean and livable.

One day I spied a lizard scurrying about the wall. After much stalking, with little thought about why I was doing it, I finally caught the lizard. "Now what?" I thought, while it squirmed, biting my finger surprisingly hard. Then it dawned on me. *A pet.* Of course. This was just what cell 39 and I needed.

Because he was always so willing to bite me, I named him *El Chingon* (the mean fucker). I kept him in a glass jar while a friend built a wood-and-glass cage. Then I let out the word to the other Mexican prisoners that I was in the market for other live lizards. Within two days I had five of them, including two over six inches long—almost as big as *El Chingon.*

And now what to feed them? I caught a DDT-immune cockroach and tossed it in. It was eaten before it could bounce twice. The first day, my lizards ate over fifty cockroaches. That was a lot of vermin, and more work catching them. So I assigned my ever-faithful houseboy Blas the additional responsibility of lizard feeding. He got a five-peso-a-week raise, and thus went about the vermin catching cheerfully.

Blas fed the lizards for a week. But then we ran into a problem: we were out of cockroaches. After months of spraying, clubbing, stomping, squashing, and mashing, we had not stumbled onto the final solution until we began lizard feeding. Blas and I made the rounds, visiting our Mexican friends to see who had the dirtiest, most vermin-infested cell. There were many candidates. We finally chose a nearby cell and asked them if we could have their cockroaches.

They all looked at us as though we were *passando la verga* (passing them the dick), which in Mexican slang means putting them on. But no, we weren't. They consulted among themselves and decided that we could have their cockroaches for *five pesos a week.* I told them that they were now trying to *passar la verga* to me. But no, they swore they had the "best" cockroaches in the entire dorm. Finally, we settled on five pesos a week for the cockroaches, but only if they would in turn pay *us* five pesos a week for the "exterminator's fee." It was a deal. We shook on it. I gave them five pesos, and they gave me five pesos.

Over the next month I added a scorpion, a black widow, and a mouse to my prison zoo. On visiting days, some prisoners would bring their children to watch the feeding of the lizards. It was a big hit. The little kids would cheer, clap, and laugh as the lizards gobbled up the roaches. Sometimes the bolder children would even throw a cockroach to them. They smiled even more when the lizard ate their cockroach.

One day I returned to my cell to find that the black widow had inexplicably escaped from her cage into *mine*. I searched all over for her, but I couldn't find her. I didn't sleep very well that night. Her freedom intimidated me.

Cages within cages; and a zoo within a zoo.

I needed money to live here. I felt like a parasite bleeding my parents of $100 a month. Other Mexican prisoners earned meager amounts by making ponchos, rugs, and other saleable items. Their families came in regularly to pick up their wares and sell them on the street.

A Mexican prisoner could obtain a "work commission"— permission to rent space in one of several supervised, antiquated prison shops to do his work. Not only could he thus earn some money to support himself, but if he was extremely industrious and frugal, he could even help support his wife and family on the street. But the best part about the work commission was that for every two days a prisoner worked, he was supposed to receive one day off his sentence.

On paper it was a very humane arrangement, and in practice it motivated many Mexican prisoners to utilize their time. But making money was not so easy. Before anything the prisoner made could leave Lecumberri, the prison taxed it for one-third of its value, so work commissions were very convenient for the prison too. Cardenas had his hand in everything.

But for the Americans it was a different story. First, nobody in the maximum security dorms "M" or "O" was allowed a commission, and "O" was where almost all the Americans were. But now that I was in the lesser security dorm "F," I applied for a work commission in the artists' shop. Cardenas rejected it. I then applied for the carpenters' and metalworkers' shops. Again both applications were rejected, as was my application to get access to a typewriter. I asked *mayor* Granados why, and he told me that Cardenas didn't like the Americans in general, and hated me in particular. Cardenas wanted me to do my sentence *a punta cola* (to the end of the tail) with no work commissions whatsoever.

I walked back to my cell. No two-for-one work commission, no way to make money. I knew Cardenas hated us, but I didn't know he would go after me with such a vengeance. Unless I could figure out some business to set up on my own, I would remain dependent on my parents and brother *a punta cola*.

Mame continued visiting the Americans in "F" regularly, each time bringing food, reading material, and living essentials. We all grew to love and depend on her in a way that even we did not realize—until the U.S. Embassy intervened.

Another American in "F" and I still had some money at the U.S. Embassy that we needed. We had personally asked their representatives, and sent letters and messages to them, requesting that they bring us our money, but either deliberately or out of their own inertia, they had refused to do it. Since Mame had retrieved money for me from the embassy before, I finally asked her if she would pick up our money.

"Of course. I'll get it this afternoon and bring it to you tomorrow."

We gave Mame written, signed notes giving her the power to pick up and deliver our remaining money. She left cheerfully with the notes.

We did not see her again.

A week later we received a letter from her. She had gone to the U.S. Embassy and presented Vice-Consul Katherine Mullins with our note.

Seeing Mame's name on the note, Vice-Consul Mullins commented, "Oh, so you're the one who wrote that critical letter about us to Senator Jacob Javits."

"Yes, and to a lot of other congressmen too."

Mame and Vice-Consul Mullins then proceeded to argue about the U.S. Embassy's role regarding the U.S. prisoners. In the end, Vice-Consul Mullins refused to give Mame our money.

The next day when Mame came to visit us, the guards immediately took her directly to Colonel Cardenas's office. Cardenas told her she was in serious trouble for slandering the prison and the U.S. Embassy. Mame began to protest, but Cardenas shouted at her to shut up right now or he would arrest her on the spot. Mame sat silently for the next thirty minutes as Cardenas quoted her conversation with Vice-Consul Mullins. Cardenas's sheer rage frightened even Mame. Then Cardenas gave her the verdict. She was banned forever from Lecumberri by orders from above, and she had to get out right now. Fearing for her safety, she immediately left the prison.

With her went the books and magazines, the fresh food full of protein and vitamins, her lively conversation and high spirits, and all the other essential things that she had regularly brought us to keep us going. In one fell swoop, we Americans in "F" were back to nothing.

More help from the U.S. Embassy.

Night was the only time when the dorm was quiet. I appreciated the 10:00 lockups because the ensuing silence and privacy allowed me to read and write. I became nocturnal, sleeping in the mornings and early evenings. With such a schedule, and by putting on mental blinders, it was possible to obliviate much of the prison. I did not see many prisoners and I talked to even fewer. I had my program—a schedule of things to do for the day—and when I stuck to it, I was much less conscious of being in prison. I began to transcend my surroundings.

The best thing I did for my mind was to read. I devoured hundreds of books, more than all I had read in my previous ten years of freedom. I came to enjoy a good historical account or profound novel as a rare delicacy, to be savored to its fullest. I discovered that when I was in the midst of an informative, or moving, or enlightening book, I was doing something I would have done regardless of where I was. Therefore, I *was not in prison.* A good book could take me beyond the walls.

Getting books in was always a chore. The guards were suspicious of contraband and drugs, and worse yet, of maps and coded escape plans. The most innocent book in English aroused the guards' darkest suspicions, for the only thing the Mexican prisoners ever read were comic books and girly magazines. Many bribes had to be paid to receive books.

But once in prison, books were valuable gems. After the original owner had read it, a book in prison became everybody's property, with a long waiting list for it. Every American had eventual rights to the others' books, and consequently, there was always a large, floating library, which worked to everyone's advantage.

One day a copy of Amnesty International's *Annual Reports 1974-75* was passed on to me. How it got in I don't know, for it was definitely prohibited material. Just to have been caught with it would have meant trouble. I had heard about AI previously, and I was interested in them even though I was not a political prisoner. Amnesty had sent a mission to Lecumberri in the summer of 1975 to investigate charges that Mexico was holding political prisoners guilty only of advocating their beliefs. I was impressed that Mexico allowed Amnesty International to visit, for no other journalists or investigators had ever been allowed to visit the *politicos* of Lecumberri. No doubt this visit was more than just an annoyance to the government. But to have denied Amnesty access to dorms "M" and "O" would have hurt Mexico more in the long run, for it would have been an implicit admission that the government *did* have something to hide in its dealings with political prisoners. After the visit by Amnesty, the treatment of the political prisoners in Lecumberri improved noticeably.

I picked up the AI *Annual Reports* with renewed interest, and read about the increasing horrors that were happening around the world to nonviolent political dissidents, violations of human rights far worse than anything that had happened to me. I read excerpts from the AI 1975 *Report on Torture*, and from my limited perspective I could finally get my head up out of my own situation and empathize with the political prisoners throughout the world. I began to realize how fragile a democracy could be, and how much constant support these prisoners need. Amnesty International might be leading a nearly impossible campaign against the increasing incidence of oppression and torture on the planet, but at least they are doing something.

I read Rose Styron's *Special Report on Chile*, a horrifying documentation of the death of a democracy. It became vividly clear to me that internationally, the United States had at times worked directly against the democratic interests of other countries.

But although U.S. activities overseas had often been less than democratic, I felt that the individual's rights within the U.S. were strong and undeniable. With the hard-earned insight of a prisoner abroad, and with publications and activities such as Amnesty International's to learn from, I began to respect and support civil liberties as if I had never heard of them before. In my mind, I felt myself fitting back into what the United States was intended to be, and what it meant for me. It was just that I had six more years to wait in prison before I could get back.

One day I received a book I had not been expecting: *Gulag II*. I had already read *Cancer Ward, First Circle,* and *Gulag I* by Aleksandr Solzhenitsyn, but I had not read anything like *Gulag II*. For the next month I read and reread it, revising my perspective of what other people had endured. My opinion of my imprisonment changed forever. With just one long, cool, objective assessment of the millions who shared Solzhenitsyn's fate, my experience seemed almost trivial.

But my body began to ache from sitting at my desk and staying in my cell all day. I needed exercise. Ever since my arrival at Lecumberri, I had watched other prisoners in the patios and courtyards walking back and forth, back and forth, silent and oblivious to everything. This struck me as strange—a serious symptom of *too much prison*. But now I found myself walking a continuous circle in the patio and enjoying it greatly. With the contrived privacy of continual motion, I would sing and think, take imaginary journeys, and dream of freedom. Afterward I would feel greatly refreshed and relaxed.

But I needed more physical exertion. There were some barbells in dorm "F," so I began working out daily. It felt good to exercise until my body was so sore that I could feel the delineation of each and every muscle. Every day I tried to break my personal weight record, to push myself beyond what I had done previously. I was lifting more than my body weight over my head, and with each additional improvement, my spirit felt more powerful. I might be wasting my life in prison, but at least I was getting stronger.

With lesser security precautions in dorm "F," I was finally allowed to go to *campo* twice a week. *Campo* was a 100-by-200-meter field within the prison boundaries, surrounded by double walls and posted with many gun turrets and guards armed with machine guns. But far beyond the walls to the north, I was amazed at what I saw. *A mountain*. What a relief. Until now, I had seen nothing on the horizon for a year except prison walls, where reality ended. My heart rushed. For the longest while I stood still, staring at it.

A few trees and some grass grew in *campo*. I was so relieved to be free of the concrete, bars, and overcrowded oppressiveness of the dormitory. To be able to lie on a sparse patch of grass, or walk in a relatively long, straight, uninterrupted line, or to run on dirt, was such a pleasure that at first it almost felt like freedom. I wanted to go to *campo* every day.

Campo was divided into a soccer field, a baseball diamond, a basketball court, and a handball court. In one corner stood a defaced, crumbling monument that had commemorated the execution of two enemies of the Mexican Revolution. Next to it was an old stone wall pitted by countless rifle bullets. I wondered how many more nameless deaths had been forgotten here.

After prolonged negotiations and finagling with Granados, I managed to join both the basketball and baseball teams. With it came permission to go to *campo* daily. Although we always had to watch out for gangs or robbers with knives there, I never missed an opportunity to go.

For my first several visits to *campo,* I surveyed every last angle and corner there. *Campo* was the nearest I had ever been to the outside of the prison, since all the dorms and work areas of the prison were located near the center. But just beyond those double walls surrounding *campo* was freedom. Surely there must be some way to go over those walls: a catapult or rope ladder, a climb, and a charge over to a getaway car on the other side. If some of us joined together, it could be done. Some would make it, some would not; but at least one way or another we would all be out of here. Every day, the prisoners in *campo* watched the motions and routines of the guards every bit as much as the guards watched the prisoners.

Then I saw a way out. Somehow I could make a uniform identical to that of the guards. Gradually I could smuggle it to *campo* and hide it there. Then one day I could hide myself in *campo* until nighttime. I would put the uniform on before the night *lista* (roll call), and with the aid of a grappling hook and rope ladder, quickly scale the wall to the guards' catwalk. From there I would only have to walk down the long catwalk to the outside wall, and then drop down to the real "outside." With a getaway car, I would be free.

I wrote up a list of everything I would need and would have to do. There would be at least one machine gun turret between me and the outside wall. I knew that if the guards did not see me mount the catwalk, they would not shoot me in my uniform. But as I walked through the turret I would have to say something to the guard manning it. He would then know I was not another guard. To escape, I would have to disarm him quietly. But how? He would shoot me first. Inevitably, I deduced what my plan was missing.

A gun.

Were these the stakes? I hesitated, not at all willing to take such a drastic risk. I would have to study the guards' motions at *campo* more, without being too conspicuous about it. Maybe I could watch the guards while running laps.

So I began running. At first it was just pain and agony—a poor way to study the guards' schedules and patterns. Then the more I ran, the less I watched the guards. My immediate interest became the running itself.

For the first two months I could not run over ten laps—four miles—even though in my mind I had already set my goal to run a full marathon (twenty-six miles) nonstop. Running now assumed primacy in my life. But every time I completed only ten laps my lungs would simply close, leaving me gasping and struggling to catch my breath. Asthma. The altitude of 5,000 feet and the foul, polluted air of Mexico City were not helping either. I had reservations about breathing that air so deeply for so long while running, but it was either that or nothing, so I kept trying to push myself further and further. I ran at eight miles an hour, so I was not overpacing myself. My kneecaps had swollen at first, but in time this pain diminished. My legs were strengthening. But I still could not get beyond eight miles; I just did not have the wind. I began to wonder if I had it in my physiology to run any further. Perhaps I just was not built for it.

Back in my cell one night, I felt I had finally found something to write to my parents about. I told them how I was running and weightlifting. I reported my progress in unnecessary detail. I also wrote of the books I had read and what I was studying. No longer did my letters dwell on the (im)probabilities of my being home, or the ennui and void of prison life.

The letters from home changed correspondingly. Since my arrest, my parents had always been astonishingly supportive, writing encouragements and sending money regularly. But now my mother's letters became more alive. She was happy to hear of my exercise programs, reading, and studying. She thought my idea of running a marathon would be impossible, although it would be a good goal to set. "If nothing else, do it by willpower alone," she said in one letter. But most important to me, she and Dad were not worrying about me as much, and I felt much better because of it.

Before I ran the next time, I concentrated for several hours on making the distance. I was going to run over ten miles. I had already tried this distance several times without success. This time I swore to myself that I was not going to yield to the pain.

I kept running and running. By now my surveillance of the guards had become secondary to my goal of running the distance. So now I watched their motions on the wall to divert my thoughts from the pain.

I passed the eight-mile mark at one hour and went on in stride to ten. Feeling a strong second wind I continued until I had run thirteen miles. I was ecstatic to have made it as easily as I had. Although my legs were so sore that I had trouble walking for three days, my spirits were so boosted that they more than compensated for any physical pain. I had run half a marathon. But then I remembered what was said about the marathon: "After twenty miles, you're halfway there." I still had a long way to go. I calculated that at the pace I was running, it would take me three hours and twenty minutes to run twenty-six miles. Since we were not permitted out to *campo* for more than two hours, I did not see how it would be possible. But occasionally on Saturdays when we had a sports competition, the guards might let us stay at *campo* for three hours or even longer.

The following Saturday, I went to *campo* with the basketball team, ready to try my own three-hour marathon. To my surprise I saw Roger sitting on the grass. I hadn't seen him in six months.

"Roger, hello! What have you been doing?"

He smiled and shrugged his shoulders, indicating with his arms the walls surrounding us. Yes, Roger, we're in prison. I'm conscious of that. Dorm "O" had managed to assemble a baseball team and get it out to *campo,* and Roger had come along. This was his first day at *campo.* I remembered him in "O," always sitting in the sun in the concrete patio. The only difference now was that he was sitting on the grass.

Then Roger's face lit up. "According to good sources, we're all going to be extradited to the U.S. by Christmas. Our people up there are working on it, with lawyers."

Jake, who had been sitting nearby, heard Roger, and eagerly came to talk. Within moments they were riding a wave of euphoria, going home and free.

"Roger, do you want to run some laps with me?" I interrupted.

He looked surprised. "Naw—I think I'm going to sit here and enjoy the sun. Besides, I just smoked a joint." He giggled.

As he and Jake picked up on the latest rumors, I took off running.

I ran and ran, stopping only to get drinks of water and then take off again—running, running, running running. After an hour I was in excruciating pain. My body screamed "STOP!" The pain welled to a certain point beyond which it couldn't get worse. It held me there on hot coals, daring me to find an excuse to stop. I was hoping for a storm, for a court summons, for anything that was beyond my control.

But despite the pain, I found I could breathe easier. My lungs and throat were wide open, working with me, gathering as much oxygen as possible. For the first time I felt a unity of body and mind.

Stopping quickly for a drink of water after one and three-quarters hours, I felt my legs begin to tighten up. Immediately I started running again, knowing I couldn't let myself stop anymore.

Two hours. It began to rain. Small, cold drops at first against my wet, oily, tanned skin. I half expected them to burst into steam from my body heat. The cold rain came down harder, driving the sports teams from the open fields to the awnings. An hour ago this would have been the perfect excuse for me to have stopped running, but not now. I had gone too far. The rain now felt soothing on my hot body. I bent my head back and opened my mouth. Sweet rain.

Slowly I realized that the pain was no longer getting worse. It had gotten as bad as it could get. And if it couldn't get worse, then it was getting better. My legs plodded on catatonically through the mud, unable to stop themselves.

Two hours and thirty-five minutes: Yes, I can. I am going to make it. A rush came over me, at last knowing that I was serious about running a marathon. Just slightly, through the pain and stiffness, my pace picked up. Forty-nine laps down, sixteen to go. Keep going.

2:45. I heard the whistle blow, then saw the crowd of prisoners begin to move to the exit gates. The guards were waving us to go back to the dorm. No. Not now. Please let me finish. I can't quit now.

As I jogged past the exit gate, a guard put his arm up, motioning me to stop, as if he were rescuing me from my self-imposed sentence.

With my body drenched by sweat and rain, heart throbbing, kneecaps and ankles swollen, legs stiff, and diaphram muscles so sore that simple breathing hurt, I threw my heavy arms over my head and stopped. Fifty-two laps, two hours and forty-five minutes, twenty-one miles. I felt magnificent. For that moment I was free.

16 Monastery

I had my regimen of running and exercise, of reading, studying, and writing. I was progressing in my own way more than I had in all my previous years of freedom. Most of the time when I remained completely engrossed in what I was doing, I could handle it. But the fact was that no matter what I might do, I was still in prison, and like every other prisoner I was susceptible to the poisonous boredom and total predictability of the day's events.

I knew what was going to happen and when it was going to happen for months and years in advance. Each day was just like the day before. I knew just where I would be and what I would be doing, because it was not within my power to change it. Prison was a deliberately programmed zero—a nonevent of suspended nonanimation where all normal living activities had been discontinued.

No women. I had never before lived with only males. There were prositutes who visited the dorm regularly, via *el pimp* Granados, but that whole scene was usually too depressing to even think about. One look at them would reinforce anyone's celibacy.

Celibacy. It wasn't my choice, but I had learned to live with it. "Don't think about what you can't have anyhow," as Hank said. But just when I would begin to get my celibacy act together, a sweet, bright, friendly young lady would visit one of the Americans. Although her visit was platonic, she would inevitably blow my delicate balance. I would listen to her words, nod at her comments, and try to sound as philosophical and positive as possible about my situation. Stoic, even. But I would dream and yearn for the delicate, soft-warm-moist, sweet-sour bouquet of a woman. Oh, I wanted her so—a lady, a representative of the grand sisterhood—to be in my arms right now. Besides freedom, the presence and touch of a woman was what I most yearned for, with her kisses and sighs and her soft, smooth, warm, wet— enough, enough.

I may have been making do and surviving ninety per cent of the time, but this other ten per cent was unbearable.

Totally unbearable. Life was passing me by. I was losing my sanity.

17 A Wisp of Hope

Then she walked into my cell on *visita* day, long hair streaming down her deeply tanned back, casually dressed and insouciant, face aglow. She radiated health and exuberance.

She was beautiful.

We made eye contact immediately. Whenever she caught me looking at her, she looked back and smiled. She did not turn away, acting as if she weren't looking at me. Her eyes were alive. I hadn't seen anyone like her, or felt such an attraction, in longer than I could remember.

I knew I should be talking to my old friend Stephan, or at least looking at him occasionally, but I couldn't help it. I kept staring at her. It was something primal. She was beautiful.

For the next three hours Stephan and I talked of Central America and Guatemala, of books and ideas, and of prison and freedom. Again I asked Stephan if he would help me escape. His face turned despairing. Without saying it, he was telling me it was hopeless. But she was listening. I told her that although it had not yet been done, it had to be possible. There had to be some way out. Her eyes were intent. We were watching each other.

The bugle blew and it was the end of visiting hours. Gates slamming, *commandos* shouting, a massive commotion of visitors rapidly clearing out of the dorm; she was caught up in the exodus, swept away from me by circumstances beyond my control. . . . And it had just begun.

But we watched each other as the crowd rushed down the narrow stairway. Then she passed through the gate and I watched her walk away.

18 Meeting

All other sounds blurred into silence. He was telling me about exploring Machu Picchu in the jungles of Peru, his extraordinarily fine-boned hands describing its steep angles. His body was so lean, his muscles taut as bowstrings; I could see him scaling the dizzy ruins like a mountain goat. I shared with him my climbing Mt. Atitlán, a live volcano rising above a vast lake in Guatemala, and his eyes sparked alive. An adventurer. But there was something more, something I didn't understand until I caught the brown intensity of his eyes. Then I knew. Looking into him, dizzy, distance telescoping crazily, I knew. This was what I had been longing, searching for, for so long, and already I felt familiar here. At last I was home.

In the spring of 1974 I had flown from Indiana to Guatemala with my then one-and-a-half-year-old daughter Gabrielle. We had rendezvoused with some friends from the States, and had spent a year traveling in Guatemala and other parts of Central America. I loved the exhilaration of exploring different places, but after a year I decided it was time to return home. I made arrangements to drive north through Mexico with Stephan, a friend from Indiana who had spent the past two years in Central America. On departing, Stephan informed me that on his way north he would be going to Mexico City to visit Dwight Worker, a close friend of his who had been in prison there since 1973. Stephan suggested I accompany him on this visit, adding that the last time he had been there he had had to pay $200 just to get into Dwight's dormitory to see him. Stephan was visibly nervous at the prospect of going there again, afraid of what he might find had happened to his friend in the intervening year.

I recognized Lecumberri before Stephan could point it out to me. The watchtowers and gun turrets, silhouetted against the dirty grey sky, completely dominated its turn-of-the-century architectural facade. Stephan disappeared through the front entrance while I hurried to find the women's entrance in the rear.

The prison was monstrous, its old central building in the front having metastasized into a vast sprawl covering twenty-four square blocks. Stretching in front of me were endless blank grey walls, thirty feet high, their upper edges sparkling with jagged shards of glass, so thick and impenetrable that I couldn't imagine any life—anything—existing inside them. It took fifteen minutes to simply walk from the front gate to the rear entrance, where guards pursed their lips and made sucking noises at me as I passed by them into the prison. I instantly regretted wearing the strappy summer dress I had thoughtlessly selected.

A guard inside pointed me toward a huge room of grey cement and garish, green-painted metal. Bewildered, I saw several short, squat prison matrons dressed in seedy grey uniforms, staring vacantly or gossiping among themselves. Behind them was a row of metal doors.

A twenty-foot gate clanged shut behind me as I approached a small cubicle marked "F." The matron lurking there grudgingly stood aside and closed the door after me. She had pinned her skirt zipper to allow for bulging flesh and her fingernails were black-rimmed. I shrank against the wall, but she pulled me toward her. *A search.* Breathing in my face, she began probing my body through my clothes. I braced myself, thankful at least that Stephan had warned me of this. After several interminable moments she sullenly waved me through.

The guard at the next checkpoint scanned his list and peremptorily told me that the name of Dwight James Worker was not on it. When I protested, he sent me to the counters for the other dormitories. "Dwight James Worker" was not on any of their lists either. Suddenly I felt as if I would never locate Stephan or dormitory "F," that I would somehow find myself inside the prison without any point of reference at all. Feeling a slight edge of panic, I returned to the first guard and *looked* at his list. I found Dwight's name on it immediately and quickly filled out a pass myself. The guard signed it grudgingly and I hurried away.

The outside world seemed nonexistent from within this labyrinth of endless driveways, passageways, cement walls, and clanging gates. Guards leered at me from everywhere like ghouls, laughing when they knew I had lost my way and making sucking sounds through wet lips. Finally a guard pointed me to the *rondin,* a circular walkway that appeared to be the hub of the prison. From its center, a machine gun tower reared 150 feet above my head. I gingerly joined the stream of guards and gangs of prisoners in the *rondin.* Its circle totally disoriented me. Twenty-five-foot-high barred gates opened onto long, narrow dormitories where prisoners leered and hissed at me, dark, broken faces pressed against the bars. I had no idea where I had entered and I must have circled around several times before I saw the letter "F" on one of the huge gates.

As I waited to be admitted, a gang of prisoners passed me at a shuffling trot. All were barefoot and dressed in tatters, four of them pushing a metal cart stacked with greasy, sugar-encrusted sweet rolls. Flies clung to the rolls and hovered in a cloud about the prisoners, several of whom had strange open wounds on their bodies. The rest were staggering under fifty-kilo sacks of flour on their backs. All of them were dusted with flour from head to foot and they all had identically blank faces. The guards kicked at them to move along, shouting threats. I stepped as far away from them as possible. Pariahs.

A loudspeaker blared unintelligibly as the guard swung open the barred gate of dormitory "F." I stepped into a sort of cement courtyard thronged with prisoners and visiting women. I saw no American face in the bewildering hubbub and felt more lost than ever. Just then I heard my name and looked up to see Stephan on the catwalk, gesturing below to my right. I saw the stairs and hurried up.

Following him, I passed through an open solid metal door, #39, and through a plastic shower curtain into a cell. A slender but muscular man closed the heavy door on the noise and turned toward me. His brown hair was cropped short and his angular face looked young, in spite of a few interesting lines—no more than twenty-six, I thought. His eyes sparkling, Dwight welcomed me to his "humble abode." His smile was singularly beautiful.

We sat down on a bunk and I told him of the obtuse guards who had delayed me. He nodded and said that I had missed my cue to "grease their palms." Oh. It hadn't occurred to me.

The cell was about the size of a suburban American bathroom, with one small, barred window set high in the wall opposite the door. The floor was bare cement. A small, crude sink had several makeshift shelves suspended above it, cluttered with plastic dishes. A tiny table in one corner served as a desk, with a jar of pencils labeled HANDS OFF and a metal pencil sharpener on a string attached to the wall. Sheets of paper taped to the wall served as a shade over a bare light bulb. Over the light was a clipped newspaper headline stating MAGRUDER FINGERS MITCHELL. Under the newsprint, written in ink, was JOHN OR MARTHA? I smiled. On one special small shelf a small glass cage contained a lizard. And taped to the walls everywhere were photos, cards, and little cut-out mementos.

While Stephan filled him in on news of their mutual friends, Dwight caught my eye. I felt a flush of warmth from head to foot. I sensed a bit of ennui in him about people he was cut off from. He changed the subject and we became engrossed in conversation about Solzhenitsyn, as all three of us had just finished reading *Gulag Archipelago I.* Dwight felt it had put his own misfortunes in perspective. No self-pity there at all.

He had read extensively and was quick and intelligent in conversation. He was a challenge to me. By the time he was finished he had actually compiled a "required reading" list for me. He had been writing six hours a day too, and he gave me a thick stack of manuscripts to take out of the prison for safekeeping. I was surprised to learn that there were no rules about taking anything *out* of the prison.

Stephan was glad to find him so much "calmer" this time than on his last visit. Dwight nodded, mentioning that it had been six months since he was last hospitalized. Here in this dormitory he had learned to stay out of "trouble" in the interest of his own survival.

Hospitalized. How could I have forgotten that Stephan had told me of the torture, the extortion, the beatings? Now I was doubly amazed by Dwight. He was strong and self-reliant, more directed and alive than anyone I had ever met. His body was fit and vibrant, his eyes flashed, his smile warmed me clean through. He was in prison, but it was clear how much he loved life.

He spoke of his exercise regimen, I of my travels; but our eyes were shining in recognition. I forgot there was anyone else there; I forgot where in the world I was; I forgot everything but him.

The sound of a bugle snapped me back. Dwight started abruptly to his feet, explaining that visiting hours were over. There would be a big crowd and maybe trouble if we didn't get out in time. I felt a chill. This was the last place in the world I wanted to get into trouble. We made sure we had our passes and Stephan and Dwight hugged quickly. Then we were hurrying out on the catwalk, down the stairs to the gate. The courtyard was thronged with people, women and children streaming around us. Dwight's hand on my arm gave a final squeeze as he propelled me through the gate. From outside I turned to get a last glimpse of him, but the crowd had closed around him and was carrying me with it out of the prison.

The very next day I wrote Dwight the first letter. It was the beginning of a chronicle of my feelings that I wrote during the remaining three weeks of my journey northward—half to him, half to myself—just trying to logically straighten myself out.

From the moment I left Lecumberri I was in a turmoil of emotion. I had never met such a vital, sensitive, fine-spirited man; he moved me unlike anyone ever before. I *knew* I had felt an extraordinary affinity between us, and I had to follow my intuition through.

19 Letters

As soon as I returned to Indiana I mailed off the thick packet of letters to Dwight quickly, before I could think twice and censor what I had written.

Gabrielle and I moved into a cabin in the woods of Brown County in hilly southern Indiana. I found an evening job as a waitress in a large inn, leaving my days free to enjoy Gabrielle and settle into the spring rhythm of planting our garden. I wrote several more letters to Dwight and watched my mailbox.

But then the letters began arriving. Many of them. She was asking me if I would mind her writing me.

Mind? Of course I wanted her to write me! I sat down and began writing to her immediately.

At first the letters were slow and searching, cautious on my part. Don't get my hopes worked up over nothing. At best I thought she might be able to send me books and writing materials. I would be thankful for that.

Several weeks passed. Just when I began to think that my intense flashes of feeling were totally unfounded, when it became clear how foolish I had been to have written so nakedly to someone I barely knew—there was a letter.

I snatched it from the mailbox and bolted back to the cabin. Gabrielle was lolling in the pine needles with the neighbor's two tawny English mastiffs. The silver-gold spring sun filtered down on them in their mindless play. I sat on the doorsill and looked at the envelope. No doubt about it—it was from Dwight, and the envelope was marked LETTER #3. I tore it open.

I was surprised by the fresh openness in her letters—almost suspicious of it. Why should she be interested in me? Her feelings rolled off her letters in probing and passionate bursts: there was a real person on the other end of this tenuous link. I would read and reread her letters four and five times, feeling like a new man afterward. Someone out there really did care about me. I was not all by myself down here. I found myself anticipating the daily mail call as my big event of the day. I began to have hope.

Eleven a.m. became the magic hour in my life. All other hours led either toward or away from eleven. Each morning at 11:00 a battered dusty station wagon toiled up our narrow, dirt road to deliver the mail. The mailbox was half a mile from my tiny cabin, so every day at 11:10 Gabrielle and I took our ritual mail walk. Down our woodsy hill, following a path flanked by a deep, slow creek and a green-gold valley meadow. We waded across the creek, emerging by the end of the road at my closest friend Anna Jane's 100-year-old cabin. By now my stomach would be churning in anticipation and dread. Would or wouldn't there be a letter? The Russian roulette of the mail.

We walked through the sensory bombardment of early summer in Indiana, the air and earth jungle-humid, moist and fragrant with fertility. Thick tangles of blackberry, masses of multiflora rose, its white, apple-scented blossoms alive with bees, and clumps of daisies and black-eyed susans lined my path. The mailbox marked the eternal resting place of a '55 Chevy which had been kindly engulfed by the multiflora and festooned by wild pink roses. Ferns were sprouting from its upholstery, and its broken headlights peered patiently from beneath the towering ironweed shooting through its hood. It was the guardian angel of the mailbox, distracting the obliterating weeds to itself.

The moment was at hand, my spirits for the day about to be determined. I opened the box—it was empty, its blank mouth hollow. Peering inside once more to make *sure*, I closed it and walked slowly homeward with Gabrielle, rewinding my anticipatory clock for the next twenty-four hours.

I opened the box. There were three! Fat, red-white-and-green airmail envelopes! I snatched them out, my heart pounding. Gabrielle skipped and laughed, picking up on my emotion. After we had gingerly ensconced ourselves among the ferns in the back seat of the Chevy, I savored the envelopes a moment longer before ripping them open. I read, reread, laughed, cried, and hugged Gabrielle. I told her that pretty soon we would take a long trip to visit someone very wonderful.

And then she said what I had been hoping to hear from the first. She's coming to Mexico.
She's coming.

A small package arrived in the mailbox. Dwight had written me what to expect: it was from a professional actor friend of his. But today there was no letter. Without opening the box, I walked back toward Anna Jane's, joining her on her shady porch swing. Anna was my one confidante, a natural consequence of my sharing her mailbox and her warm friendship. We sat together enjoying the easy rhythm of the swing, watching the children splashing in the green-dappled creek. Anna Jane was wonderfully and frankly nosy. What was in the package? I hesitated, knowing I shouldn't tell, but telling anyway.

A disguise.

Anna Jane raised her eyebrows.

Yes, okay, we'll open it.

Inside the box we found a black moustache and sideburns, special facial adhesive, and a small spray can of black hair dye. They were all of theatrical quality, Hollywood stuff. The mustache and sideburns were made of human hair woven into an almost imperceptible microfine net backing. Just in case, I explained, some opportunity arose, we were keeping that door open.

"Well," mused Anna Jane, her green-eyed face framed like a flower against the ornate wicker of the ancient swing, "Maybe you'll be back sooner than you think."

By the end of July, four months after my visit, it was clear. One hundred and fifty letters had passed between us. We had stretched the written word to its limit. We had squeezed every possible bit of communication and understanding into it, and wrung every drop of emotion and passion from it. It was time to step out of two-dimensional paper words into the warm, living, three-dimensional world of each other.

I continued working and saving money, spending just enough to live frugally for several months. In early August I invited my mother down for a weekend visit. I knew she would be hurt by my leaving so soon after my return from Central America, and I dreaded the disbelief and skepticism that would fill her eyes when I told her why I was going to Mexico. My father's reaction was apt to be volatile, and I thought it best that she tell him rather than I.

But I could postpone it no longer. After a long visit with Anna Jane (she and my mother liked each other very much), as we were walking through the woods up to my cabin, I told her everything—the meeting, the letters, the magic. She looked at me searchingly, and whatever she saw must have answered her questions about my motives. When would I leave? And for how long? How would I live there? She was calm, and in her own quiet way, affirming.

I had no words to convey my love for her at that moment.

I finished tying up my affairs in Indiana, and finally the day arrived. Anna Jane and my mother saw us to the airport. On August 23, 1975, Gabrielle and I were on a plane to Laredo, then on to Mexico City, and Dwight.

20 Arrival

We took a cab from the Laredo airport to the border. I planned to take a train from there to Mexico City, a twenty-four-hour trip costing only $24. I asked the cab to wait while I went inside the Mexican border station to get my visa. But once the guards inside learned that I was taking a train, they flatly refused to issue the visa, saying that there would be an official at the train station who would do it.

I was immediately suspicious, but twenty minutes later they were still refusing. Gabrielle was tugging at my arm and the cab meter was ticking away outside. They won.

The cab left us with our luggage at the train station of Nuevo Laredo. Inside a huge, barnlike building, I joined a long line of American tourists queued up before a firmly closed ticket window. The August heat was stifling in the airless depot.

An hour later I had given up standing in line to sit among the rows of wooden seats. In the next three hours I made several trips to the main office to find someone to issue my visa. No one there. Back to the ticket window to find out when the train was leaving. Closed. There was no posted timetable or any other clue.

Finally, I found two Mexicans in the office who told me that visas were never issued at the station, but rather on the train. Yes, they insisted, there was an official who traveled on these *turista* trains especially to issue visas. *Pero aqui, no hay.* (But here, we don't have any.)

When would the ticket window open?

Ahorita. (Right away.)

When was the train leaving?

They shrugged.

Three hours later, at 7:00 p.m., the ticket window opened. It had begun to cool off outside, but the depot remained an insulated oven. I unglued myself from my seat to purchase our tickets. After an hour we were on the train, and after another, the train was rolling, eating up the miles between us and Mexico City.

I awoke suddenly from a fitful doze. Flashlight beams flickered inside the dark car. Three dark figures were tapping on the walls and ordering people to open their luggage. The harsh Spanish made my heart thud. *Federales.* They were looking for something or someone. I froze in my seat, covering Gabrielle with my jacket. They were methodically working their way toward me. The Mexican woman behind me began to plead as they picked up her sleeping child to search underneath him. The *federales* snarled at her; she shut up instantly and her child began to cry. We had to be next.

But unaccountably and without a glance, they skipped us and continued to the seats in front of us, jerking all of the sleeping passengers to their feet. A few interminable minutes later the *federales* moved on. Fear hung thick in their wake.

I stayed wide awake until the horizon outside my window began to lighten, feeling both excitement and tension. I had sure burned all the bridges behind me; now here I was. Or here we were. Gabrielle lay sleeping easily across my lap, her cheeks flushed. How vulnerable. No one but me between her and the world. No matter what, I had to make this trip positive for her, keep her feeling secure through it all.

I spent a good part of that day roaming around the train looking for the visa official. There wasn't one, but I was told that I could obtain my visa from *Gobernación* in Mexico City. I felt uneasy. In all my travels I had never gotten into a country without a visa, but here they refused to give me one. It was beyond my control.

At ten o'clock that night, we rolled into the *Estación Nacionale de Ferrocarril.* Dwight had written me that his friend Mame Levinson would be picking me up and that we were welcome to stay with her until we found a place of our own. Mame was a wonderful, eccentric, big-hearted lady and I was sure to love her, he had said.

But what did she look like? I got off the train with two suitcases, three pieces of hand luggage, and a half-dead Gabrielle. The depot was huge, a vast network of tracks and landings all under one roof. I was surrounded by chattering Mexicans, but relieved that no official was checking tourist visas. Working my way toward a pay phone to call Mame's number, I suddenly heard a gravelly voice calling my name.

A short, fiftyish American lady with a porter in tow was pushing her way toward me. She wore an embroidered blue jean skirt, Mexican peasant blouse, wooden clogs, and Navajo jewelry. Mame! She looked like a hip version of the Broadway character of the same name, her blue eyes sparkling behind wire-framed glasses.

"Barbara! I'm Mame Levinson. Oh God, I'm so glad you're here. Am I late? Those damned freeways . . ."

She gave Gabrielle and me a big hug and steered us out of the crowd, directing the porter to bring our luggage. Her Spanish was perfectly fluent, but she spoke it with a broad Manhattan accent. Just then the porter bounced a suitcase off of his cart, bending its frame. But I found myself smiling, as Mame unleashed a stream of the foulest Spanish curses at the porter, while she scooped up Gabrielle in her arms. Gabrielle was hugging back. Never had I encountered anyone quite like Mame.

Five minutes later we were packed into her Volkswagen, and she was talking away. "God, Barbara, I don't know who's more excited that you're here—Dwight or me. I mean, he's been talking about you for weeks. Not to me directly, of course—I've been banned from there for months. But he gets messages out and every time I send one in, I have to promise him again that I'll take care of you and Gabrielle. I keep asking him what he did to get you to come down here." She grinned at me. "But you know, you really couldn't find a nicer boy—god*damn* these Mexicans! They are the worst drivers in the world."

As she slammed on her brakes, I jolted out of my basking reverie about Dwight, remembering my visa problem. I asked Mame about it; she would know what to do.

"You mean they let you get all the way down here without a visa? Jesus, I've never heard of such a thing. Yeah, I guess the only thing you can do is go to *Gobernación,* and they're such bastards. They just may send you back to the border for it."

"Back to the border!" I was incredulous. "But *they* refused to give me the visa there! I mean, it's not my fault—"

"My dear, of course not. Welcome to Mexico."

After an hour and a half of Mame's expert maneuvering and swearing in Spanish through Mexico City's jam-packed free-ways, we arrived at her home in a quiet residential area north of the city. The silence when we got out of the car made my ears ring. At the door we were almost knocked off our feet by two huge, bouncing Airedales. Mame pushed them away and led us to the guest bedroom, where I tucked Gabrielle immediately into bed.

I was dead tired, but still too wound up to be sleepy. Mame

wanted to talk, so we relaxed with glasses of Sangria and Led Zeppelin—her favorite rock group—on the stereo. Mame's warmth and humor put me completely at ease as she told me anecdotes about her "boys" in Lecumberri. She explained that she had had no idea there were so many Americans there until she went to Lecumberri to visit a young Cuban friend of hers who had been arrested. She had continued visiting him and the American prisoners ever since. It was that simple.

Mame taught me the ropes of visiting Lecumberri. She was a good friend of Dwight's lawyer and promised to help me arrange to get a *"defensor"* pass through him so that I could visit Lecumberri every day. She also explained the system of "depositing" things—such as books and clothing—for prisoners. I showed her the books and the bedding Dwight had asked me to bring.

The books would be no problem, she said, because the guards couldn't read English, but they wouldn't allow those flowered sheets.

Why not?

"Because they think the boys'll make dresses out of 'em." She laughed hoarsely. "And when you take food, don't take pineapples or more than two apples or oranges, and if you bring bananas you have to peel them before they'll allow them in."

Why?

"Because they think the boys'll make *pulque*."

"Pulque?"

"Yeah, you know—home brew. Oh God, Barbara," she sighed, "I'll tell you, I don't envy you coming down here, especially with a little girl, getting into this prison trip. It can really get to be so awful, you know, it really starts to get you down. And this whole fucking city's a mess, man." She coughed on her cigarette. "You know, when I first moved here twenty years ago, there was nothing but polo fields around this house. I used to hear frogs at night, and now look at it. Wall-to-wall houses. Too many people and it's too damned expensive. Costs me more to live here than in New York. I've got to sell this place and get out of here. I am so sick and tired of dealing with the fucking Mexicans. The only reason I'm still down here, really, is for the boys. I've been thinking ever since I got involved in this that we'd get them all home somehow. But Jesus, I've been going into those prisons three and four days a week for almost two years now, and writing letters to congressmen and making scenes at the embassy—I haven't even been able to get into Lecumberri for four months because the embassy blacklisted me. Yeah, the *American* embassy. Damn it. The kids are still here, just rotting away, man. Jesus, they're good kids and I love them all, but the prison trip just gets to be too much for me sometimes, you know?" She ground out her cigarette and stood up. "That reminds me, I have something from Dwight that he said to be sure to give you when you arrived."

Mame placed a strand of beads in my hands. They were hand-hewn of turquoise, agate, obsidian, pipestone, and shell in every color of earth and sky. They were the most beautiful beads I had ever seen. I hung them around my neck with tears in my eyes.

Mame was going to drive me to Lecumberri at eight the next morning on her way to visit another prison, so we said goodnight. In the comfort of a big, quiet bed, I fell instantly and deeply asleep.

21 Passage

August 24, 1975. Mame drove east from the Zocalo—the central plaza of Mexico City—through streets that got progessively shabbier. Several blocks ahead the street was flanked by a verdant park. Beyond that green, the monolithic Lecumberri rose in unmistakable contrast, out of a shimmering haze of exhaust fumes. A huge black sprawl, bristling with gun turrets. And I was seeing only its face. I knew its blank walls stretched out for many blocks behind it. I sat rigidly as we drove around them. We were there. Mame gave me a quick hug and deposited me at the rear entrance to Lecumberri.

Inside, I experienced none of the confusion of my last visit. My anticipation was unbearable, but I had mentally rehearsed this scene so many times that I hurried eagerly to checkpoint 1, the body search. The matron was as vulgar as before, feeling my body through my clothing everywhere, checking my hair to make sure it was not a wig, bending my sandals back and forth to reveal nothing stashed in their soles. But in my intensity of purpose I scarcely minded; impatiently I emerged at checkpoint 2, the paper pass issue. Here a guard behind a counter marked "Dorm F" filled out the blanks on a numbered pass with my name, Dwight's name, his dorm, and the date. He signed it and tore it off the pad. I hurried away with my pass into a 500-foot walled-in driveway. Guards paced the catwalks above me from gun turret to gun turret, their rifles silhouetted against the sky.

I turned left through a doorway that had the letters "F, B, G, A, L" stenciled faintly on the dingy wall above it. It opened into a narrow room, which seemed very dim after the glare of the sun in the driveway. The room had only three walls, the fourth side— opposite me as I stood in the door—opening onto a long, roofless walkway. This was checkpoint 3, the paper pass/metal tag exchange. On either side of the narrow room was a counter manned by two guards, designated respectively by the letters "I" and "F & L." These were the dormitories having general (open) visits that day.

The guard at the "F & L" counter took my paper pass, then removed a small brass star-shaped metal tag from a wire loop

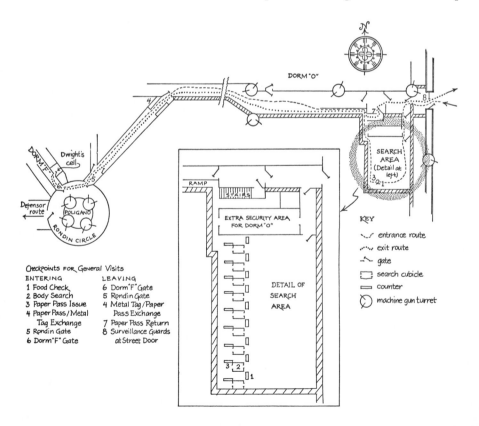

DORM "O"

SEARCH AREA (Detail at left)

Dwight's cell

DORM F

RAMP

STAIRS

EXTRA SECURITY AREA FOR DORM "O"

DETAIL OF SEARCH AREA

Defensor route

POLIGANO

RONDIN CIRCLE

KEY

entrance route
exit route
gate
search cubicle
counter
machine gun turret

Checkpoints for General Visits

ENTERING	LEAVING
1 Food Check	6 Dorm "F" Gate
2 Body Search	5 Rondin Gate
3 Paper Pass Issue	4 Metal Tag /Paper Pass Exchange
4 Paper Pass/Metal Tag Exchange	7 Paper Pass Return
5 Rondin Gate	8 Surveillance Guards at Street Door
6 Dorm "F" Gate	

strung with hundreds of identical tags. This particular one was stamped with the letter "F" and the number 32. The guard carefully wrote this number in the upper right-hand corner of my paper pass, which he kept and filed in a cardboard box, and gave me the metal tag.

From there it was only one hundred feet down the cement walkway to checkpoint 4, the gate to the *rondin,* the circular walkway at the center of the prison. Now I didn't have far to go. I held my metal tag in plain view of the attendant guards and entered the *rondin.*

I circled to the right around the *rondin* and hurried to the final checkpoint 5, the gate to dormitory "F." So far, so good; but now my heart was pounding uncontrollably, my stomach in knots. My face felt flushed, and my palms icy. I was trembling. I had dreamed of this moment and imagined it a hundred different ways and now, here I was. Five months of hopes and doubts, of agonizing internal dialogue and one hundred and fifty crazy letters. Two hours of a chance meeting and those hundreds of letters had totally uprooted my life and landed me here, in this ancient, squalid prison 2,500 miles from home.

The loudspeaker blared; the gate swung open. I showed the guard my metal tag. The cement courtyard was a sea of brown faces. The noise of chattering women, squealing children, and shouting guards blurred and receded. I looked to the upper cell tier and saw door #39 open.

He saw me instantly as he came out of his cell, his face at that moment etched forever in my mind. But he swam in my eyes, and before he could even move, I burst into tears.

22 Reunion

We stood in the stairway; she was sobbing in my arms. I led her to my cell and shut the door, first one lock and then the other, trying as much as possible to barricade the prison out.

I had so much I wanted to tell her—too much to begin now. I had gifts for her, clothes and embroidery that I had made, jewelry, toys for Gabrielle—but it all fell to the wayside. All that mattered now was holding her and kissing her, wiping her tears away, and telling her "I love you" over and over and over. Our mantra. One look into her moist eyes and I knew she loved me. She was more beautiful than I remembered her to be. We sat down, never letting go of each other, whispering assurances again and again in the cell that I had tried as much as possible to disguise into a room.

An infinity later, with our hopes confirmed and fears relieved, the bugle blew. The end of visiting hours. We kissed again. We had agreed on two things today: that we would marry; that we would not be staying here.

As she passed through the gate waving to me, her eyes sparkled. She was not crying.

23 On the Street

Through Mame's help and with considerable luck, I finally located an inexpensive apartment in the house of a middle-class Mexican family. It was a few convenient blocks away from the subway that took me to and from the prison. But we had barely settled there when, after my third trip to *Gobernación* and after filling out countless forms about why I had "neglected" to obtain my visa, I got the final verdict: I had one week to return to the border for my visa.

Mame offered to keep Gabrielle with her while I took the bus to Matamoros, but I brought her along. I was afraid that if I didn't, they would refuse to put her on my visa, even though she was on my passport, and I'd have to do the whole trip all over again. So two weeks after our arrival in Mexico City, Gabrielle and I took the grueling all-night bus trip to Matamoros, obtained visas—one for each of us—and immediately headed back to

Mexico City. We wearily staggered in our door only thirty-four hours after we had left.

I was at Lecumberri at nine o'clock the next morning, September 10, 1975, for an appointment with *Licensiado* Ferrer-Gamboa, *Subdirector Técnico de Lecumberri,* the man who could arrange for our marriage in the prison. Having attempted to handle legal transactions for Dwight's case in the court, I had been reviled, insulted, and extorted in a hundred ways by the prison bureaucracy. Now I braced for the worst as I made my way to Ferrer's office.

A smiling, fresh-faced secretary admitted me to a spacious office where a dignified, middle-aged man—more Spanish than Mexican in appearance—rose from his desk to greet me cordially, introducing himself and the pretty secretary, his wife. Pulling up a chair for me, Ferrer told me that several couples were married in brief civil ceremonies within the prison every two to three weeks, and that he would be happy to arrange our *matrimonio.* He gave me the necessary forms to fill out, promising to have their counterparts delivered immediately to Dwight in "F." After we took our physical exams and blood tests and returned the forms, he would do his best to arrange our wedding at the first possible date.

I thanked him profusely, incredulous at his courtesy. He was a true *caballero.* I left his office feeling stunned by the discovery of a sentient human in the midst of such a rotten prison.

The Mexican family from whom we rented our rooms fell in love with Gabrielle and I was able to leave her with them several days a week, so that she would not always have to accompany me into the grim filth of the prison. But the daily trek to Lecumberri soon made me realize that Mexico City was a nightmare in itself. In the Metro (subway) tunnel I would stand back, waiting for the next train, while crowds of people packed into the one already there. The automatic sliding doors would close on a bulging stomach that had forced itself on at the last instant, and the train would take off with bare flesh protruding here and there. Gabrielle was far more traumatized by these crushing subway rides than by anything she saw in the prison.

The Metro, like subways everywhere, was the favorite hunting ground of gangs of professional pickpockets, ordinary street punks, and ragged, hard-faced children whose only ability seemed to be lifting wallets oh-so-skillfully from unsuspecting passengers. But there was something far more disgusting than pickpockets on the Metro, namely, Mexican men. So many times I felt a hand creeping insidiously between my legs from behind, and when I turned around . . . identically blank faces. It enraged and demeaned and embittered me every time it happened, and especially when Gabrielle was with me. My loathing for these men was overwhelming. How could they do that when I had a child in my arms? I shielded Gabrielle from them as best I could.

Then one afternoon it happened on a relatively empty train. The only person behind me was a fairly tall, well-dressed businessman with the faintest smirk on his face. I felt the familiar surge of anger, and as Gabrielle was not with me, I told him *not to touch me.* As soon as I turned my back I felt a groping hand. It wasn't the first or even the fifth time that day. In a rush of blinding rage, I whipped around and crunched my knee upward into the crotch of his well-tailored pants. The look of shock and pain on his face almost surprised me as the adrenalin left my body and I stood there trembling. The man scuttled off the train at the next stop.

I looked around. The car was silent. A couple of squat, grocery-laden women quickly averted their eyes, resuming their impenetrable introspection. It was obvious that violence was never far from anyone in Mexico, and that was why the women seemed indifferent. I knew I would get off at the next stop anyway, so my composure returned. The train slowed and the doors whirred open. Just as I stepped down, a male voice behind me whined, *"Deja me mis huevos, puta chingada gringa."* (Leave me my balls—literally "eggs"—you fucked gringa whore.)

I didn't look back.

When I talked about Mexican men to the young women of the family I was living with, they all concurred—yes, it's disgusting, but it's the way things are here in Mexico. *Pero, tu sabes, son los indios* (But, you know, it's the Indians—dark-skinned ones), they would insist, as if this justified the vulgarity. Of course, the light-skinned Mexican men were just as bad, but this the young women would never accept. It didn't take me long to learn that in Mexico the ultimate social attribute and standard of beauty was whiteness of skin. The Mexicans with the tawny complexion so sought after by the suntan cult in the U.S. were obsessed with milk-white skin. This explained why, amid the continuous

144   ESCAPE

stream of sucking and slurping sounds that followed me wherever I went, the most common catcall was *guera*—white one. My fair skin was prized and I was resented for having it when they didn't. I knew that the leers I experienced were but a shadow of the violent hatred unleashed on Dwight for the same reason.

Entering Lecumberri on Sunday, the general visiting day for all the dormitories, and Tuesday, the general visiting day for dormitories "F" and "L," was a complicated procedure. It was several city blocks from the general entrance in the rear of the prison complex to the dormitories toward the front. But what made entering interminable were the hordes—literally hundreds—of women visitors, each of whom had to be processed through each of the five checkpoints. The lines were so long that it usually took forty-five minutes to get through to the dormitories.

But on the remaining days of the week I was able to get from the street to dormitory "F" within fifteen minutes. I arranged with Dwight's lawyer, F. Lopez-Portillo, to pay 300 pesos ($24) for a *defensor* pass that enabled me to visit Lecumberri on Monday and Wednesday through Saturday—not general visiting days for "F"—during the usual hours of 9:00 a.m. to 2:00 p.m. Obtaining this number-coded ID-with-photograph required too much money and too much legal string pulling for ninety per cent of the women visiting Lecumberri, so the crowds were visibly diminished on *defensor* days in "F."

Defensor visitors were processed through the front of the prison complex instead of the back, and even though they had to pass three additional checkpoints, they were able to enter the prison much more quickly than general visitors because there were far fewer visitors and much less distance between checkpoints.

Entering as a *defensor*, I was usually searched by the same matrons. Gabrielle and I quickly built up a good rapport with them. I dressed conservatively, observing the rules, and was calm and friendly toward the matrons, always speaking with them in Spanish.

But undoubtedly my greatest asset in this relationship with the stern prison matrons was Gabrielle. Her bright smiling innocence, her fair skin, and the fact that she, too, spoke Spanish to them, melted these hard women as much as they could be melted. They gave me the lightest of searches and scarcely patted Gabrielle's clothing.

But the matrons were characteristically unpredictable. If the food-searching matron happened to be in a surly mood, she wouldn't, for example, allow me to take in the same muffins I had taken in a dozen times before. If the body-search matron was feeling lousy, she wouldn't let me in wearing the same sandals I always had, but would revile me for going *contra los ordenes* (against the rules) when I should have known better. Of course, the rules were always subject to her whim of the moment. I knew that the very next day she would pass me in the same sandals, and I wanted to throttle her when I had to go all the way back outside to a newspaper stand that did a lively business in renting rubber thongs to visitors to Lecumberri. But even at times like this I never could bring myself to bribe the matrons, who received "gifts" from almost all visitors. Ironically, these not-very-clandestine transactions occurred directly beneath a prominent sign that proclaimed: *AL OFFRECER UN SOBORNO A UN OFICIAL SERIA UN INSULTO A SU DIGNIDAD.* (To offer a bribe to an official would be an insult to his dignity.)

The matrons' "whimsy" could have chilling consequences. Many times as Gabrielle and I stood in line before the waist-high partition of the body-search cubicle, I watched American women cringe as the matrons searched them internally, without gloves or any other sanitary precaution whatsoever. These Americans knew that such searches were the sources of chronic infection.

I could never be sure that I would receive the usual light search they seemed to have reserved only for Gabrielle and me. Ice-cold dread grabbed the pit of my stomach as I imagined the awful violation of the internal search, and the embarrassment of knowing that everyone else in line would see it happen. But the moment my turn came, I slipped on my polite veneer, automatically accommodating the routine motions of the search, ever deferring to the matron.

Mil gracias, señora. I had made it through once more.

I knew she was coming today. Where was she? Were they harassing her right now? She should be here by now, why the delay? What were they doing to her this time?

I paced around and around in the patio below, taking my usual laps. But at times like this, walking did no good. I knew that everything was probably okay, that it was just the usual delays and that soon she would be here, but I couldn't help it.

I walked to the gate and with both hands on the bars, twisting my head
around the door, tried to get a glimpse of her coming around the rondin.

After the body search, I hurried to the paper pass/metal tag
exchange, then through a narrow door behind the counter into a
long open patio. To the right I could see exclusive dormitory "I,"
reserved for very rich prisoners, always very quiet and sedate,
with none of the plebeian hoopla of the interior dorms.

This patio led directly to the circular *rondin*, where I flashed my
metal tag to the guard and was admitted. Dorm "F" was the first
gate on the left. With luck, on *defensor* days I sometimes made it
this far in ten minutes. I quickly flashed my tag at the guard as I
ran through the gate and into Dwight's waiting arms.

24 Decision

Barbara visited me every day. Every morning she arrived
before any other visitors, carrying bags of fresh fruit and
vegetables and meals that she had prepared the night before.
Sometimes Gabrielle would be standing by her side, pensive and
silent, still overwhelmed by the bizarre surroundings. I would
wait for them at the gate, waving as they approached, and after an
embrace and a kiss we would retreat to the privacy of my cell.

Gabrielle and I would wrestle, romp, and participate in our
daily projects. She was enthralled at feeding the lizards, cheering
wildly as they ate the cockroaches she tossed to them. I caught a
mouse for her, which immediately won her heart over the
reptilian indifference of the lizards; but I could not let her pet it or
play with it, even though she thought it was a cute little furry
thing. One day, with an old T-shirt of mine draped over her, she
painted a stool I had gotten for her. She was attentive and curious
as I taught her how to use my improvised tools to make and fix
things. After watching me, she always insisted on trying to do it
herself. Often we would play together and almost neglect

Barbara. But not really—the look I saw on Barbara's face as Gabrielle and I became lost in each other told me how good she felt.

One morning I found a pregnant cat in the throes of labor lying precariously on the stairway near my cell. She had been staying in another cell, but they had thrown her out the moment she had gone into labor. I quickly arranged a box lined with rags under my bed and placed her in it.

When Barbara and Gabrielle arrived I rushed them up to the cell just in time to watch the first kitten being born. By the time visiting hours were over, Gabrielle had witnessed the birth of five kittens. Every day afterward when Gabrielle arrived, she immediately wanted to see the kittens.

When the kittens were ten days old the mother disappeared. Through the prison grapevine the word came back that some prisoners had killed and eaten her. They would have killed her earlier, except that she was pregnant. I believed the grapevine.

I bought an eyedropper from a junkie and now found myself constantly feeding the kittens. Since I was the first living thing they saw when they opened their eyes, my visage must have been permanently etched onto their innocent psyches. Once they could move and walk, they regularly crawled into bed with me to snuggle and attempt to nurse on my side. During the day they followed me around, crying unbearably loudly whenever they were hungry. "MAAA! MAAA! MAAA!" they wailed. The only way to silence them was to engorge them with warm milk. I was living proof of the theory of imprinting.

After Gabrielle had finished playing with the kittens and feeding the lizards, Jaime always offered to baby-sit Gabrielle for us—strategically—so that Barbara and I could be alone.

A lady, a real lady—*my lady*. This was the best thing, the only real thing, that had happened to me here. I was unable to take myself away from her. I was ascending from out of the despair of my life, feeling positive and joyful even in the midst of this dungeon. A wonderful woman loved me, and for the first time in my life, I was in love. I was a new man.

My whole world changed. I lived for 9:15 a.m., when Barbara always arrived. She was so loyal, doing the many errands that the other American prisoners and I requested of her. Each day we talked and talked, exchanging feelings and ideas as if we hadn't seen each other in months. We explored the possibilities for our lives, mapping out how, given the circumstances, we could best merge them together. The hope in her eyes made everything worthwhile. And every day I had the joy of her smile. I was rejoining humanity after a journey to the far side. Regardless of everything else, we felt that our love could surmount all.

But then the bugle would blow, jolting us back to grim reality. We would automatically gather up Gabrielle and her things and walk to the gate. Embraces, and kisses, and a promise to be back in the morning.

One day after I hugged Gabrielle goodbye, she looked into my eyes. "I don't want to go."

Silence.

Then Barbara explained to her that they had some work to do at home.

"Dwight, come with us." Her dark innocent eyes wondering.

Neither of us answered her. I knew that some day I would have to.

After Barbara left, I went at the weights and running with renewed passion. At night I did artwork for the silk-screening business that Barbara and I planned to set up. Barbara would supply me with the materials and I would do the work in my cell. I figured I could do a brisk business in T-shirts and custom designs, and Barbara was arranging with shops to take my work on consignment. I was hoping that Barbara and I might be able to support ourselves through this. I still read and wrote diligently into the night, or made things for her and drew comic books for Gabrielle, but no longer did I stay up all night like I had before. I wanted to be rested for Barbara's arrival in the morning.

I waited for Barbara at the gate at 9:15 a.m. At 9:30 there was still no Barbara. By 10:15 I was nervous, pacing back and forth. Something was wrong. Had they planted drugs on her and arrested her? Was she hurt?

Finally, at 11:00 a.m., the guards called my name. Barbara had arrived. I ran to the gate and as I threw my arms around her, she burst into tears.

Barbara had just cashed one of our few remaining checks and was on the subway, holding Gabrielle, when suddenly two men grabbed her from behind. They yanked her purse away and Gabrielle fell out of her arms. The men then squirmed through the packed crowd as Barbara yelled and Gabrielle began to cry. Not only did no one try to stop the men, but they all turned away from her as she shouted for help. Barbara began crying again in my cell as she related the story to me.

That was the money that we had planned to use to set up the silk-screening business. Now we would be running out of money even sooner than we had planned.

I sat there shaking. Despite all of my personal admonishments to stay cool and not blow it, I found myself in an uncontrollable rage. It was one thing for me to be assaulted while I was in prison, but totally another for it to happen to Barbara. I wanted to dash out of the prison right then and kill those two men who had robbed her. As she sat there crying, I realized just how useless I was to her, and that thought drove me into a seething fury. I couldn't get control of myself for the remainder of the day.

In the following weeks Barbara guarded our remaining money more carefully. We didn't have much left. She began hitting and kicking back as men assaulted her. I almost didn't want to hear her daily tales of confrontations on the Metro, because I could not do anything about it. The rage of helplessness was too painful.

One afternoon Barbara and I were jarred from our cell by the screams of David Lopez, an American Chicano also in "F" for cocaine. We stepped out on the catwalk to witness a bunch of *commandos* beating David up while Granados cursed him. Barbara looked horror-stricken.

"What did David do?" I yelled to Jaime.

"He refused to buy pants from Granados."

"What?"

"Granados brought a bunch of lousy pants in from the street and he's making every American buy a pair at $20 apiece, even though they're just rags. David refused, and so now Granados is having him beaten until he buys them."

"Oh my God. Someone should stop him," said Barbara, looking over to me while David squirmed to avoid the kicks.

I shook my head.

Déjà vu. I had seen this movie before. I remembered how I had once charged to the rescue in dorm "O." I knew better now. The *commandos* stomped and kicked David while we watched. Through his screams he agreed to buy the pants. Granados then called off his goons. Red-faced, bruised, and torn, David paid the money. Granados threw the pants at him.

David trudged slowly up the stairs and walked past Barbara and me. We both said something to him, but he didn't answer. He threw the pants at a few Mexicans and locked himself away in the cell for the rest of the day.

From the balcony Barbara, Jaime, and I watched the pig Granados summon another American to see if he wanted to "buy" a pair of pants.

Barbara was almost in tears. I stormed back into my cell, hating myself for not having done anything, while at the same time knowing there was nothing I could do.

Then it was September 17, 1975, my birthday. I could barely remember what had happened on my last birthday here. Birthdays in prison are drab events—just a reminder of another year wasted. But today would be different. Barbara had baked two whole-wheat-crust pies—apple and raisin, and pecan—the night before, and she and Gabrielle would be throwing a birthday party for me today. Maybe I was now a twenty-nine-year-old man lost in prison with years and years to go, maybe I had blown my life and even deserved my fate, maybe maybe everything. But one thing was certain: Barbara and I loved each other and that made my whole mini-universe worthwhile. A party! I had hope.

Nine-thirty and no Barbara. By 10:00 I was pacing the dorm like a big cat in a cage, imagining every possible insult, harassment, and danger that she was now enduring. By 10:30 I was killing the imaginary assailants in my mind.

She arrived at 11:00 a.m., empty-handed and again with tears running down her cheeks. We hid ourselves away in my barricaded cell.

First the matron had refused to let Barbara enter because of her sandals, even though they were the same sandals she had worn for almost a month. When Barbara returned with her different sandals the matron inspected the birthday pies. No raisins or apples permitted, she declared, even though these same items had been routinely approved on other days. Barbara told her it was my birthday. No, I would make *pulque* with it to get drunk on. She shook her head and made Barbara wait thirty more minutes while the others went by. Finally, for the first time since her arrival in Mexico City, Barbara offered the matron a bribe. She stuffed it down her dress, then insisted that Barbara give her one of the pies. Barbara held the pies up to the matron, who chose the apple. Smiling, Barbara then dumped it into the garbage can. She gave the other pie to a Mexican lady who was leaving. Only then did Barbara enter the prison.

Again the white anger. So much for our birthday party. I was proud of her for standing up to the matron. But in spite of everything, I wanted to strike back at the guards, any and all of them. Revenge. The blind rage of those who are impotent to do anything about it. Although I knew that feelings like these could get me into real trouble, I couldn't control them. Watching Barbara get abused while being helpless to do anything about it was driving me mad. Now, more than ever, Lecumberri was taking its toll.

Barbara and I pieced together the remnants of the birthday party as best we could. At least they could not take our love away. Or could they?

It became clear to me on the night of my birthday, when I was alone in my cell. Everything pointed to it. I had initially avoided the subject with Barbara because I did not want her to think I was using her. But now it was inevitable. I knew it, and so did she.

I did not know what would happen to me after five more years of this prison. Would I still be sane? Madness could creep up so slowly in prison, and in so many guises. Madness can be sanity in prison. I knew that after five more years here I could be so full of hate that I would be warped. I was already too bitter.

And when would I get out of prison? Already I had waited twenty months for my trial, with no results. I had heard too many stories about how other prisoners who had served their full sentences still had to pay bribes to get released. Knowing the streak of cruelty and revenge in Mexicans as well as I did, along with their national resentment of *gringos*, I understood that this could very well translate into my staying here until the 1980s—a time span far longer than I could possibly conceive.

And there was always the possibility that I would be charged with some additional crime and get 3-5-10? more years added to my sentence. I had heard of Bill White, an American at Santa Marta prison in Mexico City who, while serving his first sentence, had been sentenced to thirty more years for murder. Thus far he had been at Santa Marta for twenty, and would not be released until the year 2000. Imprisonment in Mexico could be a horror story for life.

And would I even live through this imprisonment myself? I didn't know. I had already had several close calls with death. I knew that everything was up for grabs—my whole world, my own life. Visions of my mortality were haunting me.

What would happen to Barbara and me? I doubted whether I could ever manage to support Barbara and Gabrielle through any business in the prison. They would tax me to death one way or the other. And I could not expect Barbara's relatives or mine to support us here indefinitely either. Our parents just did not have enough; and I had already bled mine of too much anyhow.

And what about Gabrielle? What kind of life would this be for her, to visit me as a prisoner for our first five years together? How it would affect her I did not want to know. And although Barbara would stay in Mexico City the five years if necessary, I did not want her to. What a cruel state of limbo for her to live in, just to be with me. That would be too much for me to ask of her.

I could not bear to see her crying when she came to visit; I could not bear all of the insults and vulgarities she put up with daily just to see me. I could not bear not being able to be with her and Gabrielle, to help her, love her, share our lives together. I could no longer bear our forced partings and our fears of what would happen to us. I couldn't take it any longer. It all came down to one thing. *Escape.*

After I had been through their forced confessions and their phony legal system, after I had met their lying, ripoff lawyers, after I had lived in and suffered through their dirty extortionist feudal prison system, and after I had experienced firsthand their ruthless culture, I did not want to beg the Mexicans for my liberty. I did not want to give them the pleasure of deciding my fate, or the possibility of thinking that they were doing me a favor. I did not want to negotiate with those arrogant bastards in any way. And I did not plan on waiting for them either. I had personally broken all diplomatic relations with them a long time ago and now all I wanted to do was get myself out of prison on my own terms.

I had to escape—or at least to try. How could I live with myself twenty years from now knowing I had done all those years in a Mexican prison without even trying to get out? Maybe they would kill me if they caught me, but then, I just might make it. Maybe I could assert my free will against them and win, proving that I could be a free man by my own decision and my own acts, regardless of what they thought or did. Far beyond being an act of defiance, escape would be an affirmation of life and freedom and dignity. Escape was the only honorable way out.

Barbara's presence made it so viscerally real to me. She brought me hope.

The time had come.

"So. We're agreed."

"Yes. Agreed."

"All right, then. One plan I've been studying is to go over the wall at *campo*. I'll have to make a guard's uniform in the cell and hide it out there. Then some afternoon when things are just right, I'll stay out at *campo* and hide until nightfall, put on the uniform, and somehow get up onto the catwalk without being seen. The catwalk goes right to the outside wall. I can easily lower myself down to a getaway car on the outside wall. They won't shoot if they think I'm a guard."

"If they don't see you climbing up or lowering yourself down. But if they do, they'll shoot for sure. What if one of them passes you on the catwalk?"

"That's a problem. I'd have to say something to him. Then he'd recognize me for sure. If it came to that, I'd have to disarm the guard or knock him out."

"But wait, if you don't come back to the dorm after *campo*, won't they know that you're missing as soon as they take *lista?*"

"Not until 7:30, the same time they always do. But for a few hundred pesos I can arrange to take *lista* in my cell—then I don't have to line up. They just yell through my cell door without opening it."

"But you have to answer, don't you? And if you weren't there, you'd have to get somebody to answer for you. Who could you really trust? How dangerous would it be for him? I just don't think we should involve anyone."

"I know. I know. But the thing is, if I *arrange* to take *lista* in my cell, it buys time; I could be far away from here by the time they discover I'm gone."

"But the real risk is that they're prepared for someone to try to go over the wall. They're expecting it, they're armed to stop it. You could just be shot down off that catwalk and that would be the end of everything. God, Dwight it's so risky."

"I agree it's too go-for-broke, but—All right, let me try a second plan: you know how the lawyers and doctors come through here every day? They have to leave their photographs and identifications at the desk when they sign in. Then when they go out they have to sign out and pick up the IDs. So if one of them comes in and leaves his ID at the desk, and I go out as that man with that ID . . ."

"How would you do that?"

"Well, I'd have to change my appearance to look exactly like him, for one thing. And I'd have to learn how to forge his signature. And somehow I'd have to plant a forged ID and photo on the desk."

"But how? They watch those IDs like hawks. The guard literally holds onto the box that they're filed in. You'd have to sneak the false ID in right under his nose while three or four others watch. I know I could never get near there to do it—that's a man's checkpoint and I would immediately draw attention if I got within ten feet of it. And you know you can't bribe a guard to do it—the minute we pay him, he'll squeal."

"Yeah, but look: if I could change my appearance enough to look like the visitor, my only problem would be to leave the dorm early, to make sure that he himself hadn't signed out and left the prison before me."

"Well, then how does he get out?"

"He doesn't."

"You mean he stays here? What happens to him?"

"By Mexican law, they'll charge him with conspiracy. But if he's tied up and gagged in my cell, they'll see it's not his fault."

"Oh God, who could we possibly do that to?"

"Well, there are several people visiting this dorm with a height, build, and complexion similar to mine."

"Then you mean just an innocent visitor? Dwight, do you honestly think you can get free by risking an innocent person's freedom? Do you? Besides, if they caught you they'd charge you with assault too."

"I know that. You think it doesn't bother me just to think of doing something like that? But look, we have to try something. It's either that, or stay here for God knows how many more years."

"Well, what are the stakes for us, whatever we try? What happens if we get caught?"

"For me it could be *la ley de fuga*—the law of escape. In Mexico there is no official capital punishment, but the guards shoot prisoners in the back all the time and then say they were trying to escape. It's the unofficial capital punishment law. It's not written in any law books, but everyone knows it."

"But legally, what does the written law say?"

"According to the *Código Penal,* it says that anyone helping an escape can get from three months to seven years. But that doesn't apply to the prisoner's direct relatives."

"You mean if we were married—"

"You would be legally safe. But if I use violence against anyone, or damage state property, or bribe an official, or help other prisoners escape, I'll get from four to twelve more years. The strange thing is there's actually no law against escape itself in Mexico. Legally, if I don't do anything that is officially illegal, I can't get any more time for trying."

"Why that's incredible! You mean that if you try to escape without making trouble, then you get a fighting chance? Why, that's the first rule I've heard of in this prison that's fair. All we've got to do is think of some nonviolent way. I think that's our best chance."

"Okay. I've known that for a long time. But how?"

"I don't know. We have to be patient. Look, we can't make a split-second decision. What we have to do is to start observing everything."

"Patient? Barbara, if I don't try it someday, I'll just get so 'patient' that I'll never try. I've been 'observing' for years and I've got too many years to go."

"I know, but it's there someplace . . ."

"I don't mean to snap at you but—there's the bugle. I'll walk you down to the gate."

25 Conception

The guard at the gate of "F" had his back to me, engrossed in some transaction with a well-dressed Mexican. He didn't notice as I flashed my metal tag to his back and stepped out into the stream of women in the *rondin.* It was a general visiting day and I had to fight the crowds, but I was absorbed in thought about my conversation with Dwight, feeling a bit depressed at the discordant note it had ended on. I knew as well as Dwight did that we couldn't wait forever, but we couldn't be rash, either. We had to be careful about a decision that would mean life or death for him.

I absently flashed my tag again as I exited the *rondin*, checkpoint 4. Approaching checkpoint 3, I could see that the walkway was choked with women pushing and jostling to get nearer to the guards' counter to exchange metal tags for their paper passes. I stood at the end of the crowd (lines were unheard of) and was pressed inexorably forward by the women accumulating behind me.

They were a motley crowd: mostly mothers with clinging babies and squealing children whose stick-thin bodies contrasted sharply with their mothers' squat shapelessness. There were gnarled, ancient grandmothers with hair still long in plaits down their backs. A scattering of middle-class Mexican women in nylons and hennaed hair were recognizable by their disdainful expressions. Far ahead of me was a lone American woman, tall and wholesome looking by contrast. Glaringly obvious, as if they were carrying neon signs, were the whores, whose garishness held a morbid fascination for me. Most of them were hideously fat, swinging the ponderous breasts that were thought attractive by Mexican men. Catlike eyes, mouths painted like blood-red gashes, thick oily makeup like pale masks over brown skin, hair bleached impossibly blond—they were travesties of the unattainable *guera*—the white woman—as grotesque as drag queens on Halloween.

Body heat and smell were stifling. At last I was at the counter, extending my metal tag to the guard. Someone shoved hers in front of mine, shrilling impatiently at the guard. He was flustered by all of the women, taking the tags and returning the paper passes without looking up. He ignored the woman who, giving her tag to her friend to exchange for her, passed by the oblivious guards to wait in the driveway beyond. The idea that I could do that never occurred to me. It was amazing that the guards didn't notice, or maybe they just didn't care.

Sweating, I broke through into the wide driveway and breathing space. The sun glared white on the cement walls, glinting on the helmets of the guards on the catwalks above. I thought about Mexico's nonlaw on escape: if we didn't harm anyone or anything, or involve anyone else, then we *deserved* to make it. But how? I racked my brain, hurrying along the driveway toward the ramp that led inside, bypassing the search area. Here the crowd had bottlenecked again, but the progress was faster.

Up the ramp, three abreast to the dim landing inside, then down the stairs.

At the foot of the stairs was exiting checkpoint 2. There, the same guard who had issued the paper passes that morning now collected them from the women as they filed by. He glanced at his signature on each pass and, when he had accumulated a fistful, tossed them randomly into a wooden box behind him. I handed him my pass and walked the twenty feet past the guard head-quarters surveillance window to the street door, which was flanked by two guards. I passed between them and was on the street. Behind me, twenty guards lounged against the exterior prison wall, twirling their guns and eyeing the women.

I hurried across the garbage-strewn street to the taco stand where I had checked my handbag (prohibited inside the prison). Flies buzzed around the greasy pyramids of fried food and landed on the cook's face as I handed her a few pesos for my bag.

Glancing at my watch, I saw it had taken me only fifteen minutes to get out of the prison—less than half as long as it usually took to enter on these general visiting days, and not nearly as harassing an experience. Thank God there was no body-search *leaving* the prison as well as entering. Leaving was pretty straightforward.

Leaving was pretty straightforward.

I stopped in my tracks. It had been so easy for me to leave the prison. Those guards and the women, all those strange women. Could he, could he possibly . . . His smooth-skinned face floated before my eyes—just the faintest beard, his sensuous lips. I had often thought him *pretty*. Not too tall, slim and fine-boned—I imagined long hair, a touch of lipstick. The image hit me full force. *As a woman, he could do it, he could walk right out.*

I took a deep breath and walked on blindly. The longer I thought, the clearer it became that it was the perfect way to escape, tailor-made to our nonviolent specifications and to Dwight's physique. He'd fit right into that strange assortment of females. Why, he'd even look more normal than most of them. *If we did it right, it would work.*

I felt a rush of clarity and resolve. I hurried home on the Metro, oblivious for once to the crowds, my mind going full speed, envisioning the details, counting off the hours until I'd be back with Dwight tomorrow.

Did I have news for him.

26 **D-Day**

"A woman! You can't be serious."

"I am serious."

"But how? I'm taller than just about every man here. As a woman I'll be a giant."

"No, you don't go as a Mexican woman: you leave as a *gringa.* That way, if anyone asks you anything, you don't have to speak in Spanish."

"But they're still going to recognize me. Everyone in this dorm has seen my face twenty times a day for a year and a half, and I'd have to walk right by them."

"Forget all that for a moment. This idea is perfect for you because they won't be expecting it. Look at yourself in the mirror. You're five feet ten inches—just the height of some of the American women who visit here. You're slim. Your shoulders and waist are narrow. You have a light beard and your face is fine-featured. Oh, I can see it so clearly. Just imagine your face looking very smooth, with makeup and long wavy hair all around it."

"It's hard for me to believe. I've never dragged up in my life. What about clothes and makeup?"

"The clothes are no problem, I can wear them in. But the makeup we'll have to work on. One way or another I'll have to smuggle it in because they don't allow anything like that. It can be done, though. But no more weightlifting. Your arms and legs are too big already."

"I don't know. I just don't feel very comfortable with the idea of dressing up as a woman. I don't think I could pull it off. It's just too outrageous."

"It's so outrageous it *just might work.* They've never prepared themselves for it, don't you see? But you have to drop your mental block about it. Believe me, the problem is not going to be making them believe you're a woman. You'll be more feminine than most of the real ones I've seen here. But to carry it off, *you* have to believe it before anyone else will. Your body language, your vibrations, everything has to be feminine. For that bit of time you have to *be* a woman. That's much more important than the disguise. If it's going to work, you have to believe it'll work."

I walked over to the jagged piece of mirror glued to the wall and looked at myself. Maybe it could work. I would have to walk through the dorm for less than a minute, and no one would be expecting to see me in drag. And also, leaving as a woman was not like going over the wall. There would be less chance of getting shot, and since I would not be doing violence to people or property, less chance of getting another sentence if they caught me. But deep down, I objected to dressing as a woman. I had never done it before and I felt presumptuous and awkward at the thought of it.

But Barbara was right; I would have to discard those feelings completely in order for this plan to work. All right, I would be open to the idea. With that, a hundred other questions came to my mind.

"What about the metal tags, the paper passes, the signing in, the guards? This has to be planned out perfectly, no surprises, because once I leave this cell dressed as a woman, there can be no turning back. No dress rehearsals or second chances."

"Right, there are hundreds of logistics that we'll have to figure out. The paper passes and metal tags we'll have to forge, but we can do it. What we have to do now is start observing and watching everything—you in here and I coming in and out. The dorm gate, the guards, how things change from day to day. We'll begin today."

With that Barbara took out a marked string, instructing me to take off my shirt and hold up my arms. She wanted to take my measurements. She wrote each one down studiously: arms, legs, neck, head, (for wig size) waist, chest, hips, everything. I wasn't too sure exactly what she had in mind, but she was very thorough.

Leaving the prison every day became a rehearsal for escape. I moved through every checkpoint as if I were Dwight. Some days I "made it" easily; other days were so disastrous I was certain Dwight would have been caught—or shot. It quickly became obvious that the most dangerous part of the plan was checkpoint 3. It was there that the exiting women visitors had to exchange their metal tags for the coded paper passes they had deposited on entering. The pileup of women there was fierce, because for each departing visitor, the guard would take the metal tag, find the paper pass in his file that matched it, and give that paper pass back to the woman, who would then show it to the next guard at checkpoint 2.

But Dwight, of course, would have a forged metal tag, and there would be no paper pass in the file to match it. So if he gave the guard his metal tag and the guard couldn't find the nonexistent paper pass, Dwight would undoubtedly be pulled out of the crowd for questioning. If, on the other hand, Dwight sneaked by the guard at checkpoint 3 without giving up his metal tag, he would not have the paper pass to show the guard at checkpoint 2.

Obviously, we would have to forge both the metal tag and the matching paper pass. Then, in the confusion of the crowds clamoring around checkpoint 3, Dwight would hide the metal tag, sneak past the guard, and pull out the forged paper pass as if the guard had just given it to him. Then he could move right along and flash the pass to the guard at checkpoint 2.

Very risky. I continued to study checkpoint 3 with such obvious scrutiny that I began to worry that the guards were suspicious of me.

Over the next few weeks, Barbara and I wrote down everything we could think of that would be needed for the plan to work. The list continually changed and grew, but it finally settled down to the following:

MAKEUP	CLOTHES	ACCESSORIES
lipstick	36B bra	Mexican shopping bag
foundation liquid	long skirt	metal tags (perfectly forged)
mascara	nylons	
rouge	lady's belt	paper passes (perfectly forged)
eye shadow	sandals	tweezers (for plucking eyebrows)
eye liner	blouse	
eyebrow pencil	sweater	
fingernail polish	butt pad (to swell my hips)	metal dies (for stamping letters and numbers onto metal tags)
"cover-up" stick makeup		
face powder		bracelets, earrings, rings, necklace
		wig
		lady's prescription tinted glasses

But these were only the essentials. Before we knew it, details piled on details and our lists had to be rearranged in dozens of new categories. We deliberately calmed our excitement to remain as objective as possible: step by step, first things first.

I quit shaving and cutting my fingernails. Moustaches were permitted in prison, but beards were prohibited. I wanted as many whiskers on me as possible, so that people would forget what my face looked like clean-shaven. The plan was to shave immediately before the escape. I told the guards that it was an American tradition to grow a beard for Christmas, *"como* Santa Claus."* They didn't go for it, so I had to shave. Then I tried another angle. The guards knew that Barbara and I were trying to get married, so I told them that it was an American tradition for the groom to grow a beard before his wedding, to show how *macho* he was. The chief of the guards listened intently to that one, because anything that was *macho* made sense to him. *"Sí. Hombres son machos,"* he commented, although he still was not sure about the beard. But when I said that I would give him one hundred pesos a week for the next few months until my wedding *if* he would permit me to grow my beard, my offer quickly tipped the delicate scales of his logic. Inside the dorm I also had to pay the *commandos* fifty pesos a week in order not to shave my already thin beard. Every day after that I felt better knowing that my beard and nails were growing longer and longer.

And now, timing.

There were three twenty-four-hour shifts of guards in the prison—the first, second, and third. Every day the shift changed, and within each shift the guards were constantly rotated to supervise different locations. In this way the guards were continuously moving around the prison, a system that prevented any familiarity between guards and prisoner and reduced any possibility of bribery. But bribery was out of the question anyway. We didn't have the money to start with, and even if we did, a guard would just take the money and then turn us in.

The men in the first *guardia* were sharp: competent and very vigilant. They were used for show and to clamp down whenever necessary. They could be killers. The second *guardia* was moderately vigilant. But the third *guardia* was an assembly of slack morons who would do almost anything for money, including beg for it. It was on third-*guardia* days that most of the prison *transas* (illegal business dealings) took place. The third *guardia* brought in and sold all manner of contraband, including heroin, in prearranged runs from the outside. What they lacked in standards, the third *guardia* made up for in money, and that was why Colonel Cardenas needed them. They earned Cardenas a lot of money.

Then there were the two shifts of gate *commandos* working on alternate days inside the gate of dorm "F." I knew I couldn't trust either shift, but the first shift appeared to be more lax. An enemy of mine, Tierno, worked on the second shift, and he was especially vigilant. He thought he was a prison guard himself. Tierno would stop me and turn me in if he suspected anything was going on. The other *commandos* would most likely do the same thing, but Tierno would be the worst. So I would have to avoid the second *commando* shift.

The *commando* shifts, like the *guardia* shifts, were regularly rotated, so it was possible to determine months in advance what shift would be working on what specific day. This was a crucial factor, for besides sneaking by checkpoint 3 (where metal tags and paper passes were exchanged), the most difficult step in the escape would be this one, checkpoint 5—getting past the *commandos* inside the dorm gate and the regular guards outside. Walking out under the noses of potentially 200 people who had seen my face every day for one and a half years, and then passing the *commandos* at the dormitory gates as an unfamiliar woman visitor, would be a major risk.

Barbara had already confirmed that the main requirement for getting past checkpoint 3 was to hide myself in the crowds of women who would pile up there soon after the bugle sounded at 1:45. But the bugle was also a cue for extra *commandos* to rush over to the inside dorm gate at checkpoint 5 and inspect exiting visitors. This meant that over a dozen of them would be waiting for me by the time I got there. It was a painful dilemma: if I left too late, the *commandos* would catch me: if I left too early, there would be no crowds to hide in at checkpoint 3.

I began to observe the dormitory gates from 1:30 to 1:45. After three weeks, I found the hole I was looking for: every day, a few minutes before the bugle sounded, a handful of women visitors left the dorm early enough to create a distraction for me to get past the guard outside the gate. So if I left my cell at exactly 1:42, I could arrive at checkpoint 5 one minute before the bugle sounded at 1:45, and one and a half minutes before the *commandos* lined up on the inside to examine departing visitors. Then, if I stalled for five minutes between checkpoints 5 and 3, the crowds would catch up to me and provide my cover for the metal tag/ paper pass exchange.

Close, close timing. But it could work.

My cell on the upper tier was, fortunately, only one door away from the stairwell that descended right to the dorm gate. Thus my exposure on the catwalk would be minimal; once on the stairs I would be concealed from view except by anyone on the stairs at that moment. Under the third *guardia* the dorm gate, although closed and monitored, would be unlocked. Most exiting visitors could pass through without much delay. My total exposure to the dorm could be as little as thirty seconds, if everything went right.

Now that we knew the best time to make the attempt would be at 1:42 p.m. of a third-*guardia* day, we turned our attention to deciding the best day of the week. On Sunday the *lista* (roll call) was taken as the visitors were leaving. They would discover my absence before I was even beyond checkpoint 3. Sunday was out. No general visitors were allowed in Lecumberri on Monday, so that too was out. Barbara had thought that I should leave the dorm on a Tuesday, which was a general visiting day for "F." But after observing the gate on three consecutive Tuesdays, I noticed that the *commandos* patrolled the gate of dorm "F" and inspected the visitors with extra caution, so Tuesday likewise was out.

Wednesday through Saturday were *defensor* days for dorm "F," although general visiting days for various other dorms. On *defensor* days, visiting women had to sign in and deposit photographic identification, picking it up when they left. It would impossible to leave the prison as a woman *defensor* visitor on these days because there was no way we could forge a photograph of me in drag. The more I studied the days, the more they pointed to the inevitable conclusion: *no day worked*. Everything was covered.

I watched the patterns and shifts again and again for two more weeks, first observing that on *defensor* visiting days for "F," security at the gate was lax because there were so few visitors. I might be able to get out of the dorm, but not the prison. On general visiting days, Barbara told me that if I had been outside of the dorm as a woman, I would have a decent chance to leave the prison because of the crowds. But never did the two occur together.

For another week I studied the patterns, drawing elaborate

prison maps and timing charts, studying them over and over late into the night. Finally late one night the missing piece to our puzzle appeared to me in a flash. Although I could not leave the prison as a *defensor* visitor, *I could leave dorm "F" as a defensor.* Other dorms would be having general visiting days, so I could then sneak around to the general visitor exit gate, checkpoint 4. There I would have to present the guard a metal tag from a dorm having general visiting on this day. After that, the critical point would be sneaking by the guards at checkpoint 3, where the metal tags and paper passes were exchanged. To get by them, I would need to have the biggest crowds possible as the visitors exited.

For the next three weeks, while I investigated the general visiting days for other dorms, Barbara observed the size of the crowds. Thursday and Saturday were not crowded at all, she said, and Friday was erratic, sometimes crowded, sometimes practically empty. Wednesday would be the day.

So I knew that I could only leave on a Wednesday at 1:42 p.m., with the third *guardia* shift and the first *commando* shift. That meant that the crucial factors of the escape boiled down to once every Wednesday, once every third-guard shift, and once every other *commando* shift. $1/7 \times 1/3 \times 1/2 = 1/42$: once every forty-two days would the conditions coincide to be ideal. I got my calendar down. The next possible day would be November 5. Too early, we would never be ready with the forged metal tags and forged paper passes by then. It would have to be forty-two days later, on December 17, 1975. The next available date would be January 28, 1976. Too late, for we would have run out of money by then.

I circled December 17 on the calendar.

27 Accomplice Number One

One general visiting day Barbara and I were jostled out of our plotting by a loud banging on the cell door, accompanied by a raucous voice.

"All right, you guys. Open up. Make room for a *ménage à trois!*"

I rushed to the cell door and unlocked it. That voice could only belong to one person. The door swung open and there she was, grinning triumphantly at the surprise on my face.

Mame Levinson came swaggering in.

I squeezed my errant mother-away-from-home like never before. I hadn't seen her since her run-in with Cardenas and the U.S. Embassy six months ago and I had not known if I ever would again.

"How did you get back into Lecumberri?"

"I broke in."

"Mame . . ."

"Oh, I had a cozy chat with the colonel and turned on the charm. I even suggested that I might let the goddamned bastard have the honor of taking me to the best restaurant in town! Anyway here I am—God, I hate to admit it but this stinking hole feels like home."

I sat down between Mame and Barbara with my arms around both, listening while Mame launched into a diatribe covering herself, Mexico, and life. Sitting there gazing at Mame, I realized that since she would be a regular visitor again, I would have to tell her the truth. She would need to know it for her own protection. I was certain that we could trust her—she would not be so unthinking as to blurt out any part of it to anyone. So without even discussing it with Barbara, I plunged.

"Mame, can you keep a secret?"

"Is it a dirty one?" Her eyebrows arched.

"A very serious one. You should know this so you can be far away from here when it happens. Mame, I'm going to try to escape."

She stopped right in the middle of a drag on her cigarette, her face losing its levity. "Oh . . . you are."

I nodded, not sure what her reaction would be. She sat unusually silent for a moment, then took another puff. "Well, it's about time one of you guys got off your ass and did something. Do you need any help?"

Barbara and I breathed a heavy sigh of relief and gratitude.

"Yes, I sure do," Barbara volunteered.

"Well, I've never engaged in this sort of thing before, but I'm very versatile, you know."

"Now, look Mame, if they find out you helped us in any way—"

"Right. Cardenas will take me to dinner. Come on, spill it."

Barbara and I told her the complete plan. She listened carefully, asking questions about details, offering advice when necessary. As we continued, I felt a great sense of relief in having her on our side. Her help and insights would be invaluable.

Barbara told Mame that she needed her help in making an observation at checkpoint 3. Together they would test the security there. Before the bugle blew, they were ready to go.

As Mame and I approached checkpoint 3, I prepared to give her my metal tag to exchange for me so that I could continue on through to the driveway beyond. I felt a flutter of nervousness: this wasn't the best time to try it. Today was a first-*guardia* day, and since we had left the dorm a couple of minutes early, there were only a few women at the counters to provide the distraction for what we were about to do.

I had seen it happen many times during my observations of the last three weeks: hoping to avoid wading through the crowds at the counter, a woman would give her tag to a friend and move along toward the next checkpoint. Her friend would then exchange both tags for paper passes and catch up with her in the driveway. It was like moving away from a crowded bar while your escort got you a drink—simple and efficient. And so common, I thought, that the guards had gotten used to it and didn't mind. If Mame and I got away with it on a first-*guardia* day, when there weren't too many women around, we would know for certain that Dwight could succeed with his own version of the practice on a third-*guardia* day, when there would be a huge crowd.

I gave Mame the tag and walked on through, without glancing at the guards. Ten feet, twenty feet ahead, almost into the driveway, I heard running footsteps behind me.

"Pssst! *Guera! Ven aqui!*"

I froze. Roughly spinning me around, the guard steered me quickly back to checkpoint 3. I could see Mame ahead, standing with her hand on the other guard's arm, talking to him in her most syrupy voice. He was smiling and slyly winking at her, but he stopped abruptly when his partner approached with me. Then both men started in. Loudly and with threatening voices they announced that we had broken the rules and could be arrested right there for such an act. I tried to speak, but the guard ordered me to be silent. Mame, soothing and calm, instantly became remorseful and explained how deeply sorry she was, it was only because I had been feeling ill today that she herself had suggested I move ahead and leave my tag with her. I looked pained. The guard released us with a lecture on the importance of returning my *own* metal tag in exchange for the paper pass. Those were the rules, they said, turning to Mame, no matter how sick anybody was. The next time it would go badly for me.

"*Muy bien,*" soothed Mame, grateful and secretly patronizing all at once, "*Claro que sí, jefe.*" And finally we were on our way. My heart was pounding. Had it not been for Mame's perfect act with the guards, things could have taken an ugly turn. But as we continued down the driveway toward the ramp, Mame reassured me.

"Relax, will you? All it means is that he'll have to do it on a third-*guardia* day. You knew that anyway. I mean, the third-*guardia* are so old they're all half blind. Jesus, they don't know their asses from food on the table."

I knew she was right, but I felt weak and shaky as I imagined Dwight hearing those running footsteps behind him. I kept reminding myself that I had tried it under the worst possible conditions. With a crowd, on a third-*guardia* day, it should be much easier. I forced myself to calm down as Mame steered me up the ramp and down the stairs.

Here at checkpoint 2, a crowd would again be helpful. If there had been a crowd at the last checkpoint, there would now be a steady stream of mothers, children, housewives, whores, and an occasional *gringa* filing past the guard at the foot of the stairs. The guard would simply take the paper passes from the women's outstretched hands and throw them in a box behind him. But today the guard looked carefully at his signature on our passes and asked us our names before letting us go by. I again reminded myself that this was the exception.

From there, Mame and I walked the twenty feet to the street door and checkpoint 1. The guards flanking the doorway looked us over without stopping us and we were outside. I asked Mame if she would like to see the spot where I planned to be waiting in a car with Enrique, a neighbor, when Dwight walked out.

"Yeah, sure, I've got time for a little walk."

We crossed the street behind the prison and walked one block along the north side of a huge shoe factory, turning behind it into a narrow alley which dead-ended in an immense hill of stinking garbage. Mame sniffed distastefully.

"Jesus, not a very romantic spot for your rendezvous, is it?"

"No, but it's the first place that's beyond the line-of-sight of the machine gun towers. That factory blocks their view."

"God, Barbara, I've heard so much talk from those boys about how they're all going to break out of there, you know?" Mame narrowed her eyes at me over her cigarette. "But you two are really going to go through with this, aren't you?"

I smiled at her without answering.

"Yeah, well, if anyone can do it, you can. D'you already have the makeup and the clothes and all that for him? And a wig too. Oh Jesus, Barbara, this is so exciting. I mean, I just get chills . . ."

"No, I was going to begin buying those things this week so I can figure out how to smuggle them in. It'll be easier when I see what I have to work with."

"Why wait? I can drive you to that gorgeous new shopping mall we've got up in Echegaray. And listen, did I ever tell you about my friend Ginger? Well, she has the most marvelous wig store—"

At that point, I interrupted her with a giant hug.

I sat before a huge mirror, trying on wig after wig. Mame's friend Ginger flitted around me, proclaiming each one more "darling" than the last. Most of the wigs looked ridiculously unnatural, except for a brunette one that was cut in a long, wavy shag. I studied myself carefully in the wig, imagining it on Dwight instead. The color was different enough from Dwight's own hair to be distracting, but not so different as to look impossible with his complexion. Its waves were unexaggerated and natural and would soften the angles of Dwight's face, and it was long enough to cover his ears and his fifteen-inch neck.

"What do you think, Mame?"

"Don't you think that platinum afro would be better?" She was grinning, but her eyes were narrowed appraisingly in the mirror.

Gabrielle was watching me intently. "You look different, Mommy."

That decided it. I paid for the wig and we left.

I found myself enjoying the colorful glitter and bustle of the shopping mall. As I followed Mame through the huge department store—a Mexican equivalent of Macy's—I realized that this was the first time I had gone out anywhere since we had arrived in Mexico City. It was a relief to be away from the prison for a change, to be out shopping with my "girlfriend" for an afternoon.

My girlfriend had stopped under a strobe light in the record department to riffle through the latest rock album releases, but I dragged her away to ladies' sportswear. After much deliberation, we chose a conservative white blouse, size 38, and a soft grey sweater that would be big enough to camouflage the lady's considerable biceps. Then, up the escalator to the yard goods department, where I bought enough pale green cloth to sew two long skirts. Now the hard part: lingerie.

After I chose some panty-style nylons (size tall), we moved on to the bra section. Mame and I compared Spandex, foam-padded, and underwired pointy ones for "extra support." That the lady wouldn't need, not for her breasts anyhow. Mame finally drifted off to another counter as I settled on a plain white, foam-padded, 36-B bra that looked as if it would take well to stuffing.

I was paying for the bra and stockings when Mame nudged my arm. She dangled a pair of bikini panties in front of my face. They were strategically adorned with a patch of transparent pink lace.

"Hey, don't you think she'll need a pair of these? Or maybe a girdle would be better. Jesus, Barbara, she's apt to get so excited walking out of there, she's liable to have an erection, for God's sake. Maybe you'd better tie it to her leg—I mean, you know, just to make sure she doesn't give it away at the wrong moment."

"Mame! Ssh!"

The sales clerk was looking at us strangely.

"No, Barbara, I'm serious—you've got to take every precaution, you know. Masking tape might not be strong enough. How about heavy twine? Adhesive, maybe. This is a toughie . . ."

That night at home, with Gabrielle asleep, I locked my door and spread the day's purchases out on my bed. Except for the paper passes and metal tags, we now had all the raw materials for escape. I put away all the makeup and the inexpensive jewelry that Mame had helped to select, and carefully hid the wig in a locked suitcase, with a shiver of fear or excitement. The escape was suddenly much more real to me.

I spread out the length of green cloth on the floor and set about cutting out two simple long skirts. I sewed them up on the sewing machine that Mame had loaned me to make a shirt for Dwight to wear on our wedding. I put a zipper in only one of the skirts, hemming the other one to fit me at angle length, sewing on some snaps at the waist, and fitting it like a lining inside the zippered skirt. I sewed the edges of the waist opening flush with the zipper of the outside skirt. Then I machine-basted the two skirts together through their waistbands to look like decorative stitching, and turned the hem of the outside one over the hem of the inside one. The final touch was a detachable ruffle basted along the hem on the outside.

I tried on this creation and studied myself in the full-length mirror. The skirt was a bit heavy, but otherwise it seemed perfect. I would have to add a belt to cinch in the waist to fit me. As soon as I got into Dwight's cell, we would rip the two skirts apart. I would wear the "lining" and Dwight would hide his. The skirt would be just long enough to cover his large calf muscles, and it would look perfectly Victorian and feminine.

The clothing would be the easiest part of the smuggling, but because its bulk made it hard to hide in the cell, it would have to be among the last things I smuggled in. First things first. Before anything else, somehow I would have to get ten items of makeup into the prison.

I got out the wedding shirt I was embroidering for Dwight, and climbed into bed to think it over while I stitched. Hiding things in my clothing was out of the question; even the most casual matrons were careful to feel all seams and linings. No matter how I tried to avoid it, there was only one method of smuggling items of makeup into the prison: internally. I had never yet received an internal search from the matrons. Although I was quite squeamish about the thought, I would have to risk it, but only on third-*guardia* days when the matrons were most lax, and with Gabrielle along as a distraction at the *defensor* entrance where the matrons knew us.

The problem of the paper passes nagged at my mind. Forging them perfectly was the most critical thing I would have to do, and it was time to start thinking about how to do it. The passes were issued in a different color every day, and I could never be certain which of eight possible colors would be used on any given day. As the colors of the forgeries would have to be perfect matches to the real thing, I had already begun tearing a minute corner off of each different paper pass as I left the prison, and these tiny samples were now taped to a large sheet of paper for safekeeping.

But the more difficult problem was printing the correct information on the passes. Not only would I have to memorize all of the words and numbers, but also the exact typeface used, the margins and spacing of the lines, and the size of the passes. Somehow I would have to do all this before I could have a printer forge the slips.

So much to do, and only ten weeks before December 17. I heard the silence of my room. It was late; I was tired. I picked up the half-done embroidery to put it away. Tonight I had finished the detailed central figure of one panel: a white, silver-winged Pegasus prancing from the night into daylight. But the figures of Dwight and me were still only faint pencil outlines on his back.

The next day, Barbara and Gabrielle came through the gate in a bolt. As I leaned to kiss her she rushed straight past me up the stairway.

"Hurry."

I followed her into my cell, carrying Gabrielle. Before I could embrace her she commanded, "Lock the door!"

I did so, not understanding why. As soon as the cell door was sealed, Barbara reached under her skirt and pulled out two wrinkled blue paper passes and handed them to me. Her face was aglow. They were the paper passes used for entering visitors!

"The guard was being deliberately slow, hoping for a bribe. When I didn't give it to him, he walked over to another counter to check another woman. So while he wasn't looking, I *stole* these!"

Magnificent. Authentic passes. I examined them. Complicated printing, but not impossible to duplicate. This pass was for Tuesday, though, and we needed one for Wednesday. But at least now we had something.

Barbara and I sat down on the bunk to discuss the plan while Gabrielle fed the kittens. Elated by Barbara's pilfering the pass, we turned to the most dangerous aspect of the plan, smuggling the items of makeup past the matrons. Barbara calmly explained her decision about carrying each one in internally. I hesitated. It had been a third-*guardia* matron who had made the fuss about the pies on my birthday not long ago, and any of them could suddenly decide to give Barbara her first internal search.

We were pondering this problem when suddenly the cell was filled with the scent of a French boudoir. Gabrielle, who had been playing quietly, approached us to show us something. It was a glass vial of perfume. I asked her where it had come from, wondering where she could have come by such a strange bit of contraband in prison. Gabrielle calmly told me that she had *brought* it herself.

"Brought it? HOW?"

With a conspiratorial little smile, she matter-of-factly patted the hammer pocket of her Farm Bureau Co-op overalls.

"Right there."

Barbara and I looked at each other in simultaneous revelation. That was it! That was the way to bring in the makeup: put a little bit of lipstick on Gabrielle, then put it in her overall pocket. We quickly conjectured: Barbara could pull a wooly poncho over all of Gabrielle's clothes to pad any telltale bump from the matron's touch. She was sure that at the *defensor* entrance, the matrons would never detect anything in the cursory searches they gave Gabrielle. And if they did find it, Barbara would just feign surprise, scold Gabrielle for picking up her makeup when she wasn't looking, and tell the matron that she would leave it outside.

An innocuous smuggle. We were confident that this would work for most of the makeup, and for the things that weren't feasible—well, Barbara still had her own hiding place. By the time the bugle blew, we were jubilant.

28 Accomplice Number Two

We would try it today. I dressed Gabrielle in her Farm Bureau Co-op overalls and let her touch the lipstick to her lips. Then I put it in one of the pockets in the bib of her overalls, explaining to her that we were going to sneak the lipstick in to Dwight, just as she had done with the perfume. She giggled in conspiracy with me. I layered a shirt, sweater, and bulky wool poncho over her overalls, and then felt her chest carefully for the lipstick. It was barely noticeable, and I was pretty sure that the matron wouldn't detect it in her usual light search. Nor would it seem unusual to her that Gabrielle was heavily bundled up; to the Mexicans the early morning chill in the city was severely cold.

At ten minutes to nine, we were first in line at the front door of Lecumberri. I felt a tingle of tension, but I was not nervous or jittery, knowing that my attitude would have to be perfectly normal to carry it off, and taking my cue from Gabrielle, who was her usual smiling self.

When the door opened, we rushed in and were first to get to the body search. I greeted the third-*guardia* matrons warmly and respectfully. It was early in the morning and their teeth were chattering. I sympathized in Spanish, while one matron felt my clothes and body, and checked my hair as always to make sure that I wasn't wearing a wig. As I was speaking, the matron turned to Gabrielle. I kept talking, hoping to distract her. She passed her hands down Gabrielle's back and chest, patted her bottom, and waved us through.

I scooped up Gabrielle in a hug, grinning from ear to ear, singing inside, feeling a building momentum. *It was going to work.*

I picked Gabrielle up at the gate and began carrying her up the stairs. She reached beneath her poncho.

"I have a surprise for you," she said, handing me a tube of lipstick in front of a Mexican prisoner. I quickly stuffed it into my pocket. "Wait, honey, not here," I whispered.

Safely within the cell, I explained to Gabrielle that the lipstick was a secret surprise just for me, and that no one else should know our secrets. She listened attentively. Then she spoke.

"Put it on."

"Not now," I said, shaking my head. "Let's hide it first."

I had a five-inch-thick foam mattress on my bunk. With a razor blade I carefully sliced into the edge of it until I had a pocket six inches deep. Holding the gash in the foam open, I let Gabrielle put the lipstick in. I released the foam and the cut disappeared. Later I would glue it shut. Gabrielle smiled, enjoying sharing a secret.

I squeezed the mattress. Only with firm direct pressure could I feel the tube of lipstick. For now, this would do.

I turned to Barbara.

"Smuggle number one."

"*Twenty* more to go." We hugged anyway.

"I had my blood test taken yesterday, and Ferrer-Gamboa gave me the forms to fill out for the wedding."

"Good. My blood tests are scheduled at the infirmary tomorrow. When does Ferrer-Gamboa say we'll be married?"

He says he'll have the date within a week or two. Soon, anyhow."

"And in the meantime we can keep on smuggling the makeup."

Every third day, when the third-*guardia* was on duty, Gabrielle brought me a new "surprise." She pulled it out of the bib pocket or hammer pocket of her overalls and together we stashed it within the hidden pockets of the foam mattress. Mascara, eye shadow, stick makeup, eye liner, foundation makeup, fingernail polish, rouge. Gabrielle spoke in a soft, secretive voice, while Barbara, the true risk taker in this venture, remained cool, calculating the logistics of the next smuggle. And with each successful smuggle, Barbara became more confident that the next one would succeed.

Three weeks later I had all the makeup in the cell. Now I had to learn what to do with it, so Barbara gave me my first lesson. I retrieved all of the makeup from the mattress and spread them on my desk. Then she directed me, piece by piece. First stick makeup, then foundation, then the four eye makeups, rouge, powder, and lipstick—a long and complicated process.

The eyes were the most difficult. Every night for two weeks I practiced, after the 10 o'clock lockup. Not only was I aiming for quality, but for speed of application too. And each night after I was done I had to scrub my face with soap to get all of it off. Once already a Mexican prisoner at *campo* had detected a trace of mascara on my eyelashes and had begun to say something. I had quickly walked away. Now, after each makeup session, I washed my face twice. In time I was finally able to do a quality makeup job in forty minutes.

But no matter what I did, my growing beard and moustache protruded through the makeup. With the whiskers and makeup, I looked like a creation of Hollywood or New York City nightlife and nothing more. Although I kept telling myself that it would be different after I shaved, all I saw in my mirror was a blatant drag queen.

29 The "Object Lesson"

"WOR-KER, WOR-KER! *SUBITE! VAMOS! VAMOS! EL EMBAJADOR DE LOS ESTADOS UNIDOS ESTA AQUÍ EN LECUMBERRI A VISITARTE! VAMOS!"*

I jumped up, jolted abruptly from my studies of the escape plan, and looked out the door. Sure enough, there was the U.S. ambassador to Mexico, John Joseph Jova, standing below my cell, looking around at the dorm. I recognized him immediately, having seen his face in the Mexican newspapers many times. A grey-haired, slender, and dignified-looking man in his mid-fifties, he was a man appropriate in appearance and manner to the role of ambassador. Jova was supposedly the most popular ambassador the United States had ever sent to Mexico. And he was here to see *me*.

He was surrounded by an entourage of bodyguards and prison officials. I worked my way up to him and we finally spoke for perhaps ten minutes. He was cordial and nondescript—the way ambassadors are supposed to be.

I first told Jova that I was guilty and that perhaps I deserved what I was getting. But I insisted that there were many other Americans here in prison who were innocent and serving long sentences.

He listened, but said nothing. I imagined that the major goal of an ambassador is to not commit himself or say anything controversial, to maintain a low profile without offending anyone.

Jova avoided commenting on the innocents in prison, but he did commend my "honesty" in admitting my guilt. He felt that, although my situation was unfortunate, drug smugglers should be punished. I did not dispute with him, but I told him what had happened to me, including the torture, forced confessions, violations of rights, and extortion.

He said nothing.

We shook hands and he left.

Later, John Joseph Jova would say that although ". . . torture is repugnant to me personally, a little torture, and a little suffering for impudent criminals who are a blight on our society might serve as a nice object lesson for their long-haired pals back in the U.S.A."

That statement did not surprise me. I didn't expect him to defend me. I wasn't even defending myself. I would not have paid Jova's visit any further attention, except that a short while later, Jova's son was arrested for smuggling two and three-quarter pounds of cocaine into England.

Well, well, well. I guess I didn't serve as enough of an object lesson for Jova's long-haired pals.

I quickly wrote a long letter to Ambassador Jova. In it I told him that at least young Jova had the foresight to get himself arrested in a country with a long tradition of civil liberties. Ambassador Jova would at least not have to worry about phone calls at 3:00 a.m. from a screaming son begging for more extortion money to end the torture. Then I got personally nasty. I wrote a make-believe transcript of a vile telephone conversation between Jova and son. As I ended the letter I wished I could see the expression on Jova's face as he read it.

The next morning I got up and reread the letter. Then I remembered Barbara's description of my father. She had visited my parents before she came to Mexico City. My parents loved her from the start, although they could not completely understand why she wanted to visit me. Barbara described my father as pale and distraught, ill-at-ease whenever I was spoken of. Once, in the middle of talking about me, he broke down crying. Although Barbara avoided saying it directly to me, I knew that Dad was taking it really hard. My imprisonment was a heavy mental and physical burden for him. When Barbara left my parents, both Dad and Mom were crying.

I realized that John Jova was now a part of the same unfortunate club that I had put my parents in. I had written a sick letter from a vengeful, compassionless mind. Even now, deeply involved in the escape plan, in love with Barbara, and feeling more respect for myself than ever before, I had fallen prey to the poison of Lecumberri.

I tore the letter up.

30 Confirmation

I was called to the *polígano* late the next afternoon by a small, officious Mexican government lawyer. He handed me a sealed envelope and then rapidly read a legal document aloud. The Spanish legal jargon was too complicated for me to understand completely. He finished his statement in a flourish, then nodded his head. Meeting over. I was escorted back to dorm "F."

In my cell I read the statement I'd been given. It said that I had been pronounced officially guilty of *importación* and sentenced to serve six years and nine months. Six years and nine months. I had never seen the judge or prosecutor, or entered a courtroom, or made a plea of guilt or innocence. But at least I hadn't gotten fourteen years like some of the other Americans were getting. My trial was finally over. I saved the paper to show Barbara when she returned.

If everything went right, I would be free in September 1980.

The next morning Jaime burst into my cell.

"Hear the news? The guards killed Miguel Dominguez Rodriguez last night. They caught him trying to escape on the roof of dorm "L." I was at the hospital this morning and talked to a doctor there. He says his body had been stabbed thirty to forty times."

I had met Miguel Rodriguez once when I had been in the hospital. He had been arrested as a *politico* in the aftermath of the student massacre in Plaza de las Tres Culturas in Mexico City in the summer of 1968. Five years in prison for organizing a demonstration, and now he was dead.

In the *rondin* later that day Ron Hunter, an American in Dorm "L," called me to the gate. He whispered that he had witnessed the whole thing last night. Ron had been awakened by bright lights and shouting guards. Peering through the edge of his cell door, Ron saw Miguel Rodriguez on the roof of dormitory "L," surrounded by armed guards with fixed bayonets. The guards continued stabbing Miguel long after he had fallen and stopped moving. Only then did they lower his body to the floor by a rope.

Barbara came into dorm "F" the next day more nervous than usual. She handed me a headline article from an October 12,

1975 Mexico City newspaper. Before I began it, I gave her my sentence to read.

In Spanish the headline read:

PRISONER DIES IN ATTEMPTED ESCAPE FROM LECUMBERRI
Agreed on Mutual Suicide Pact

The article explained that two Mexican prisoners had attempted to escape by climbing up on the roof of dormitory "L." They were discovered, but before the guards could intervene, one of the would-be escapees, Miguel Dominguez Rodriguez, stabbed himself to death. Later the investigators found out that he had previously arranged a mutual suicide pact with his partner in the escape. The other would-be escapee, although critically wounded, was still alive, according to the article.

The state-controlled Mexican press.

Now we had seen the unwritten law of escape—*la ley de fuga*—in action. The stakes became frighteningly clear.

Barbara handed back my sentence. In one hand I held the newspaper article; in the other, my sentence—six years and nine months. September 1980.

I tore up the sentence. Our plans were unchanged. The escape was on.

I fasted twice for five days each time to lose some of my shoulder and arm bulk. Although I was no longer weightlifting, I continued running. One day, while jogging at *campo*, I felt a bowel movement coming. Since there were no toilets here, the prisoners always used the far corner of *campo* to relieve themselves. This foul area was covered with little piles of dung and swarming with flies. But like a cat I always made sure to bury mine.

I had no toilet paper, so I looked around for a newspaper or a bag. Instead I found a charred pile of paper that had just recently been burned. A guard had ignited it with fuel. I searched through the ashes until I found a handful of partially burned paper slips. As I squatted, I idly looked at the paper.

Oh my God—used paper passes!

Evidently the guards got rid of them by burning them here. I finished up my business as quickly as possible and rushed back to the pile of charred paper. Halfway up to my elbows in ashes, I sifted through the remains for any more intact passes. I found a handful. None were perfect, but by pairing the different remaining parts, I could construct whole slips. I searched and searched, finding eight different color samples. Finally I found one that said *MIÉRCOLES* (Wednesday). That was the essential day we needed.

"*QUE HACES, GRINGO?*"

I jerked my head up. A machine-gun-toting guard on the *campo* wall had been watching me search through the paper.

"*Tengo disentería, jefe. Necessito papel higiénico*" (I've got dysentery, chief. I need toilet paper), I said with forced urgency in my voice.

"*OKAY, GRINGO. CAGARLE!*"

I squatted again, fanning through my "toilet paper." Pretending now to relieve myself, I couldn't wait to get back to Barbara.

Sitting at the desk, piecing together the charred bits of paper passes, we patched up a complete pass for *MIÉRCOLES,* and samples of the eight possible colors of paper it could be printed on. We had already made paper rubbings from all of the possible metal tags. Now all we needed were the real blank passes and the metal tags themselves. The paper passes would have to be counterfeited, the tags forged. Barbara would have to go to a shop someplace and have the work done—but not in Mexico City. Everyone here knew of Lecumberri, the Black Palace, and no doubt many people visited relatives imprisoned here. There would be no one, even outside Mexico City, we could trust.

Barbara sighed. After her exhaustive trip back to the border with Gabrielle to obtain their visas, she had sworn she would never again travel north except to get out of the country for good. But we had no other choice: it would be safer to have it done in the United States, and the quality of the printing would undoubtedly be better, too. Barbara left early to make arrangements for the trip, while I scanned the calendar for the thousandth time: her trip would mean a loss of one week of preparation for the escape. November 25, 1975: three weeks to go.

31 Counterfeit

It took two days of searching in Brownsville to locate a rambling, run-down metalworking shop on a dusty road on the northernmost fringe of town. In a makeshift office inside the corrugated metal building I found an elderly Chicana. In Spanish, I described to her what I needed. She called her son who, after half an hour's poking around through piles of old dusty metal, came up with two scraps that were perfect. One was of brass, and the other of a nickel alloy, and because they were old, they already had the tarnished appearance of the metal tags for dorms "F" and "C."

I was jubilant with his discovery. Giving the Chicano the paper patterns for the tags that I had made from our pencil rubbings, and explaining thoroughly what I needed, I promised to be back early the next morning to pick up the finished tags.

When I left the shop it was already 4:00 p.m., but if I hurried, I could check out the last printer on my list. It took an hour's walk to find the tiny printing shop on the opposite end of town; to my relief, it was still open. The sky had darkened and fat raindrops began to splatter in the dust as I walked in the open door. The shop was humming with the rhythmic clatter of the printing presses, while the blades of an old ceiling fan turned ineffectually against the thick, humid air. The tall, rangy printer straightened up from his presses with a smile and introduced himself.

I got out the worn envelope containing two authentic paper passes—one for Wednesday and one for Friday (as an alternate day)—and the color samples, explaining for the fifth time that day what I needed, stressing that the copies had to be exact to the finest detail, and that the colors of the paper had to match perfectly.

The printer surprised me by holding one of the passes to the light, explaining that the watermark in the paper was indicative of its grade. He had noticed a detail that I had missed. Then he got out a thick book of paper samples and was able to match every color perfectly. The passes, he said, would be ready on Friday morning.

It was now Wednesday. I was impressed with the printer's efficiency and precision; he was going to do a good counterfeit without even realizing it. I walked back to the hotel through the pouring rain, feeling good: I had gotten everything going within eight hours of my arrival in Brownsville. If all went right, I should be back in Mexico City on Saturday morning in time to see Dwight.

When I awoke at 7:00 a.m., it was already steamy hot. After a cold shower, I walked to the metalworking shop to find twenty perfect metal tags waiting for me: ten brass diamond-shapes for the dorm "F" *defensor* visit, and ten nickel rectangles for the dorm "C" general visit. I gratefully paid the Chicano eighteen dollars, complimenting him on his good work.

On the way back to the hotel, I stopped in a hardware store and bought a set of metal dies to stamp the necessary letters and numbers on the metal tags. I was careful to match the type and size of the letters to the pencil rubbings of the real tags.

Back in my room, I realized that I had all my business taken care of. All that remained was to pick up the paper passes from the printer in the morning. For the first time in three months I had a whole afternoon free. I quickly changed my clothes, walked to the nearby terminal, and took a bus east toward the gulf.

The driver let me off by long, deserted sand dunes, explaining that his bus, the only one, would be returning to Brownsville at 4:00 p.m., and that I should be waiting at this spot on the highway to catch him then.

As the sound of the engine died away on the flat, empty highway, I heard the waves crashing unseen on the other side of the dunes. With a rush of excitement, I took off running, scrambling up a dune to its crest. Before me, the ocean stretched to the sky, and the beach curved away empty on either side. There wasn't a soul in sight. I tore off my clothes and ran down to the water, jumping through the waves, gasping from the chill, to swim beyond the breakers.

I rolled and played mindlessly in the waves for a long time before staggering out onto the hot sand. My body glowed and tingled. The relief from the sun and wind and water—the release of the tension—overwhelmed me. I reveled in the solitude after the hordes of the city, but the joy was hollow. How long would it be before Dwight, Gabrielle, and I could run together on a beach like this?

At 10:00 the next morning the printer was cutting the passes to size. Without pausing in the rhythm of his motion with the huge paper cutter, he handed me one of the newly printed passes, along with the original of the same color.

I gasped. Even to my hypercritical eye, the two passes were perfectly identical. I had expected good replicas, but the forgery far surpassed my expectations. Even to the darkness of the print, the forgery was perfect to the last and finest detail. Except that the original was dog-eared, I could not have told them apart.

I wanted to jump up and down and hug the tall printer. But I settled for telling him again and again what a beautiful job he had done. He separated the passes into those for Wednesday and Friday and then packed them in a bag for me. Although I had told him that I needed only ten or twenty of each color, he had printed literally hundreds of them. I would have enough passes to help half the inmates of Lecumberri escape.

How much did I owe him?

Twelve-fifty.

For all those? I was incredulous, but the printer insisted that the expense was not in how many were printed, but in setting the type. He steadfastly refused to take a penny more.

What a joy to be in the U.S. again! I paid the printer and thanked him over and over again.

As the bus pulled out of Brownsville at 6:00 that evening, my spirits were high. I had gotten the forgeries done in two and a half days when Dwight and I had estimated it could take as long as a week. We were ahead of our schedule and the forgeries couldn't be more perfect. I could hardly wait to report all the good news to headquarters.

32 Return

I settled back into my seat as the bus left Brownsville and passed through the squalid border shacks of Matamoros. The desert swallowed the outermost fringes of the town and stretched out empty in all directions, its harsh edges softened by the rose-gold of sunset.

November 30: the escape was only seventeen days away. Not much time left—where did we stand? The makeup was all smuggled in and hidden. I would still have to wear in the tinted ladies' glasses that I had had made to Dwight's prescription. The clothing was ready for me to wear in, which I thought should be relatively easy. All that remained was for me to stamp the metal tags with the numbers and letters, and for Dwight to corrode them and otherwise make them look old and worn. The paper passes were complete. I felt a thrill of satisfaction at the thought of how perfect they were. Because of their small size, neither the tags nor the passes would be any harder to smuggle than the makeup, but they would be the most deadly to get caught with. I would wait until the very last few days to smuggle them in.

That left the bulky wig. The question of how to smuggle it had been nagging at me for weeks. With only seventeen days to go, I had to figure out a way. I couldn't *wear* the wig in; the matrons always felt my hair to make sure that I wasn't wearing one. And no matter how I compacted the wig, it was still the size of a softball. It was just too bulky to hide on my body.

Dwight had mentioned that we could conceal the wig inside a radio and bribe a third-*guardia* official to bring in the radio from outside, but I had an instinctive feeling against using the guards for anything. I was sure it would blow up in our faces if we did.

There remained only one avenue for smuggling the wig: to hide it in something that was allowed for "deposit" to a prisoner. I had previously taken such things as books, bedding, certain clothing, and writing supplies to an office near the *defensor* entrance, where a guard had searched through them and then typed an itemized receipt for the goods with Dwight's name and dormitory and my name. I then had to put my thumbprint on his copy of the receipt. The things were delivered to Dwight in his dormitory later the same day, but not before they were searched again by another group of guards in the interior of the prison.

With so many security checks during the deposit, I'd have to think up a foolproof way of hiding the wig. I thought about all the things I had deposited to Dwight over the past months: books, writing and art supplies, mousetraps, pillows.

Pillows. What if I hid the wig loosely in the middle of a well-stuffed pillow? The wig would be soft like the foam stuffing and undetectable no matter how the guards punched the pillow. Surely the only way they would find it would be if they tore all the stuffing out, and they wouldn't do that without due cause for suspicion.

I felt a rush of excitement. The only hitch was that *if* somehow they discovered the wig, they would know who to get. Dwight would at very least be thrown into heavy punishment, and I—well, Dwight and I would have to talk about it.

The bus sped through the desert twilight into night. I switched on the light above me and got out my embroidery for Dwight's wedding shirt. I had begun the second panel. On it, Pegasus had metamorphosed into a phoenix high in the sky, with rainwater streaming from one wing into daylight, and comet fire from the other wing into night. The volcano that had been quiescent in the nighttime background of the first panel was now erupting and spewing fire in the second. I was absorbed in this cosmos growing under my needle as the bus roared southward.

33 December 1

Sixteen days to go. What Barbara had accomplished in forging the passes and metal tags now made the plan more real to me than ever before. It was as if I had spent every day in this prison preparing for the escape. And now I allowed myself the forbidden luxury of imagining what it would really be like to be on the "outside"—the thought of actually going swimming . . . in the ocean . . . under a hot sun . . . with Barbara . . . almost brought tears to my eyes.

But I was very worried about the wig. Of all the items Barbara had so ingeniously smuggled in, the wig was the most dangerous and, if discovered, the most damaging. To hide it inside a pillow and deposit it at the gate was, of course, the only way we could get it in, but if the guards did happen to open it and find the wig, both of us would be in deep trouble.

"It's not the pillow itself that bothers me," I told Barbara, "I just don't want *you* to deposit it, or *me* to receive it. But"—I was thinking aloud—"if someone else who had never before visited this prison were to deposit the pillow for another prisoner whom I had never met, there would be no risk to us. Do you see what I mean?"

"Yes. A person named A deposits the pillow under his name and leaves his thumbprint on the deposit receipt, requesting that the pillow be sent to B, who knows neither of us."

"Right."

"Okay. If the wig is found, A never returns to the prison anyway and has left a phony address, so he can't be located or charged. But what about B?"

"B simply denies knowledge of the pillow or its contents, having never heard of or seen A in his life, which is absolutely true. It will be an obvious attempt at smuggling, but nobody'll ever get caught."

"Okay. But now how does B, someone you've never met, get the pillow to you?"

"Through an interceptor."

"Dwight, we can't—we'd have to tell somebody and we can't risk—"

"No, wait, Barbara, wait: I have a plan."

Later that day I approached my closest friend Jaime with a request that would have seemed outlandish to anyone outside of prison, but that, inside Lecumberri, was treated with the respect and confidentiality of a high-level business deal (which for me it was). Jaime only needed to know that the item inside the pillow was not a weapon or a drug—contraband the guards always looked for—and that I could not meet the prisoner receiving the pillow. Asking no further questions, he did some checking and figured out on his own that for whatever reasons we wanted the pillow, it was so dangerous that it should not come into my dorm at all but into "G," where a prisoner named Raul Aceves would receive it and get it to Jaime with no questions asked for 500 pesos.

I looked at Jaime and couldn't believe it. Five hundred pesos was *nothing* for what we were asking either of them to do, and yet Jaime stood there as if the transaction had no risk at all. I gave him the 500 pesos, and promised him 500 more upon receipt of the pillow safely within dorm "F."

34 December 4

Licensiado Ferrer was smiling when I entered his office. The date was set for our wedding: December 6! That was only two days away! After the weeks of waiting, I was astounded at the sudden decision. But the timing was perfect: it would leave us a week and a half before the escape. Ferrer told me that I should come to his office early the next morning for the final details on the exact time of the marriage. I thanked him for his kindness and was on my way.

In Mexico, there is a specialized store for everything. Walking home from the Metro terminal, I stopped at an *acojínamiento* (a "pillowery"), which sold only foam pillows and mattresses. Inside, I noticed that they had casings made of thin foam sheets sewn together on three sides, which were not yet stuffed. If I bought one of these and the foam shreds to stuff it with, perhaps I could return to have it sewn up on the special machines here, so that the stitching would match the outer edges. I asked the clerk if that would be possible.

"*Como no, señorita?*" (Why not, Miss?) She clearly wondered why I didn't want one of the hundreds of already-finished pillows in the store, but I confused her with an explanation that was half Spanish and half English, hoping she would be too busy to try to understand every word. She was.

I left with the foam casing and a big bag of shredded foam.

At home that evening, Gabrielle helped me to stuff the pillow. When it was half full, I laid the wig loosely inside. We finished stuffing the pillow firmly, and packed it away in a large bag to return it to the *acojínamiento* the next day.

December 5. Carefully, I inspected the pillow. The fourth edge was now sewn with a machine-overcase stitch that was identical to the other three edges. It was indistinguishable from a regular factory-made pillow. No matter how I punched or squeezed it, I could feel nothing but soft foam inside it. Noticing that the other ready-made pillows in the shop had a case of cotton ticking sewn over them, I asked the clerk to do the same to mine. Five minutes later, I left the *acojínamiento* with a perfectly normal blue pillow under my arm.

I dropped the pillow off at home, and rushed to the prison to make my appointment with Ferrer, in high spirits over my success with the pillow and our marriage scheduled for tomorrow. I looked forward to breaking all the good news to Dwight.

Arising from his desk to greet me, Ferrer said dolefully that he had just gotten a call from the *Registro Civil*, the governmental agency that performed legal marriages. The date had been postponed. He was sorry, but it was beyond his control. I should return to his office on the seventh; he would know the new date by then. And one more thing, added Ferrer. By the time the next date arrived, our medical forms would have expired. It would be necessary to get another physical exam and blood test. Those were the rules, he apologized again.

My spirits took a nose dive, my exuberance giving way to the old familiar frustration of dealing with the Mexican bureaucracy. *Mañana.* Ferrer was personally a decent man, but he was part of the same rotten system. I continued on into the prison, subdued, to tell Dwight the news. I wore his new glasses in.

She walked into the cell with the glasses on! "You wore the glasses and it isn't a third-*guardia* day! Didn't anyone notice, didn't they ask questions?"

"No, no one noticed anything different about me at all. But I didn't have to wait until third-*guardia*, Dwight—after all, they're women's glasses and I *am* a woman, remember?"

Strange how it had hit me. After smuggling everything else in so carefully, suddenly Barbara just walked in with the glasses on her face for all to see. Of course she didn't have to wait for third-*guardia*! They were her glasses and anyone who asked would be told that. Perhaps I was becoming paranoid, an easy thing to do in prison. Or perhaps I was more worried than I knew about Barbara taking so many risks. Thank God we were really going to do it. I had to get out before I lost my mind.

I put the glasses on. I could see well. The tint was dark enough to obscure my eyes, but not so dark as to cover them entirely. Perfect. Then Barbara quickly took off *my* bra and *my* panty hose and handed them to me. We folded them strategically so they could be hidden in my special cache, the padding in the kittens' box. I was very protective of my kittens and I hoped I could use this guise to keep people's hands away from the box and the contraband at the bottom of it. Then I told Barbara that I had arranged a safe way to receive the deposited pillow-wig. The only problem was, we still didn't have the person named A to bring the pillow to the guards at the gate. We couldn't ask anyone we trusted because then that person would be in jeopardy if the wig were discovered.

"It has to be someone who is Mexican, who doesn't know us, who wouldn't be suspected even if the wig were found. I just don't know anyone—"and then she looked at me with a grin, and we almost said it in unison—"but Mame will!"

35 December 6

Mame was all business.

"Now look," she whispered, "it's no sweat depositing the pillow. You know how a visitor is only allowed to deposit things to one prisoner at a time?"

Barbara nodded.

"So. I'll tell my maid to go in and deposit Dwight's pillow because I already deposited something for somebody else. Believe me, she's perfect—pretty, shy, honest, dutiful. Doesn't speak a word of English and won't be noticed."

"Mame . . ."

"And if I thought they'd harm a hair of her head I wouldn't have her do it, see? Jesus, best maid I ever had; you think I'd jeopardize her for a goddamn pillow?"

"Yes."

"Maybe, but not this time, it's too well-covered. She'll never come back to the prison again, and she'll leave a phony address."

"They'll have her thumbprint, Mame."

"Well, so hooray for them—who are they going to match it up to, the Pope?" She grinned and dragged on her cigarette. "Now let me ask you something that *is* important: what are you going to do afterward, you know? I mean, God, Dwight, you may bust out of here but once they discover you're gone, they're going to be searching for you *all* over the damn country."

"I know, but I think we've got it figured out: we know they'll look first at the border, then at the northern checkpoints—and they'll be looking for Barbara, too. So instead of going north like they expect me to, I'll go straight south and hide out somewhere for a week or two while Barbara and Gabrielle go north."

"Say, that's pretty good. But where will you hide out?"

"Well, I don't know. I'll keep moving around the rural areas, I guess, maybe hide out in the hills for a while."

"How much money have you got?"

"Enough."

"I'll bet. Well, look: here's an idea. I know this American fellow who lives just outside of Morelia. You can trust him, and the location is perfect because it's 200 miles west of Mexico City and it's way up in the mountains away from everybody. If you went there immediately afterward, you could stay with Andrew until you thought things were safe. That is, if he agrees, and I'm sure he will—he'll be visiting me in a few days and I can ask him then. But how does it sound to you?"

"It sounds great!"

"Mame, that would be wonderful!" said Barbara. "But let me ask *you* something: aren't you going to be in real danger if you stick around this prison when Dwight escapes? I think you've got to be far out of town or something so that when they discover him gone, you'll have an alibi."

"Yeah, I've thought of that," she answered. "I've already told everyone that I'm going out of town, but actually I'm going to hole up at home and stay away from Lecumberri for a good long while. On the seventeenth, I'll be with someone who can vouch for my alibi. No one'll ever know I had anything to do with it. In fact today, I have already announced, is my last day in Lecumberri for at least two weeks."

"You already announced it?"

"Yeah. I told the other boys and the guards—it'll spread around soon enough. And in the meantime I brought you this early wedding present. Here," she said, shoving a huge bowl of jello toward me, "check it out."

I took a bite of it. It tasted like ordinary jello to me.

"No, you've got to dig deeper. This is three-layer jello-jello."

I scraped the top two layers away, my spoon working down the jello like a spade until it hit—

"Water?"

"No, you idiot. Vodka. I mean, God, is this a wedding or is it a goddamn—" her voice turned back to its raspy whisper—"you-know-what?"

The sound of the 1:45 bugle pierced through our laughter and we quieted down at once. I put my arms around Mame, knowing there were tears in her eyes. This was the last time we would meet for—I didn't know how long.

"I'll see you in the States one day, Mame, that's a promise."

"You bet your ass," she said huskily, hugging me harder. "You sure you got enough money? Do you want me to call anybody? I mean, God, if I can—"

"Mame, you've done everything there is to be done. I can't thank you enough, it's meant so much to us just to know you. . . ."

"Well, you can quit with all that," she said, grabbing Barbara's arm. "I don't know why we're all standing around here bawling when there's work to be done—come on, Barbara, let's go."

I walked them to the gate and waved goodbye until I could no longer see them and they couldn't see the tears in my eyes.

That evening Jake and Willis came into my cell, wildly exuberant over a newspaper article that Jake waved over his head.

"Look here, skeptic, look at this article!" Jake shouted.

I read the article in Spanish. A prisoner named Steven Jones had won his *amparo* (the Mexican equivilent to *habeas corpus*). The court had concluded that he had not done a criminal act, but only attempted to. Thus Jones would be released soon.

"And if Jones is leaving, then we'll all be going home free soon too!" Jake concluded.

Other Americans heard the shouts and came into the cell to find out what was going on. Within a minute there was a group of dancing Americans planning on getting drunk together for Christmas. *Déjà vu.* I was quickly barraged with a number of requests by the other Americans for Barbara to telephone their parents and tell them to send money quickly because they were ". . . coming home for Christmas!" This wasn't the first time they had asked Barbara to make embarrassing and misleading phone calls. Many other times she had dutifully read such messages in a dispassionate monotone, explaining afterward to the now-confused parent that the opinions expressed were not her own. I personally felt that sending such messages was unfair to the parents. Why ruin their Christmas by giving them still more false hopes that their son would be home so soon.

"Who is this Steve Jones guy anyhow?" Jake interrupted the festivities for a moment by asking aloud to anyone.

Since I was the only American in "F" who had ever been in dorm "O," I was the only one who knew Steve Jones. I told them that he was an Australian who had been arrested with less than one ounce of marijuana at the Mexico City airport almost three years ago. He had wealthy parents who had spent upwards of $75,000 for his freedom, and more importantly, a consul from the Australian embassy in Mexico City had visited him regularly and had actively pressured Mexico for his release. So it seemed to me that there were many many differences between our cases and that of Steve Jones: money, political power, constant attention, and severity of charges.

Smiles dissipated, eyes hardened into tight beams focused at me—I was raining on their parade once again. They began to file out of my cell to a more receptive one where they could resume their rejoicing without any further encroachments by reality.

"Fuck you, Worker. You *want* to stay here."

36 December 7

I met Mame outside Lecumberri at 9:00 a.m. to give her the pillow. She was excited.

"Oh, Jesus, Barbara, I talked to Andrew when he was in town. Now I didn't tell him Dwight's name, just the circumstances, and he's agreed to let Dwight stay at this house in Morelia for however long he needs. All you have to do is let him know a day or two in advance; and he'll pick Dwight up in Morelia. I'll give you his address and two phone numbers where he can be reached, just in case they get their signals crossed, and a map of how to get to his place from Morelia. It's way up in the mountains—be a beautiful place for Dwight to hide."

I squeezed Mame hard, without words for my gratitude.

"Okay. Look, Barbara, tomorrow is the third-*guardia* and the deposit should work out just fine. I'll give you a call tomorrow evening and tell you—oh man, I don't know who might be listening in on my phone. I know, I'll tell you that I got the wedding present, okay? That is, if it works . . . "

"You're really getting *into* this, aren't you, Mame?"

"Well, I'll tell you this, Barbara. I think you two are going to fuck those bastards over good, and I just want to have a hand in it."

As Mame swaggered off toward her car, a policeman hissed at her, calling her *mi mamacita*. I watched Mame get into her car without a glance at him, and then roll down her window to swear at him, so luridly that he actually looked shocked, turned on his heels, and slunk away.

Barbara arrived to tell me that Ferrer had finally set the wedding date for December 13. Good. Tomorrow Mame would have the pillow-wig deposited by Maria Sanchez-Perez. I would give her name to Jaime to prepare him for the deposit. I advised Barbara not to visit me tomorrow, so that if the wig were discovered, they could not blame it on her.

Another item: I did not want to be a fugitive on the streets of Mexico without a tourist card. The paper-loving bureaucratic police would throw me in jail even if they did not know who I was. I had suggested to Barbara that she try to borrow or buy a tourist card from a U.S. tourist, but she thought that would be difficult, and would risk exposing us too.

Barbara had another plan. When she returned from Texas to Mexico City the second time, she and Gabrielle had been given separate tourist cards. Mame said that this was highly unusual, for the names of mother and child were usually on the same card. After studying the cards, Barbara realized that she could add her name to Gabrielle's card and alter the name on her card into a fake name for me. Leaving Mexico, I would be that person, with a valid tourist card.

Barbara showed me how she would alter the name.

"See? *Roaland J. Addoake,*" she announced proudly.

"What? Who?" I started to laugh. "What kind of a name is that?"

"I don't know, and the Mexican authorities won't either. All I know is that changing Barbara S. Chilcoate to Joe Jones would have been quite a bit more difficult, Dwight."

"Barbara, I don't mean to make fun of Roaland J. Addoake. I know how tough it is to forge a name out of another name . . ."

"Very tough."

"It's just that—well, Roaland J. Addoake—you have to admit it's just so *funny.*"

"I think it's a handsome name," she said, grinning. "Much more interesting than Dwight James Wor—."

"Yeah. By the way, did you talk to Mame about Andrew?"

"Yes, everything's all set. I'm going to get the tickets tomorrow, since I'll be staying away while the pillow gets deposited. You all set for that?"

"Sure. We've thought it through too well for anything to go wrong now."

37 December 8—A.M.

As I wouldn't be going to Lecumberri today, I planned to take care of a lot of preparations. After breakfast, Gabrielle and I took a bus to the *Terminal del Norte,* the immense bus terminal on the north side of the city. We would be traveling out of Mexico during the holiday season, and I wanted to be sure to have reserved seats to Morelia for Dwight, and to Arizona for Gabrielle and me.

Most of the bus lines running north to the border were already booked full for December 17. I was finally able to get tickets for Gabrielle and myself on a bus leaving at 10:00 p.m. to Santa Ana, a Mexican town in the Sonora desert about fifty miles from Nogales. I would have to take potluck to get us from Santa Ana to the Arizona border.

The tickets to Morelia were easier. There would be a bus leaving at 2:45 p.m., and another at 3:45 p.m. I bought a ticket for each, so that if Dwight were able to make the 2:45, he could get out as quickly as possible; but if he missed it, he could take the 3:45 bus. Either way, he would be assured of a seat.

As Gabrielle and I left the terminal, I felt buoyant and excited by the bustle of arrival and departure. It gave me a taste for travel, and I couldn't stop myself from imagining how it would feel to be rolling out of this city for the last time, knowing that Dwight was free and on his way to the mountains.

At home that afternoon, I put the finishing touches on the wedding shirt, appliquéing the solidly embroidered panels to the front yokes of the shirt. I embroidered our intertwined initials and the year, 1975, inside the collar, and then I looked at it in amazement. After the countless hours I had spent on it, I could hardly believe that it was at last complete.

38 December 8—P.M.

"DE-WITE WOR-KER. *VEN A LA PUERTA!*"

I ran down the stairs to the gate and looked through the bars to see Jaime *being held by the elbow* by the gate guard. In the guard's other hand was *the pillow.*

Dread horror. As I started to turn back up the stairs, Jaime whispered in English, "Hurry! The guard wants a tip and I didn't have any money with me."

I checked my pockets. All I had on me was a fifty-peso note. I couldn't give the guard that much or then he would be suspicious. The guard began to toss the pillow into the air.

"Jefe, usted tiene cambio?" (Chief, do you have change?)

"No. Pagame la plata ahora." (No. Pay me now.)

They never had change when you owed them money. I rushed to the dormitory to get change. They wouldn't give it to me unless I bought something, so I did, waiting forever to get my change. I then rushed to the gate again.

The guard was patting the pillow between both hands, feeling it for anything inside. Jaime was frozen.

"Jefe, here's your tip." I handed him five pesos.

"Mas." His greedy hand was still open.

"Pero Jefe, cinco pesos es sufficiente," I play-bargained, careful not to seem too desperate.

He pulled the pillow away from the gate.

"Okay," I said resignedly. *"Usted es muy cabrón, pero usted gana."* I handed him five more pesos.

He smiled, and then opened the gate and handed me the pillow. I could almost feel Jaime sigh as I turned with the pillow and climbed the stairs. I felt sick to my stomach.

Late that night I opened the pillow. When I pulled the wig out, with it came a thousand pieces of finely chopped foam. I spent an hour gently picking all the foam from it and brushing out all the knots. When I finally put it on, it fit well. I put on my prescription glasses and covered my moustache and beard with my hand while looking into the mirror. I was surprised at how different I looked.

Then I hid the wig with the rest of the clothes beneath the padding of the kitten's sleeping box. There were just nine more days to go, and if they found one piece of disguise, they would search the whole cell until they had found it all. I packed the wig with the clothing beneath the disturbed and whining kittens.

That evening, I stamped the metal tags with the appropriate numbers and letters, making several of each kind so that Dwight could experiment with heating and corroding them to make them look old and worn.

Although they were small and not difficult to smuggle, the tags would be the most incriminating things I had smuggled in yet. It was imperative that I find the perfect hiding place, and I discovered that spot to be in my shoes. I had a pair of Mexican *huaraches*—woven-strap sandals with soles made from rubber tires—that I had purchased especially to conform with visiting regulations at Lecumberri. The leather innersoles were fastened to the rubber soles with only nails placed at intervals of about three centimeters. I pulled several nails out of each shoe and pushed the tags through the spaces between the nails, forcing them in between the leather and rubber soles. I stuffed both sandals, heel and toe, with a half-dozen tags. When I carefully replaced the nails, the metal tags were imperceptible inside the *huaraches.*

I flexed the soles back and forth to see if I could *feel* a difference, but they were perfectly flexible. I was ready for the next third-*guardia*.

39 December 11

I woke up early and dressed quickly, pulling Dwight's wedding shirt over my blouse, stepping into the long, ruffled double skirt, and slipping my feet into the loaded *huaraches*. I knew it was risky to try so many things at once, but time was running out. Today was the third-*guardia*.

Gabrielle and I arrived at Lecumberri at 8:30 a.m. in time for an appointment with Ferrer to get the final details for the wedding on December 13. But when I entered the office, I stiffened at the apologetic expression on his face. A horrible *déjà vu*.

Ferrer shrugged hopelessly. The marriage was postponed again.

I stood silently for a moment, gathering my self-control. I told him that I had been trying for three months to arrange this marriage. Now, I lied, my father was ill, and I had a flight booked back to the U.S. within a week. I could wait no longer.

Very well, sympathized Ferrer, he would try to arrange the marriage immediately.

I left Ferrer's office feeling angry and tense, definitely not in the right frame of mind for smuggling in the tags and the double skirt. But I couldn't waste this third-*guardia* day. I went back outside the prison to the park across the street and pushed Gabrielle on the swings for a while, forcing myself to relax and regain the calm nonchalance that I would need for the smuggle.

We re-entered the prison. We were later than usual and there were no lines at the *defensor* checkpoints. The matron waved us into the search cubicle.

I was calm and detached. The matron began to search my torso.

"Hace frío, verdad?" (It's cold, isn't it?) she said, noticing the two shirts I wore.

I nodded benignly.

The matron moved down the double skirt, carefully feeling all the seams and the hem, spinning me around as she did so. So far, so good. Then she straightened up, and asked me to take off my sandals. I did so, talking to her now in nonstop Spanish about the weather and the cold and the problem of bringing children outside in the cold, and as she bent one sandal in half I noticed one of the nails in the heel slip halfway out.

"Muchas gracias," I said, as she handed the sandal back to me, watching the other one to see if it were similarly falling apart. No nails appeared. I put the sandals on and stomped on the floor to pound the nail back in, appearing to be chilled.

"Sí, hace frío," she agreed.

As soon as Barbara and Gabrielle came into the cell, Barbara kicked off her sandals. I removed the nails from her sandals while Barbara removed her thick skirt and began dividing it into two thin skirts. I pried the metal tags from her sandals and dumped them onto the floor. They were perfect counterfeits, although too new and shiny. I would have to take care of that later.

Barbara had been wearing in my escape clothing every day now, regardless of what *guardia* was on duty. We were running out of time, and she felt confident. And every day she left the prison with an unnoticed shopping bag of my books, clothing, and other belongings. My prison possessions were dwindling rapidly. We didn't want to leave them a thing.

After I had repaired her sandals, Barbara informed me that the wedding had been postponed yet again to an undetermined date. Would they ever let us be married? We would just have to let it happen—or not happen—when they chose it to.

Dress rehearsal. All of the woman's clothes, along with the wig, metal tags, and makeup, were now in my cell. The only things left were the paper passes. Although they were small, if we were caught with them it would be lethal.

As Barbara watched, I applied all of the makeup. Then the clothes, article by article, and finally the wig, jewelry, and prescription glasses. While Barbara encouraged and directed me, Gabrielle squealed with delight, thinking I was the funniest looking thing she had ever seen. So did I. We had to join in her laughter.

I turned to the mirror. Even with my moustache and beard protruding, the effect was startling. For the first time I began to believe in my credibility as a woman. Barbara was ecstatic about my transformation, and Gabrielle, well, she just wouldn't shut up.

Now the walking lessons. I moved back and forth in the cell as Barbara coached. "Small steps, toes forward, don't swing your arms, smooth, continuous motions, float as you walk, lower center of gravity, womb consciousness."

I walked and walked and walked in my cell in full drag array as Barbara corrected and guided me; all of this to the background of Gabrielle's laughter. By the end of visiting hours Barbara thought that my body language was feminine, although I needed to practice on it every night. I "dedragged" and rehid the clothes and wig under the kittens' padding. As the bugle blew, she remembered to tell me that she had altered her tourist card to the name "Roaland J. Addoakes." That was taken care of.

December 11, 10:00 p.m. I had to make the metal tags look old and used. I rubbed and scraped them over the cement, and then nicked them on the corner of the bunk until they appeared worn. They were still too shiny, so I mixed a strong saltwater solution and boiled the metal tags in it over my improvised electric resistor coil. An hour later both the brass and nickel tags were thoroughly oxidized, indistinguishable from the real ones. I hid them away.

December 12, 2:00 a.m. The electricity had been turned off so I lit a candle. I took out the wedding shirt that Barbara had sewn and embroidered for me. We had been so busy today that I had not really looked at it. There were two large circular embroideries on either side of the front. On the left yoke a multicolored phoenix rose from the ground to the background of a volcano, a lightning storm, and a rainbow. Hope. On the right yoke a blue-winged, white Pegasus carried Barbara and me away from the darkness of night to a rising sun. I stared at the embroideries for a long time.

I thought of Barbara spending the hundreds of hours embroidering these messages to me, while at the same time risking everything she had to be with me and to free me from here.

One day I would deserve her. And I would deserve that freedom.

40 December 13

Luis Perea, a wealthy Chicano prisoner, came to my cell with a large brown paper bag. Out of it he pulled a small Smith-Corona portable typewriter.

"You've been telling me for months that you wanted a typewriter. So would you want to rent this one—or buy it?"

Three months ago I would have jumped at the chance. I had tried in vain for a year and a half to receive a typewriter in prison, but every time Colonel Cardenas had vetoed it. I had often told Luis that I would pay his price for one too. And now, four days before D-day, Luis calmly brought one into my cell.

"Oh, I . . . don't have the money with me right now, but when I do . . ."

"Okay then, I trust you. This one is $100 if you want it. I'll leave it here with you for a while so you can test it out."

He left the typewriter on the bed and walked out. I could have used it a year ago—even three months ago—but not now. Still, I could not tell Luis that I would not be needing it anymore, because that might sound suspicious to him. So I pushed the typewriter far under my bunk and went back to my planning.

"LISTA! 'LISTA!" The *commandos* shouted throughout the dorm. What? It was only 4:00 p.m., three and a half hours before the nighttime body count.

Everybody in the dorm rushed down below in chaotic disorder to line up in formation. As we stood still, twenty jackbooted guards filed through the now-open gate. Oh no, an *esculque* (search). I froze. The head of the guards went up to Granados and demanded Luis Perea.

Obediently, Granados pointed Luis out.

"Da nos la máquina de escribir!" (Give us the typewriter!)
"El lo tiene." Luis pointed to me. The guards ran up to me. I was petrified.
"DÓNDE ESTÁ LA MÁQUINA?"
"En mi celda," I said, pointing above.

The guards took off up the stairs as if the typewriter might escape them any moment. I stood shocked as the guards filed into my cell, knowing that right now they might be finding the makeup, wig, clothes—everything. Instinctively I bolted out of formation and ran upstairs against the shouts of the *commandos*. I slipped into my cell while the guards were busily tearing everything apart. The mattress was on the floor, chairs overturned, and boxes of books scattered. One of them had just dragged the box of kittens from under the bed.

"Cuidadosiamente, por favor, mis Jefes! Son muy jovenes y su mama gata es muerte." (Please be careful, bosses. The kittens are young and their mother is dead.)

At the sight of the five disturbed kittens, the guards immediately paused in the search, giving me time enough to reach under the bed, pull out the typewriter, and put it in the hands of the boss. Furious, he ordered his men to work me over and wreck everything in the cell. *"Soy Canadian! Soy Canadian!"* I lied, moving in front of the kittens. The guards stopped, then marched out of my overturned cell victoriously, with the typewriter and me. They rushed Luis Perea, me, and the typewriter directly to the colonel's office.

Am I going to be moved—sent to castigado, beaten? I was so afraid that I almost urinated in my pants.

"Whose typewriter is this?" Cardenas bellowed.

"Mine," Luis admitted.

"Why was it in this *gringo's* cell, then?" Cardenas pointed accusingly at me.

"He was going to test it out, and maybe rent it from me. But he didn't know. He's innocent."

Thank you for your honor, Luis.

Cardenas then wanted to know how Luis had gotten the machine into the prison. He admitted having paid a bribe to a guard to bring it in.

"What guard?"

Luis named him, knowing that Cardenas already knew who he was.

With that, the problem was now that of the guards and of Luis. Cardenas waved me to be taken back to my dormitory. In my torn-up cell I numbly reassembled things as best I could. Then I lay down on my bunk, only now realizing how close it had been. If they had found anything, they would have locked me in solitary confinement for a year. And they would have given Barbara a complete body search tomorrow and found the paper passes that she was planning to bring in. She would have been arrested on the spot.

How stupid I had been. I lay in bed trembling in fright. My whole world of hope had almost come crashing down.

41 December 14

I awoke before dawn. Today I would do the last and most dangerous smuggle: the paper passes. For the final time I would have to play the odds against receiving an internal search. If I were caught now, all my other successes would mean nothing.

It was still dark outside as I got up to switch on a small light. Being careful not to wake Gabrielle, I quietly opened the desk drawer where I had hidden the hundreds of passes, and selected one of each color—eight in all. Rolling them up, I slipped them inside a tiny cardboard tube, like a miniature mailer. After I carefully wrapped up the tube, the passes were ready for hiding.

I did it quickly, almost unconsciously shifting into the calm, practical detachment that insulated me from my fear and nervousness. By the time the first sunlight poured in my window, I was impatient to be off to Lecumberri, to get the passes in and know that the last preliminary step had worked. I woke Gabrielle and cuddled with her in bed for a bit before dressing her and giving her breakfast.

We were ready to go. My nerves were taut, but I was not nervous. I couldn't be—I had some final business to take care of.

Gabrielle and I joined an unusually long line waiting for the body search. To my horror, I saw that the matron was checking most of the women internally. Only a couple of well-dressed, middle-class Mexican women, whom I recognized from their frequent visits to the prison, had gotten by without the internal search.

I swallowed my panic and forced myself to close it off in a corner of my mind. If she tried to check me there, I would be outraged that she would do that in front of my daughter. I would refuse and walk out.

I had never seen anyone successfully back out of a search.

Our turn. Gabrielle told the matron *buenos días* and I smiled hello as she impatiently waved us inside the waist-high partition.

The later Barbara arrived at dorm "F," the more nervous I became. By now I had learned how my biorhythms changed with the timing of her arrival, but self-understanding is not self-control. I still grew nervous.

When Barbara finally walked through the gate, businesslike, with Gabrielle in tow, I knew that she had succeeded with the last smuggle. Relieved, I ran down the stairs. Now only one thing remained.

Inside my cell, Barbara and I embraced, but she was still too tense from the search to relax. While Gabrielle and I romped on the bed, Barbara quickly pulled out the eight different-colored *MIÉRCOLES* (Wednesday) paper passes. We spread them out over the desk top and I examined them. They seemed identical to the paper passes that I had found at *campo* and the ones that Barbara had stolen from the guards.

"Any more news about the wedding?"

Barbara shook her head. "It's still postponed. I'm supposed to check with Ferrer again tomorrow, but I doubt that we'll get married."

I was disappointed. Besides wanting to get married for every other natural reason, I wanted Barbara to be married to me because of the protection she could receive under Mexican law. A wife was legally exempt from prosecution for aiding in her husband's nonviolent prison escape attempt. It was almost as if she were *expected* to help him try to escape, and that was one law of Mexico I liked.

I hid the paper passes in the padding of the kittens' box, and then we went over the remaining steps of the plan. On December 17, Barbara would enter the prison on a general visit to dorm "C," in order to verify the color of the paper pass being used that day. We would need to know this to select the right color. Barbara would then come to dorm "F," even though she had a metal tag for "C," and pay the gate guard a bribe to enter "F." Only with the third-*guardia* could this be done.

Barbara told me about buying the bus tickets and arranging to pick me up with her neighbor Enrique in his car. Enrique would not need to know who I was until we were far away. By car we would go to the bus station, where Barbara and I would separate. I figured that they would be looking for me, not her; but if somehow they found her with me, they would arrest all of us. Mame had confirmed that I could stay with Andrew in Morelia, and that he had volunteered to meet me at the bus station. Barbara and I would rendezvous in Tucson, Arizona. I would find where she was by a letter waiting for me in general delivery.

But all of this secondary planning seemed very remote to me. Getting out of the prison was the obstacle, for this was the supposedly escape-proof Lecumberri. Hank's words rang in my ears, "No one has ever escaped from here since Pancho Villa."

Only after all of the last minute arrangements had been discussed in detail and each procedure reviewed by rote, could Barbara and I begin to relax. We never discussed the possibility of the escape not working. Besides being so involved in working out the details and logistics, we feared that thinking along those lines could make failure a reality.

Today would be the last day that Barbara would be bringing Gabrielle to Lecumberri. I would not be seeing our little confidante and smuggler again—until we met again on the outside. I passed the remaining moments of the visiting hours romping and cuddling with Gabrielle, and holding Barbara. In the crystal silence between Barbara and me, I felt an unspoken understanding as the immense question mark in our lives loomed ever closer.

9:00 a.m. "I have good news," beamed *Licensiado* Ferrer. "We have arranged the marriage to take place immediately. I have the final date."

I knew what was coming.

"December 17, at 11:00 a.m."

Visions of the officials' being late; of Dwight getting called to the gate in the middle of painting his fingernails; of four months' planning jeopardized by this fluke of fate.

I launched into a rapid stream of Spanish. I had come to Mexico to arrange this marriage and I had been trying for three months now. But three months apparently wasn't long enough. Now my mother had called to tell me that my father was *critically* ill and I already had a flight back to the U.S. booked for 10:00 a.m. on the seventeenth. I had waited three months and I could wait no longer.

Ferrer jumped up to calm me. I just couldn't leave now, not when I was finally to be married. I had his word as a gentleman that it would not be postponed this time.

"But my flight! I have to get home immediately, before it is too late."

"Change the flight!"

"I can't—all the flights are booked for Christmas."

"Yes, yes you can. Tell the airlines to call me. I will tell them you have official business with me and that they *must* give you a later flight. Or, if you prefer, I will call them right now."

Oh, God. "No, no, that won't be necessary. I'll try myself. But tell me this: do you promise that the ceremony will take place at 11:00 a.m. *al punto?*"

"Yes, yes, anything. Go now. Call the airline. You can't give up just like that after all this time. You want to get married, yes?"

Yes. I felt a twinge of guilt for my act. I could see that all of the postponements really had been beyond Ferrer's control, and that he actually did want our marriage to go through.

I told Ferrer that I would let him know that afternoon whether I had gotten a later flight, and hurried out of his office and through the checkpoints to Dwight.

Oh no. Of all the possible days! But then, of course.

If they had chosen December 16, we could be married; or if it had been December 18, we wouldn't have been there one way or another; even if it had been 9:00 a.m. on December 17, I would still have had time. But 11:00 a.m. on the seventeenth was just as bad as 1:42 p.m. itself.

Maybe they would postpone it again. If the past was any indication, the odds were that they would. I estimated that I would need at least one and a half uninterrupted hours to prepare myself for the escape. If the ceremony proceeded on time and finished by 11:30 a.m., as Ferrer had guaranteed, then I should have enough time. Any later and it would be borderline. But I had no reason at all to suspect that they would be on time.

"What will we do?" Barbara looked at me gravely. One thing was certain: if the ceremony was delayed beyond twelve noon, we would have to postpone the escape for at least forty-two more days, to January 28. Our money would then be gone and Barbara would have to either go back to the States and get a job or try to find work in Mexico City. But even worse than that was a very real fear, shared by both of us, that if we did not do it this time, we never would.

But if by some bizarre chance Ferrer was right and the ceremony did proceed on schedule, then both wedding and escape attempt would be possible. Again our fate and even our plans to change it were totally in their hands.

I wanted to cancel the wedding. It would most likely ruin the escape attempt, or disrupt it so that it couldn't be executed perfectly. We couldn't afford anything less than perfect conditions, so we would have to wait. But that would give them more time to discover the disguises, or change their procedures.

What should we do?

Sitting still, looking down at our tightly clasped hands, I slowly felt a feeling overwhelm me and gain in clarity with each moment. *This was no accident.* For whatever reason we were to get married and then try to escape from prison on the same day, it was no accident. As our hands squeezed tighter and tighter, a feeling of faith in ourselves and our hopes prevailed.

We would go through with it.

2:00 p.m. When I entered Ferrer's office, he arose anxiously from his desk.

"Well?"

"The absolute latest flight I could get on the seventeenth was for 12:30 p.m. If you can guarantee that the marriage will take place on time at 11:00 a.m., we can go through with it. But, if the officials are very late, please do not even call us from the dormitory. It will be too late."

"*Muy bien!* I personally will make sure that you and your *novio* are married first of all the couples. And the ceremony is very brief: sign here, sign there, that is all. You will see. It will work out, and you will get on your plane as a *señora.*"

As soon as I got home, I explained to my landlady that because of a family emergency, I would be leaving for the States on the seventeenth. I arranged to leave Gabrielle with her until 4:00 p.m. that day, when I would return to pick her up with our luggage to take a bus to the airport.

In our rooms upstairs, I methodically packed up our belongings. When I returned from the bus terminal on the seventeenth, I wanted to be able to pick everything up and leave within a few minutes. I had always given a false address to the prison, but I couldn't be too careful.

Having finished packing, I got out the phone numbers for Andrew that Mame had given me. It was time to alert him to his guest's impending arrival. I called the first number. No answer. The second number. No answer. After several tries, I gave up, planning to call again a few hours later.

At one of the numbers, I finally reached a Mexican who said that he knew Andrew and would give him a message. In slow, clear Spanish, I asked him to tell Andrew that *Señora* Levinson's friend would be arriving in Morelia either at 10:00 p.m. on the *Tres Estrellas* bus line, or at 11:00 p.m. on the *Dorado* bus line. If *Señora* Levinson's friend was not on the 10:00 p.m. bus, then he would be on the 11:00 p.m. bus, I reiterated.

"*Está importantissimo, señor, que usted lo dar esto mensaje. Por favor, señor, y mil gracias.*"

I hung up wondering if Andrew would indeed get the message, and wondering about Andrew himself. I had never met him, but Mame's judgment had always been excellent. And if, for some reason, Andrew did not show, there were always the mountains outside Morelia to hide in.

43 December 16

2:00 p.m. From Lecumberri, Gabrielle and I took a bus to Chapultepec Park. We had arranged to meet Mame outside the Museum of Natural History there for a quick and final farewell.

Mame was waiting when we got off the bus. She scooped up Gabrielle, who twined her arms around her neck and squeezed her tight with both legs. I mentioned that I had not been able to reach Andrew directly; Mame thought that he would receive the message.

Mame disengaged Gabrielle and rummaged around in her huge purse made of llama fur.

"Here's your wedding present, by the way. Did you think I'd forgotten?"

Mame thrust a white cloth into my hands. When I unfolded it, I saw that it was an antique embroidered table runner that I had often admired at her home. It was a Levinson family heirloom.

I hugged her hard.

"Listen, Barbara, you've got to let me know afterward if he made it. I've got to know, and I don't want to wait for Colonel Cardenas to tell me. I'm not going to be home that day of course; I'm going to be with someone who can verify that I was nowhere near you two. Like I think I'll go to a big party. But call and leave a message with Maria."

"But Mame, even that's risky."

"Well, we've got to do it in code, that's all. Let's see now, if he makes it, ask Maria to tell me that you've gone home to buy a Christmas tree. Okay? But if he doesn't, then don't call at all. That way I'll know, one way or the other."

"For God's sake, please be careful, Mame. You know them—they'll have to have someone to blame, and you're already notorious."

"Yeah, I know them all right, I know them better than they know their own asses. And believe me, I've got myself covered. I'm not going to stay down here much longer myself, you know. You two'd better be ready to take me out drinking when I come north. Speaking of which, I've got one good-looking dinner date in about forty-five minutes. What can I say, Barbara? Good luck, and give 'em the finger for me too, will you?"

After one last hug, I watched my one and only Mame drive

away. All of the farewells were said, all of the preparations complete. All that remained was tomorrow.

44 Escape

December 17, 1975, 6:50 a.m. I did not sleep at all last night, and it wasn't because I was getting married today.

The kittens were clamoring all over my bed and me, screaming for milk. I dug the eyedropper from my foam mattress and began injecting them with milk. Gradually, their cries subsided.

I had a lot to do before Barbara arrived. I retrieved the tweezers from beneath the kitten box and propped a piece of mirror on my desk. Time to pluck my eyebrows. I grabbed a hair and pulled. Owww. I sneezed. I yanked another and another. Large tears ran down my eyes while I sneezed away in protest. This was sheer masochism. I stopped. What else could I do?

I got out my razor and busied myself shaving the backs of my hands. Maybe I could shave my eyebrows too. I spread soap over my forehead and gently tried shaving each brow into the fine, arched shape that Barbara had described to me. I wiped the soap away and examined them. Asymmetric.

7:20 a.m. I began shaving the edge of the thicker brow, hoping I would get them to match, when there was a knock at the door. Oh no. Who?

"*Que quieres?*" I asked.

"*Quiero ver tus gatitos.*"

It was Jose Castillo, the chief *commando* of the dorm. He wanted to see the kittens and I had to let him in—with shaved eyebrows. I quickly rubbed soap all over my face and then opened the door, while continuing to wash my face. I kept the washrag in front of me while Castillo played with the kittens.

"*Tu me debes cinquenta pesos para tu barba.*"

"*Sí.*" I quickly fished fifty pesos from my hidden pocket and gave it to him. This would be the last installment on the right to grow my beard. Castillo played with the kittens some more and finally, after the third washing and hair combing, Castillo left. I bolted the door shut.

7:45 a.m. I rubbed shaving cream all over one of my hairy legs and began shaving it. The kittens interrupted by attacking the razor and my leg. I had to shave my leg up to my thigh and I had never done such a thing before. I cut myself several times, and the razor continually clogged from all of the hair. It took much longer than I had planned.

Finally, I felt that I had done an adequate job. I pulled on my pants and socks. No one would be able to see that beneath them were two shaved legs. But what would happen if, for some unexpected reason, we had to cancel the escape attempt today? What would the Mexicans think when they saw me in the shower room with shaved legs?

8:55 a.m. I fixed a cup of coffee and tidied up the room. No time to eat, and I had no appetite anyhow. I lay down in my bunk to relax, but that was impossible. Waiting waiting waiting. Soon Barbara would arrive just like she always did, except there would be tears of fright in her eyes. We would first hide ourselves away and embrace. And then, if everything went right, we would be married.

I stood at the door, peering down at the gate, waiting for my name to be called. Would she be late? Not because of anything she might do. We had talked about and planned on this day for nearly a year.

The kittens began to cry. I warmed up some milk and fed them with the eyedropper. In a few minutes their cries had ceased. Bloated with milk, they began licking themselves. While I was putting away the milk, I dropped the dish. It shattered. My shaved hands were shaking uncontrollably. I busied myself by cleaning it up.

Today—my wedding day. A rite of passage. A year in the waiting, and now it was time. We should be happy. We had both wanted this so. But only the coldest dread rose up within me today. Trembling at the door, waiting waiting waiting for her, I had never been so afraid in all my life.

9:25 a.m. "DE-WITE WOR-KER. *VEN A LA PUERTA. TIENE VISITA.*"

Barbara. I was out the door in a flash as she passed through the gate and ran up the stairs, her face all business. I barricaded us into our cell, but before I could hug her, she demanded a pen. Grabbing a piece of paper, she quickly wrote down the guard's signature from memory. She wrote it again and again before she was satisfied with her forgery. She had had only one minute to remember it.

"Dwight, you have to get me a blue felt pen; that's what the guard used to sign my paper pass."

I didn't have one. I would have to search the dorm. I combed my hair as far down to my eyebrows as I could, and pushed my glasses as high up as possible to cover my brows. Then I stepped out of the cell and began checking with neighboring cells for blue felt pens.

Seven cells later and no luck. I feared that if I continued, someone might see my eyebrows, so I returned to cell 39.

"No luck. We'll have to use blue ballpoint instead."

"No! The felt pen was too obvious."

"It's that or nothing."

"I hate to," but she reluctantly agreed. "The color of the slips today is yellow."

I retrieved a counterfeit yellow paper pass from the mattress and gave it to Barbara. She signed the guard's signature as best she could. The whole escape would be contingent upon the quality of this forgery.

After Barbara had written it to her satisfaction, she turned and hugged me. I felt her trembling—us trembling. Then she pulled her head back and looked into my face.

"Your eyebrows are lopsided."

I told her of my agony in plucking them earlier today, while I handed her the razor. She delicately sculpted my brows until the arches balanced. They were thinner and more feminine than we had planned.

10:00 a.m. Barbara wanted to inspect my legs. Off with my pants. She shook her head, laughing nervously at all the nicks. I lay back on the bunk while she shaved off the remaining stubble.

After my legs were finished, I dug out the nail polish from the mattress and Barbara began painting my toenails. I held my feet over my electric resistor coil to help them dry faster. Then she gave them a second and third coat. It seemed to take hours. I pulled a pair of long socks up to my knees and then put my pants back on. Fully covered, my feet and legs looked normal.

10:25 a.m. The kittens began crying again, so I fed them with the eyedropper while Barbara re-examined the forged paper passes.

10:45 a.m. All of the prewedding preparations were complete. Barbara and I went over the plans again and again, having them so memorized by now that it only made us more nervous to hear them. We lay down on the bunk and tried to rest, but we couldn't at all.

11:05 a.m. We clung to each other, waiting for them to call us to get married.

11:10, 11:15, 11:20: They're late. Of course they would be. *El tiempo Mexicano.* I walked to the cell door and peered down to the gate—but still no summons to be married. *What was taking them so long?* If we weren't married soon, I would not have time to drag up after returning to the dorm, and we would have to postpone our escape attempt for another month. Postpone, and perhaps cancel it entirely, for someone would surely see my shaved legs and eyebrows and get suspicious. I turned nervously, helplessly, to Barbara. We were still completely under their control. There was nothing we could do but wait.

11:30 a.m. "WOR-KER WOR-KER *VEN A LA PUERTA A CASARSE.*"

Finally, thirty minutes late.

Barbara and I rushed down the stairway to the gate. Outside the gate stood three guards, instead of the usual one, and they were *body searching everyone.*

They had never done this before. Did they know something? Was our cover blown? I approached the gate and they let me out after searching me, but one obnoxious guard now refused to let Barbara go with me to the wedding area. I explained to him that I was *marrying her* today; but no matter, the guard refused to let her go with me. Then the other two guards quickly escorted me away. I turned and saw Barbara standing against the bars inside the dormitory, her face horror-stricken.

11:31 a.m. *I had never been treated like this by a guard. He would not let me out of the dormitory. For the first time, I felt the terror of being a prisoner. It was all too strange. They knew something. But how? How? Where were they taking Dwight?*

Blindly, I climbed the stairs to the catwalk. From there, I could see the glassed-in polígano *in the central tower. They knew, and they were taking him to the* políg*ano to beat the truth out of him. I strained to discern what the silhouettes moving behind the glass were doing, watching for the white of his wedding shirt among the grey uniforms.*

As I walked between the guards, a cold chill ran through me. The guards *knew* that I had planned on trying to escape today. They were leading me off to body search and then beat me up. They would then search my cell, where Barbara was now waiting, find the wig and other contraband, and arrest Barbara and throw *her* in prison. My only hope for freedom, and with it my world, was collapsing around me. I felt so weak with fear that I was dizzy and sick to my stomach as I was led away.

11:41 a.m. *I had been waiting for ten minutes. Wait much longer and it would be too late for anything. I was numb with disbelief and terror. I watched the guard search a visitor, then strained my eyes to the* políg*ano until my vision jumped out of focus. The scene below me reeled. Panic rose in my throat. No. I breathed deeply, forcing back my old neutral control.*

They walked me around the *rondin* and took me into the large room where the weddings were usually held. I looked around and to my great relief, I saw a number of other prison couples waiting to be married.

I went up to the *Director del Registro Civil,* Ferrer, the man who would marry the couples here in the prison, and explained to him that the guards had refused to let my fiancée out of dorm "F" to come to *our* wedding. He looked surprised and angry. He got up and walked off with the guards who had escorted me to the wedding area. I realized suddenly that it was going to be all right—they *didn't* know. Trembling, I waited for Barbara.

11:43 a.m. *Ferrer came hurrying around the* rondin. *I went weak with relief. He spoke rapidly to the guard, gesticulating angrily. I ran down the stairs and out the gate with Ferrer.*

Several minutes later they returned with Barbara. Her face was flushed, as if she were on the verge of tears. I heard her explaining to the director that her plane left for the U.S. in an hour and a half and could he please marry us first. He agreed. It was already 11:44.

The ceremony proceeded immediately. There wasn't very

much to it. Barbara and I had to sign our names in several ledgers that were then notarized and *"ya estuvo,"* that was it. They said Barbara's name was now Barbara Chilcoate de Worker.

Jaime was attending the wedding as my guest. He came up to kiss the bride. Then in the Latin custom of *abrazos,* he hugged me. As we separated, his eyes caught mine with a stare. He then pointed to his eyebrows with a puzzled look. I froze and then acted as if I didn't understand. He whispered in my ear,

"If you are doing that to your eyebrows, just why are you getting married anyhow?"

I tried to answer him, but I couldn't. He had me.

"Jaime, remember the pillow?"

He nodded.

"Well, I'm leaving today."

"Today?" He looked amazed. "How?"

I shook my head.

"When?"

"Just before the bugle." The guards called at us impatiently.

"Buena suerte, hermano. Vaya con dios." Jaime looked at me once more and we both realized that no matter what happened, we would never see each other again. He gripped my arm and walked past Barbara, who had heard me whispering to Jaime. We knew we could trust him. He saw the tension in her eyes and he knew it was for real. The guards moved us out of the room.

Back at the dorm gate the three guards were still there, searching everyone who passed through the gate. *Why?*

They must know something.

As we were searched, several *commandos* began humming "Here Comes the Bride," adding to the incongruity of the wedding. Having passed through the gate, we went quickly up to our cell. I locked us in, and the moment I turned around, we both burst into tears, sobbing openly as we held each other. We lay down, still crying, but softer now.

11:55 a.m. If security remained as it was now at the gate, I wouldn't try it. To do so would be disastrous. I opened the door slightly and peered down at the gate. Now there was only one guard there, and he wasn't being as vigilant as before. Still, though, I was near panic. I watched him for a few more minutes until I felt that he was not acting differently from normal. Although I could not be sure, it now seemed okay. I told Barbara that I would have to hurry if I were to be ready by 1:40 p.m. She nodded and quickly got her things together. We synchronized our watches and then exchanged them. She asked me what was going on at the gate now. I told her it looked normal.

I walked her down the stairs to the gate. We held each other tightly, beyond emotion. Several people were looking at us. We kissed once more. I told her that I would see her in a few hours outside. She nodded, eyes brimming, then turned and walked out of the dorm. I'll never forget the look on her face as she departed—tense, yet strong; crying, yet determined. Then she was gone.

Would I ever see her again? It could only be one extreme or another. No middle ground. *Don't think about it.*

12 noon. One way or another, this was the last time I would have to go through these checkpoints. I would never see the inside of this prison again. It was early and there were no crowds. I was through in four minutes. I had at least an hour and a half to connect up with Enrique.

At the taco stand, I picked up the canvas bag packed with Dwight's clothing and hailed a cab.

12:02 p.m. I double-locked the door and barricaded myself in. If anyone came to my door, I would have to keep them out one way or another. I put a new blade in my razor and began shaving off my beard and moustache. I shaved it a second time to rid myself of any telltale stubble. After I had finished, I dug all of my makeup from the mattress and from the padding in the kittens' box. First the stick makeup. I rubbed it under my eyes and where my whiskers had been to cover up any stubble. Then the foundation makeup. I smeared it on all over from my neck to forehead. It was gooey, sticky, revolting stuff—thick enough to catch horseflies. But it did the job of changing my complexion. Then the eye shadow, eye liner, mascara, and eyebrow pencil. I powdered my cheeks and chin thickly enough to cover my pores and any surviving stubble. It looked ghastly.

12:25 p.m. I smeared on the pink-red lipstick perfectly and puckered my lips in the mirror. And then the rouge on my cheeks—vague little circles of red, just enough to remind people of the inner color of a woman. I checked it out in the mirror. At first I felt like something between a Babylonian whore and a circus clown.

But I was also surprised. This was the first time that I had put on the makeup *without* my whiskers. In my previous drag rehearsals, whenever I saw myself with the makeup *and* the whiskers, I just could not take myself seriously. But now, even without the wig on, *I was looking like a true woman,* far more so than I could previously have imagined.

12:30 p.m. I was downtown at Enrique's door. I knocked.

No answer. I knocked again, louder, many times. After several interminable minutes, Enrique opened the door, disheveled. He had been asleep. He was sorry, he said, but he'd been unable to borrow the car for me.

I looked at him for a moment in disbelief, then turned and walked away. It was 12:38. I ducked into a café and opened a book to think. Every step had gone so perfectly until today. With a shudder, I remembered the guard thrusting me back inside the gate, saw him searching, searching. And now Enrique: a final lesson in self-reliance.

A detached, neutral calm spread through me, the same feeling that had allowed me to smuggle the paper passes. I was beyond nervousness, strung tight into the hyperawareness I would need to avoid false steps. I watched the minutes crawl by one by one, with a strange mixture of anticipation and dread.

12:41 p.m. I polished my fingernails and waited for them to dry. It took forever. I had grown to hate these long, awkward extensions of dead skin that I had been growing for three months. They had gotten in the way of everything. Only now did I realize what a burden it must be for a woman to have to continuously maintain herself as "conventionally beautiful." It wasn't worth it. Never again would I do this. I might not ever get another chance.

1:00 p.m. Now the clothes. First, some ridiculously tight, bright-colored panties. If they ever searched me down to my lingerie, I wouldn't have a chance. I was pulling up the panties when someone pounded on the door. I froze.

"DE-WITE WOR-KER!"

"*VISITA CONJUGAL CON MI ESPOSA!*" I shouted. "*NO ME MOLESTE!*"

"*MENSAGE!*" (Message)

"*DESPUÉS DE MI VISITA!*" I yelled angrily, letting whoever it was know that he was bothering my wife and me on our wedding day.

"Okay."

There was a long pause. He must have left. I was trembling uncontrollably.

I finished pulling on the nylon panty hose and checked out my shaved legs. They now looked like *women's* legs. I slipped on the 36B bra the way Barbara had shown me and filled each side with a pair of socks. I would need these socks on the road. I checked out my tits. One of them looked bigger than the other, no doubt about it. Lopsided. I stuffed a handkerchief behind the smaller one to give me bilateral symmetry. It worked. I looked balanced.

1:10 p.m. *I could sit still no longer. I walked out of the café and stood on the curb to hail a cab. The street was choked with lunch hour traffic. Cab after cab, already full, crawled past me. Oh God, a ghastly vision of being trapped here by the snarled traffic.*

1:13 p.m. *A cab! I jumped in quickly, pulling in the bulky canvas bag after me. Horns blared behind us and the driver took off before I could shut the door.*

"A dónde va?"

"Cerca de Lecumberri—por atrás de la carcel. Tengo encontrarme con una amiga allí."

1:15 p.m. I slipped on my conservative, long-sleeved blouse. It fit tightly, but would not draw any undue attention. That was why I was not a 36D. Now I put on the foam pad that I had so precisely cut and contoured for my ass. Over that I pulled the full-length skirt that Barbara had so carefully made to my measurements. I tucked in the blouse and pulled the belt tight. A nice hourglass effect. I was coming along.

1:22 p.m. I stuck on the clip earrings and strung the cheap, brassy necklace around my neck. Next I put on the copper bracelets and the tawdry rings for my fingers. I looked again at my hands and the skin looked a bit rough, so I rubbed some foundation makeup onto the backs of them. Perfect. No one could ever tell if I had been washing dishes and scrubbing floors—or weightlifting and getting into fist fights. My hairless hands, with their smooth skin and long, pointed nails, looked almost dainty.

1:29 p.m. Hurry. Now the big operation: the wig. It was hidden under the padding in the kitty box where the five kittens were now sleeping. Gently I lifted up the folded blanket and fished through it for the opaque plastic bag in which the wig was hidden. I felt the bag and slowly tried to pull it out without disturbing the sleeping kittens, but to no avail. All of the kittens woke up. I took the wig and began brushing the tangles out and setting the hairpins in properly, while off to the corner the kittens were beginning to cry in chorus. They were hungry.

1:30 p.m. I directed the cab driver down a narrow dead-end street one block behind and parallel to the prison. I had him park behind a large pile of garbage and told him my girlfriend would arrive sometime in the next half hour. We would wait here. "I'll pay you," I said, when he looked incredulously from the garbage piles to me. He turned resignedly and opened a Kaliman comic book. I tried to believe a cab would work as well as a borrowed car.

It would be at least half an hour. I glanced to my right at the forty-foot-high wall of the factory. Double-checking. Yes, I was out of sight of the gun turrets. Flies droned and heat shimmered in the air above the mountain of refuse choking the end of the street. I felt surreally remote, like a visitor in my own skin. The driver swatted the flies absently, absorbed in the adventures of Kaliman. I opened a book and stared at the page sightlessly.

1:33 p.m. Slowly, I looked at myself in the mirror. I was stunned. I was stunning. It wasn't me at all, but the lady that Barbara had dreamed up from the beginning. I quickly got out the prescription tinted glasses and put them on. Even more amazing. I could now see myself clearly in the mirror and I didn't believe what I saw. *It wasn't me at all.* I slipped on my lady's sweater and grabbed the shopping bag. Then I got my little coin purse of the type that women are allowed to carry in Lecumberri. I put the two metal tags in it along with the forged yellow paper pass.

1:35 p.m. Seven more minutes to go. I knew that the most perfect disguise would not mean a thing if my body language was wrong. I had to *become* a woman now in spirit. I had to manifest myself as a woman with every step and action during every moment along the way; or they would recognize me as easily as if I were nude.

I began walking back and forth in the cell as Barbara had coached so many times before, concentrating. Walk slowly—take small steps—no angular, jerky movements—lower my center of gravity—move steadily from the hips—womb consciousness.

But with every step I took, the kittens followed, meowing at me, screaming at the tops of their high-pitched lungs for milk. My disguise hadn't fooled them in the least. I had to be careful not to step on them as they scurried back and forth after me, attacking my sandals, protesting in such a loud, dissonant chorus that I was *sure* they could be heard outside the cell door.

"No, no, kitties, no time to feed you now. This momma's going to fly the coop." Here I was trying to make jokes for a bunch of cats, I was so nervous.

Just then one of the kittens jumped on my sandal and began climbing up my nylon. I reached down to sweep the kitten off, and RRRIPPPP. I had the first run of my life. Another one was working its way up my other leg. In a few seconds both my nylons had long runs in them. It was impossible to walk in my cell with the kittens in their milk delirium now, so I stood next to the door.

I slipped the bolt quietly out of the lock and ever so slightly eased the door open. Directly in front of my door stood Maru and Tierno—Tierno, the *commando* who had always had it out for me in "F." Disaster. What were they doing here? If they saw me come out of *my* cell like this, they would recognize me immediately, and of course they would squeal. I shut my door and locked it. I could not leave as long as they were there.

1:42 p.m. *No bugle yet, no commandos. Now. Now he is stepping from the cell.*

1:43 p.m. I eased the door open again, and Maru and Tierno were still there. This time Tierno looked directly at me through the crack in the door. I pulled it shut and locked it again. I had to leave before 1:45 p.m.

Then I suddenly found myself doing something I had not done in as long as I could remember. I got down on my knees and prayed. I prayed to God—to the forces that be—to allow this to happen. My lips were moving soundlessly. I was asking the universe for another chance. I was pledging that I would carry myself more positively in the world than before. I knew that my life was up for grabs right now, and that I would have to deserve this chance.

1:44 p.m. *Through the gates now, into the rondin.*

I stood up. I brushed off my knees, straightened my skirt, inhaled deeply, and threw out my chest. I felt much better. I opened the door, quickly stepped out, and closed it behind me. Maru was nowhere to be seen. Tierno looked directly at me, blocking my way. Trying to pass him on the narrow catwalk, my face a few inches from his, I carefully turned my head, hoping he would only see my wig—at this close range, I was certain he would see through the makeup. He stepped aside.

I began walking steadily toward the stairway, looking straight ahead and slightly downward. I held my *defensor's* metal tag in front of me as I descended the stairs. Two prisoners moved aside in deference to the "lady." Again!

A number of prisoners were at the dorm gate, including four or five *commandos.* Far too many—if any one of them recognized me, he would immediately grab me and turn me in.

No honor among prisoners here. I held out the metal tag and the *commandos* moved aside. One of them, Yaqui, looked me directly in the eyes as I passed him no more than a foot away.

"*Bien,*" he said.

He recognized me. He must have!

But he didn't grab me as I walked out the gate. I saw the uniformed prison guard standing to the side facing away from me, *talking with Jaime.* This was the same guard who wouldn't let Barbara out of the dorm this morning. Busy with Jaime, he did not even look at me as I passed. But for a fleeting instant, Jaime and I made eye contact, and I had an eerie feeling as he recognized me. I instantly thought that he was deliberately distracting the guard. And then Jaime and the guard faded into the periphery as I swept forward. Checkpoint 5 down.

1:45 p.m. *Through checkpoint 4, stalling now in the long walkway, waiting for the bugle and the crowds.*

At this point my vision through those tinted lady's glasses became otherworldly. It was like a silent color movie rolling slowly and animatedly in front of me. Although there were sounds, I did not connect them to anything that I was seeing. I was dissociated from everything around me. No one was looking at me, or even registering that I existed. At least *I* thought no one acknowledged me—it could just as easily have been the other way around. In my mind I had made this walk a thousand times, and now here I was actually *doing* it. Suddenly I felt tranquil and detached from everything, as if I were watching myself float through it all. But simultaneously I felt the dread physical terror of knowing that this too was for real; that in an instant I could be smashed out of this illusion.

I was convinced that Tierno or Yaqui had recognized me—Dwight Worker—and would soon tell the guards. They would just wait for me to get to a certain point to catch me, perhaps just beyond the walls so they could machine-gun me down. *La ley de fuga.* My back tingled.

I continued walking slowly in the opposite direction around the *rondin,* leaving the *defensor* route to join the general visitors. I put my *defensor* metal tag into the coin purse and got out the general *visita* tag for checkpoint 4. I held it out before me as I approached. Miraculously, there were *no* guards there at all. They were over to the side advising a mechanic who was fixing the colonel's car, which was parked next to the checkpoint. I walked slowly past them. They did not look up. Checkpoint 4 down.

1:46 p.m. The bugle blew. Perfect timing. Soon the crowds of women would come swarming down the walkway to checkpoint 3, one hundred meters ahead of me. I moved down the walkway toward checkpoint 3. I had never seen this area of the prison before, for all prisoners were prohibited here. Ahead of me I saw two guards, each sitting at one of the counters. I would have to wait until the women came, so I pretended to search for something in my coin purse.

I panicked at the thought of Yaqui. He had told the other *commandos* and now they were surely checking my cell—or telling the guards, who would now be running ahead to catch me. At any moment I expected them to swarm up behind me. Nearby, the three guards continued arguing over what they thought was wrong with the car. I was standing too close to them. I looked behind me again for the *commandos* and guards, but they were not coming.

1:48 p.m. I looked down to the metal tag/paper pass exchange point. Only two women were there and they passed quickly. Two more minutes before the crowds that Barbara had told me about.

With my face to the wall away from any passersby, I continued searching through my coin purse for something. I fumbled through it again and again. Then I began searching inside my shopping bag which was filled with odds and ends. I sat it on the cement and went through it with both hands, acting busy while quickly stealing glances at checkpoint 4 behind me to see if an onslaught of *commandos* and guards were leaving to look for me. Where were the women?

1:49 p.m. *Checkpoint 3, standing in the crowd of women, moving forward, slowly.*

1:50 p.m. I wanted to run. Too close to the guards at checkpoint 4, too close to Yaqui and dorm "F," and too far from the street. At checkpoint 3 a few women were there, but no crowds.

1:51 p.m. Barbara had said the crowds would be building up by now. But until they did, I had no choice but to wait. I meandered a few steps closer to checkpoint 3, still searching within my coin purse for the time I was stalling for. Had the guards noticed me yet, standing still for so long a time? I heard them still talking about the colonel's car.

1:53 p.m. A small but steady trickle of women began passing by, looking directly at me. *Could they tell?* Surely to them I must be so obvious. I watched them go to the counters at checkpoint 3. The guards were handling them as fast as they arrived so that no crowds were building up. And still no *commandos* came charging up behind me to drag me to the colonel's office. For the first time since I walked out of my cell I began to feel that maybe, just maybe, no one had recognized me. As calmly as I could, I continued searching through my shopping bag.

1:54 p.m. *He has put away the tag. Now he has the paper pass, getting ready to press on through. Oh, do it just right . . .*

1:55 p.m. More women came hurrying by me, trying to get to the exchange counters before the others. I looked ahead and for the first time I saw a line of women building up at one counter. But none were at the other one. I would have to wait until there was a crowd at both tables, and then try to sneak by.

Just then two Mexican guards who had been looking at the car came walking by. One of them saw me. He reached with his hand as if he were going to pinch my foam-padded ass.

"*Oh, mi bella gringota! Quiero cojerte!*" (Oh my beautiful big *gringa* lady. Do I want to fuck you!) I quickly stepped to the side away from his hand. *Did he know?* Cold fear. *No, of course not.* In the strangest way, that insult gave me a boost of confidence.

I walked a little farther on, getting nearer to the exchange counters. A Mexican prisoner who worked in the adjacent print shop saw me through the open door. He came to the door and began begging for money and cigarettes. By the bulbous growth on his neck and the tissue deterioration on his ear I could tell he had dry leprosy. I turned away and did not look at him again.

1:57 p.m. *He has to have made it past checkpoint 3 by now. It's downhill from here on. He's out in the driveway, moving toward the ramp. Quickly now.*

1:58 p.m. For the first time there was a small crowd at both counters, enough of a crowd to perhaps block that guard's view of me. I queued into the longer line of women, noticing that I was at least a foot taller than any of them. I felt as if I were visiting a junior high school; I must be so conspicuous. Through my tinted lenses I looked at the top of the woman's head in front of me. On the white parted line of her scalp I saw a *piojo* (louse). I glanced at the women around me scrambling and pushing for position. Some of them were cutting in front of me, adding to the confusion as I stood there holding out my metal tag. They were too busy trying to exchange their metal tags first to pay any attention to me. The guards were busy moving as fast as they could, trying to accommodate the horde of women.

1:59 p.m. Now must be the right moment. But if any guard saw me do this or step out of line, I would be finished. With a forest of raised arms to cover me I quickly opened my coin purse and dropped in my metal tag. Then I pulled out the paper pass and held it inside my hand. I smoothly stepped out of the line, turned my back to the guards, and then opened my hand with the paper pass showing. I turned toward the opposite guard and slowly walked by him. He looked at me, and saw the paper pass in my hand. For an interminable moment, he continued looking at me, and then went back to his business. I glided slowly forward, away from him. Checkpoint 3 down.

I came to a narrow door. Next to me there was an elderly Mexican lady. I automatically stopped and let her step through the door in front of me. Ladies first. Oh Jesus, what a stupid thing to do. But she only looked at me a little strangely. Then I followed her.

I was now walking down a long, walled driveway, into another area of the prison that I had never seen before. I was awestruck that I was here with no *commandos* or guards charging behind me. One hundred and fifty meters ahead of me were the final two walls and checkpoints. I moved slowly and rhythmically, feeling more and more confident of myself. Overhead stretched a catwalk. In the middle of it was a guard armed with a machine gun, looking down at the flow of women leaving. I walked on beneath him, and came to a little outdoor table behind which sat a prison employee selling handmade prison trinkets. As I passed him, he made a lewd sucking sound with his mouth, the kind Barbara heard daily from Mexico City's finest. But to me, that sick, slurping leer from that half-brained cur at the table was just the kind of reinforcement I needed right at this moment. *I had fooled him too.*

2:00 p.m. *Down the stairs, now checkpoint 2—oh God, the guard's signature in the wrong color ink. Will he notice, will he . . .*

2:02 p.m. Other women were walking along with me as we queued to go up the ramp to checkpoint 2. The line was a long one. Good. Enough for the guard to get used to women filing steadily past him. I climbed the ramp with the other women, and then began descending the stairs. I watched the women in front of me handing their paper passes to the guard at the base of the stairs. As he collected them, he examined the signature on each paper pass, and then the woman before she passed. This was the same guard who had previously signed them. Closer and closer I approached.

2:04 p.m. I handed the guard my paper pass.

He looked at it, staring directly at his own forged signature. He looked at it longer than he had the one before. *The ink color.* Then he looked directly into my eyes. I couldn't wait. Another moment and he'd realize—I had to move as if nothing were wrong. I took a step, and then I continued walking, expecting an arm to pull me out of line any moment. *He had to know.*

But no one stopped me. Checkpoint 2 down. Just twenty more feet to go.

I followed the woman in front of me through a narrow passage where some guards were standing about, talking. Then I saw it— *daylight*—a small, open metal door—flanked by two guards armed with machine guns. Beyond that door I could see the street. The woman in front of me walked between the guards and stepped through the door. The guards looked at her as she passed, and then they both looked directly at me as I moved between them.

2:05 p.m. *He's walking quickly, get out of sight. One more minute before I look over my shoulder to the corner. He'll be there. One more minute before I see him.*

2:06 p.m. I stepped through the narrow doorway onto the street. There were a dozen armed guards lounging around the exit. I walked between them out to the middle of the street. The sun hurt my unaccustomed eyes. If the guards were going to do something now, it would be with their machine guns to my back.

2:07 p.m. *Look again. Empty corner. Ice cold sweat trickled in terror. Suddenly I realized that for all our meticulous planning I had never figured out what I would do—how I would even know—if it didn't work. I could sit here in this taxi for hours. No. Don't think about it. Why, why doesn't he appear?*

2:08 p.m. I dared not look behind. I stepped between parked taxis and avoided the rapid traffic until I reached the opposite curb. I slipped behind a greasy-looking taco stand and turned the corner, out of sight of the prison.

2:09 p.m. *Hadn't arranged how I would know—if he didn't try or tried and got caught. Over my shoulder again, still no one. Panic rising, dizzy eyes swimming, cab meter ticking, ticking . . .*

THE STREET! It was dirty and slummy and crowded with all of the rotten organic smells of refuse and open marketplace and trash and IT WAS THE MOST BEAUTIFUL STREET I HAD EVER SEEN IN MY LIFE!

Having walked away from the prison, I never once turned around to look back at it. I turned the corner to where Barbara was to rendezvous with me in the borrowed car. Except for one whistle, the people on the sidewalk looked at me as if nothing was unusual.

2:10 p.m. *No one.*

Fifty feet ahead of me I saw Barbara sitting in a car, except it was a taxi. Oh no. She couldn't borrow the car. Still not safe.

2:11 p.m. *OH MY GOD, halfway to the cab! "Ya viene mi amiga. Abre la puerta!"*

She saw me approaching and opened the door. I looked into her face and saw the biggest, maddest, most delirious smile ever shown on the face of this planet. I squeezed her hand as she told the taxi to go to the *Terminal del Norte.*

45 The Weirdest Honeymoon Ever

The taxi driver turned around and drove directly toward the prison. I was too afraid to say a word to Barbara for fear that he would notice my voice. As the massive blank, grey-walled prison loomed ever closer, my terror grew. This was the first time that I had ever seen the outside of Lecumberri. Machine-gun turrets loomed overhead and a myriad of armed guards were standing about the entrance with "business as usual" expressions. Just you wait.

I expected to see a group of guards charging out of the entrance right now, shouting and warning the other guards. I froze up, staring at the immensity of the prison, while the cab rolled by. Then I quickly jerked my head away from the guards across the street, grabbed the newspaper Barbara had with her, and held it up in front of me.

"Don't worry," Barbara whispered. "He doesn't suspect a thing. You look disgustingly beautiful."

I did not know how to take that.

The taxi charged through a red light and screeched to the right. Barbara slid over against me. I took her hand. The prison was out of my sight. A wave of relief came over me. Barbara leaned forward and told the driver that our bus would be leaving soon, so if he could hurry, he would get *una buena propina.* He sped up even more. With each minute, each block, each turn of the wheel away from Lecumberri, I felt less and less paranoid. The driver did *not* know. From behind my wall of newspaper I stared at the unfamiliar street and the traffic flowing by. For the first time in two years there were no walls. My God, it is working. *It is working!*

I had not said a word to Barbara since I had entered the cab, having been too stunned and too distrustful of my falsetto English to speak in front of him. But we kept staring at each other in awe, until I began worrying whether the cab driver thought our silence strange. Almost on cue, Barbara said.

"How do you like Mexico City?"

"I'm happy to be leaving," in my softest falsetto English. I distrusted my voice. I squeezed her hand again, and then realized that the cab driver might think it strange that we were holding hands. I let her hand go.

"Don't worry. Mexican girls hold hands together all the time." We intertwined our fingers together again.

The cab rolled on, farther and farther from Lecumberri, closer and closer to the terminal. Our plan had been to get off at a gas station near the terminal where I could de-drag in the washroom. The only problem would be which washroom I would use. We hopped off at a Pemex station and tipped the driver generously.

"*Muchas gracias,*" he said, putting the money into his wallet.

"*A usted también,*" I returned. If only he could know how true those words were. As he drove off, more relief welled through me. Now no one around us knew that we had just come from Lecumberri.

2:55 p.m. I had missed the first bus. We started walking into the Pemex station, but stopped in our tracks when we saw a motorcycle cop cleaning off his bike in the station. Turning away, we began searching the streets for a nearby hotel. We turned up and down the blocks of the middle-class neighborhood we were in, looking for a place where I could change, while we carried a double-handled suitcase between us. We were wasting time. Finally, after five or six blocks and fifteen minutees, we found a cheap rooming house.

3:10 p.m. Barbara checked in as I waited off to the side. The lady led us up the stairs to the room and opened the door for us to inspect. Anything would have been fine with us.

As soon as we had locked the door behind us, we embraced. Finally in this temporary privacy, we could speak.

"WE DID IT WE DID IT WE DID IT!" We were whisper-shouting through our incredulous smiles. I started to kiss Barbara, but she pushed me away.

"Take the makeup off first. We have to hurry. They may already know that you've gone."

I first pulled off that constricting, suffocating wig that I had been sweating under and threw it on the bed. Then the earrings and wristlets. I broke off the necklace and let it drop to the floor as I slipped out of the hot sweater. I unbuttoned my blouse and let it fall. Then I asked Barbara if she would please help me with my—bra.

The bra slid down my front like the beginning of an avalanche, ending up on the floor like a used parachute. My long skirt fell from my hips like a circus tent collapsing. I yanked off my ass pad and then skinned my panty hose down to the floor. And then, finally, I pulled off those tight, strangling panties that had been squeezing my balls up to my kidneys. In a minute I was naked.

I was free of the clothes too! I hugged Barbara again, quickly, and turned to my hated fingernails. Growing them had been a three-month project and they had been in my way the whole time. So many times I had poked myself in the eyes or cut myself when all I had wanted to do was take care of an itch. And scratching my balls had been near catastrophic. In a moment I snipped all ten of them off and there they lay on the desk top like some small, exotic seashells at the Smithsonian. I made a fist with my hands again and again. At last my nails did not cut my palms. I was becoming normal again.

Barbara handed me the Nivea cream and I smeared it all over my face, especially on the eyelids and lashes. Then I hopped under the cold shower and sudsed up. Barbara inspected me after the rinse.

I failed.

More Nivea cream and soap with vigorous scrubbing. This time Barbara said that I now looked like *any* plucked-eyebrowed man. Finally we kissed.

We had to hurry. Soon Lecumberri would confirm that I was missing, and an all-points bulletin would be sent out. I got dressed quickly into my own clothes and repacked the suitcase Barbara had brought. My skirt, blouse, and underwear were scattered about the shabby room. Let them figure it out. This had to have been the tackiest bridal suite ever. Barbara handed me my forged tourist card, bus tickets, and $200—the last of our money. I was now "Roaland J. Addoake." I started out the door, but Barbara stopped me. My fingernails were still red. Jesus, how could we have overlooked *that?* Barbara handed me the polish remover and the last traces of the escape were wiped away.

3:30 p.m. Down the stairs and Barbara and I, as man and woman, walked right past the lady who had checked us in. No one else was there. It was still *siesta* time. We didn't pause to watch the expression on her face. Fifteen minutes to go before the second bus departed.

We quickly walked a few blocks from the hotel and hailed a taxi.

"We need to catch our bus. Please hurry."

3:45 p.m. Before getting out of the cab at *Terminal del Norte*, we surveyed the bus station to see if the police were conducting an inspection of outbound travelers. Everything looked normal, even through our paranoid eyes. I tipped the cab driver and we ran off to the bus line going to Morelia.

3:50 p.m. "Are we late? Has it gone?"

"No, of course not. We haven't even begun loading up yet. It'll be leaving in fifteen minutes."

Good. For once we could use *el tiempo Mexico* to our advantage.

We sat in the lobby holding hands, alternately scanning about us for guards. Nothing unusual, but still—deep fear. I was in shock at the unfamiliar surroundings: newspaper stands, cafeteria, store. No one was yelling. There was open space and bright sunlight and a myriad of colors. Barbara was sitting at my side with the most beautiful smile in the whole world. *My God.*

Over the intercom the departure of my bus was announced. With a tense, careful hug and a kiss, Barbara and I parted.

"Meet you in Tucson." I watched her walk away from the bus window. I'll never forget her smile.

The bus pulled out of the terminal into an incredible traffic jam. Slowly we inched out of the foul, polluted northern section of Mexico City toward the highway to Michoacán. I chatted in fluent Spanish with the people sitting around me. Very friendly souls. They all complimented my Spanish.

"Where did you learn it?"

"Visiting Mexico."

I couldn't get over the amazement of seeing him outside, free and functioning. He was radiant. I watched him get on the bus, turning away only after the last possible glimpse.

What I wouldn't give to talk to Mame right now! I walked quickly to a pay phone, dialed her number, and asked Maria to please tell the *señora* that I had gone home to buy a Christmas tree.

There was no sign of anything unusual in the terminal. I caught a local bus outside to go back to my apartment at the opposite end of the city—an hour's trip. I gazed out of the window at the twilit city, but everywhere I looked I saw that empty corner of the garbage-strewn alley where everything had hung in the balance. I felt the growing horror; and then I relived the sight of the tall woman who had suddenly materialized, whose every step pulled me out of the horror into unbelievable joy. Oh my God, my God.

I turned my face to the window as tears streamed down over my uncontrollable grin.

5:00 p.m. Farther and farther we rolled away from Mexico City. What was happening in Lecumberri right now was their problem, not mine. I didn't care. But ahead of me I saw it: a checkpoint manned by *federales*. Cold fear surged through me as I got out my tourist card. *Please don't look at it too closely.* As the armed guards boarded the bus, the reality hit me again that I was a fugitive in Mexico, and I would not be safe until I was out of here. The *federales* walked by me, glancing at my card, but they didn't stop. In a moment they were off and the bus was rolling again. Relief.

Gabrielle and I were back at the *Terminal del Norte* by 7:00 p.m. I checked our luggage into a locker, and then Gabrielle and I went for a long walk outside the terminal. I didn't want to spend the three remaining hours before our bus left waiting in the terminal for the police to show.

On my occasional glimpses into the terminal I could see no sign of anything out of the ordinary—no police, no inspections, nothing. I checked the departure gates of several northbound buses. Nothing. But I was still too nervous to sit down. I carried the sleeping Gabrielle in my arms as I paced up and down the length of the terminal.

The bus kept rolling through the Mexican countryside, but it was nothing like the euphoria rolling through my soul. I looked at my watch. 7:45 p.m. The guards must now be frantically looking for me in Lecumberri.

Fuck them. Fuck the sentence. Fuck the time. Fuck the charge. Fuck the *commandos*. Fuck the *mayor*. Fuck Colonel Cardenas. Fuck Echeverria. Fuck Lopez-Portillo. Fuck all of them. FUCK OFF TO IT ALL!

I quit.

I sat alone in the bus, smiling uncontrollably.

I thought about the political prisoners I had left behind. I wanted to do something for them, to expose their plight and denial of rights. I thought of Jaime and I felt sadness. I wanted to help him.

All of the Mexicans I met and talked with on this bus were very cordial and friendly and even helpful to me, a total change from my prison experience. I wondered about that for a while, as the bus kept rolling farther into the night. I lay my head back to rest.

That evening, for the first time in two years, I watched the sun go down on the horizon and the stars appear in the sky. Oh, did it feel good! I held my hands together in my lap prayerfully, thanking the universe, God—the whole works. I would not forget my promise.

At 9:45 p.m., the loudspeaker blared that the 10:00 p.m. bus to Santa Ana and all points between was now boarding. On time! I quickly ran to the locker, got out our luggage, and called a porter. In five minutes we were on the bus without a trace of a policeman anywhere around us.

The big diesel engine roared out of the terminal toward the highway as the last lights of Mexico City diffused into a fading mist behind us. I could see the stars glittering in the black square of desert sky outside my window, and I knew that at this very moment, for the first time in two years, Dwight was seeing them too.

Late that night, the bus pulled into Morelia. I had all but forgotten about Andrew. It seemed just too improbable that on the basis of one phone call he would be here, so I planned on staying in a small, inconspicuous hotel tonight. Next morning I would get moving again.

But when I got off the bus, a moustached American man was standing directly in front of me.

"Are you the one?"

I looked at him and then looked around. No one else was there.

"Uh—yeah," I said, hesitating. "I guess so."

"Welcome!" He slapped me on the shoulders. "I'm Andrew." And he steered me to his car.

A half-hour later I was on a small mountaintop, in the middle of a large orchard. The change completely overwhelmed me. I was too far away from Lecumberri—with its stone and cement and bars and walls and guards and machine guns and its resignation and horror and despair and death—to believe that it had ever existed. I did not understand it at all.

In every dream I had ever had in my two years at Lecumberri, I was free. Now at last I actually *was free* and I was not dreaming. My God.

Was I hungry? No, not at all, even though I had not eaten all day. Andrew then wanted me to explain to him in detail what had happened. I started to, but could not. I was incoherent.

I apologized to him. He said that it was all right, he could understand. I excused myself to go outside and carry in some wood for the fireplace.

Above me were thousands of stars, and their light was all shining down on *me.* I was shivering beneath the mountain pine trees, once again in awe of the universe. I lay on the ground and put my cheek to the earth. It was covered with pine needles. At that moment there could have been no sweeter scent in the world.

I sat up again and folded my hands in my lap, remaining still except for an occasional shiver.

I thought of Barbara, who was now traveling with Gabrielle across northern Mexico by bus to the border. Her beautiful face appeared before my eyes just as I had last seen her, smiling deliriously at the bus station. Then I thought of our wedding and how we had felt when we had just returned to the cell. I put my head in my hands on that pine-covered mountainside under the soft, cool starlight, and I cried and cried and cried.

46 Fugitive

December 18. Early in the morning Andrew and I went swimming under a nearby sixty-foot-high waterfall. I basked euphorically in the sparkling exuberance of the water. During the following two days I took long solitary walks all over the isolated mountainside, submerging myself in the natural beauty of this earth, not yet completely believing that I was free, or even that I had ever been in Lecumberri. Each day Andrew would bring all of the Mexico City newspapers to his home and I would search through them for articles. But for two days the papers mentioned nothing. Andrew began wondering if I had in fact escaped, or was just a strange imposter with a very bizarre story. I began to wonder what was going on.

December 20. All five of Mexico City's Saturday newspapers announced the escape in banner headlines.

AMERICAN ESCAPES LECUMBERRI!

Seeing it there, in the headlines, finally and loudly announced for all the world to see, I was terrorized. The articles stated that not only had the police launched an all-out search throughout Mexico City, but also that agents from the DEA, Interpol, and the Mexican Army had placed roadblocks and inspection points all over the country. My mind was spinning. I wanted to force the hair on my eyebrows and legs to grow out. I had to think, I had to act before they caught up with me. I wanted to run and hide—literally go underground—anything.

Andrew grinned broadly as he read the articles.

"Boy, are those bastards upset. You really screwed them. Are they mmmmmaaaaadddddd!"

I folded the paper so that no one else could read it, even though there must have been hundreds of other papers on the newsstands in Morelia. Get rid of the evidence. No matter what I told myself, I felt horribly conspicuous. My hands began shaking uncontrollably.

"Calm down," Andrew stressed. "They don't even know I live here. There's no one around. The safest thing to do is just sit still."

He was right. But as I read the *Excelsior,* a wave of panic hit me. *THEY HAD ARRESTED MAME LEVINSON.*

Andrew stopped cold.

"Jesus, they may be torturing her right now," I whispered. "She may already have been forced to give your name."

For the first time I saw an expression on Andrew's face like the tense, hunted look that had been on Barbara's and mine for all too long. It was not pleasant.

"All right, it's time for you to leave right now. I'll take you to the bus station."

As we drove along I worried about Mame. Although she had her alibi together and was too smart to be frightened into signing any confession, their form of torture was unknown to her. But perhaps they were only questioning her as a matter of formality. I could not take any chances.

"Where's the most remote place you can think of?"

"Go to Paricutín. They'll never look there."

Eyeing the Morelia bus terminal with renewed paranoia, I bought a second-class bus ticket for Paricutín. I decided I would travel on the rural backroads where surveillance would not be as tight.

In the privacy of the back of the bus I reread the newspapers. What surprised me about them, along with their confusion and inaccuracy, was that the escape had only made news in the Mexico City papers. All of the newspapers outside of Mexico City were strangely silent about it. Either Mexico had no national manhunt coordination, or they were deliberately silent about the search in the other areas. I suspected the latter.

Later I would learn that the prison officials, after discovering my absence, first announced that I had been murdered in the prison and that they were checking all the sewers for my chopped-up body. They were so convinced that I had been killed that they even told the U.S. Embassy I was dead—because "no one escapes from Lecumberri."

The U.S. Embassy apparently agreed, because for three days they told visitors that I had been murdered in Lecumberri and they were looking for my body. Thank God they didn't find it.

As the bus wound through the beautiful Michoacán mountains, I became more relaxed again. My main worry would be an all-points bulletin on all highways, railroads, and airports north. They could do it. But it was Christmas season. Millions of *gringos* were now in Mexico spending hundreds of millions of dollars. To check every one of them would be very difficult. More seriously, it could hurt Mexico's tourist trade.

I arrived at a remote village at the base of the volcano Paricutín in the early afternoon, hired a guide, and rode a mule up to the top. They wouldn't be looking for me on the top of Mt. Paricutín. By now I was calm enough to appreciate its raw, violent beauty. How wonderful it was to be alive and free and traveling, even if I was a fugitive—especially since I was a fugitive.

At the roadside again, I caught a bus to Guadalajara. Keep moving moving moving. All along my exodus I met Mexicans who were kind and helpful, especially the *campesinos*. They were totally different from the people of Mexico City. It was good for me to meet Mexicans in other contexts, good to lower my anger level and rehumanize me. I was finally getting it together. But I had to keep moving.

Late that night I arrived at Guadalajara, slipped off the bus, and quickly obscured myself in the pandemonium of the station. Thirty minutes later I was asleep in a small, inconspicuous hotel nearby.

December 22. I realized I was starved, not having eaten all day yesterday, so I ordered a large American breakfast at the train station, while waiting for the train to Hermosillo. In the restaurant I bought all the newspapers available. There were many articles about me in the Mexico City papers, but nothing in local ones. Good. I carefully stood in line and boarded the train. It pulled out at 9:00 A.M.

The train was old, dirty, and so crowded that people eventually began lying down in the aisles. By nightfall there was no more food or water on the train. The only thing to drink was booze. Enjoying the novelty of real, cold beer, I drank several. Good stuff. Eventually, they ran out of that too. I didn't care.

The car was unbearable—packed, smelly, and uncomfortable— so I climbed down the open steps all alone and sat in the gusting air, watching the dark land sweep by me. Keep going. I was nice and drunk. Whenever I had to urinate, I just sprayed it across the Mexican countryside at 100 kilometers per hour, expressing my sentiments for the Mexican government better than anything I could ever have said.

December 23. Sunrise. The train stopped abruptly in Obregon. Through the windows stretched the parched Sonoran desert. By now the aisles were filled with paper, bottles, and organic refuse, along with several uncleaned splatters of vomit. The bathrooms had long been out of water and the toilets filled up. The smell reminded me all too much of where I had just come from.

Federales boarded the train and searched all of the luggage—for drugs and guns, I figured. I opened my suitcase and they checked through it. They asked for my tourist card. In cold terror, I automatically handed it to them. They stared at it and handed it back.

10:00 a.m. I got off at Hermosillo and taxied to the bus station. There I bought a second-class ticket to the Lukeville, Arizona, border crossing. With an hour to kill, I went to a Mexican bank and bought some traveler's checks with only my tourist card as identification. I signed them "Roaland J. Addoake." My plan was to use these, along with my tourist card, to get back into the United States.

I rode in a rickety school bus with tall, handsome Yaqui Indians over the backroads of northern Sonora until the bus came to the last stop. I hopped off and approached the remote Lukeville border crossing by foot, in the late afternoon. Nothing appeared unusual, but at this, the last moment of escape, I felt suddenly clutched by terror.

I walked past the Mexican checkpoint without stopping. Fifty feet ahead I saw the U.S. flag and America. It was so beautiful. The Mexican guard was watching me go by. If he said a word, I was ready to sprint into the U.S. in high gear.

I kept on walking toward the lonely U.S. customs station. The two U.S. guards searched me and then asked for my identification. I handed them my tourist card and traveler's checks, explaining that I had been robbed in Mexico.

"Yeah. It happens all the time." The guards did a computer check on Roaland J. Addoake, but found him innocent of everything. Then they waved me through. We wished each other happy holidays.

I walked off of the pavement to the edge of the desert and dropped to my knees. A customs agent saw me and looked puzzled. I didn't care. I brought my face down to that dry Arizona sand and kissed it again and again and again, grabbing handfuls of earth and squeezing it through my fingers. I was crying silently, tears streaming down my face into the dirt in my hand.

Home. Here I was—tired, broken, penniless, lying on the

ground. I knew that at this moment I was the happiest, wealthiest man in the world.

I got up and walked slowly to a pay phone to call my parents and share with them our Christmas present. My father and I cried tears of joy over the phone. It was the first time we had talked in years. Then I walked over to a little restaurant for my first meal since yesterday morning. I had a cheeseburger, a slice of apple pie, and coffee. It was the best food ever served on the planet.

The sign said TUCSON 119 MILES. Just desert between here and there. I would hitchhike. It was getting dark and no cars at all were passing by, so I began walking. While passing through the outskirts of this small town, I heard the sound of Christmas carols carrying through the desert night air from someone's home nearby. Their songs and voices made me feel very good and warm inside.

I kept walking, miles into the desert. It was pitch dark now. No moon, just stars. I heard coyotes yapping in the distance. I began running and jumping and shouting as loudly as I could. I had not screamed in years. If it was necessary, I would *walk* to Tucson, where Barbara was now waiting. I would have *crawled backward.*

Much later I heard a vehicle coming from miles away. I stuck out my thumb and waited. A van came by at eighty and took a quarter of a mile to stop. I had gotten a ride from the first car. A good start in America. I ran up to it and hopped in.

Two long-haired, bearded men greeted me. They had been smoking pot.

"Want some of this?"

"No, thank you."

"Whatya doin' in the middle of the night in the desert?"

"Going to Tucson."

"Where you comin' from?"

"Mexico."

"What ya been doin' there?"

Then, in one nonstop, one-hour, *manic* monologue, I told them THE WHOLE STORY.

They sat there taking tokes, shaking their heads, rolling their eyes. They exchanged subtle, private expressions.

They didn't believe a word of it.

I didn't care.

I arrived in Tucson late at night but went to the post office anyway, hoping there might be an all-night clerk who could give me the letter Barbara would have waiting for me there. In it would be the address where she and Gabrielle were staying. Closed. No way to find Barbara. After a restless night in a nearby hotel I woke up on Christmas Eve and ran to the post office to wait for it to open. The clerk handed me her letter. It was only supposed to contain an address, but it was fifteen pages long. Laughing in spite of my anxiety to find her, I sat down on the bench and combed the letter for her address. Finally I found it—a small hotel only a block away from where I had been last night.

Down the street through the door to the hotel desk.

"Yes, I'll ring her room."

In a moment she was standing at the top of the stairs in Levi's, a western shirt, and a glorious smile. I had never seen her in Levi's before.

In that frozen moment that we stared at each other as if for the first time, a small figure scurried out and gazed down at me, frowning.

"Dwight!" said Gabrielle, "where have you *been?*"

Epilogue

Mame Levinson was interrogated for a day and then released. Fifteen guards were arrested for aiding my escape. *Licensiado* Ferrer-Gamboa was imprisoned and charged with accepting $80,000 in bribes from me and conspiring in my escape. A photo of his battered face appeared in a Mexico City newspaper, accompanying an article explaining that Ferrer had signed his "confession."

In a major purge of Lecumberri prison in the spring of 1976, Colonel Cardenas was arrested on charges of accepting bribes and taking part in corruption, extortion, and multiple murder. He has been in a Mexican military prison ever since, and has been confined as an invalid because of "injuries."

Fernando Gardner-Pasqual was murdered in prison shortly after Cardenas was arrested.

The Mexican lawyer, Jorge Aviles, was arrested and charged with fraud by Mexican authorities in April 1975.

Dan Root, vice consul of the American Embassy, was accused by Aviles of conspiracy to defraud, but was quickly transferred out of the country.

Lecumberri prison was closed forever in the late summer of 1976.

And Barbara and I are free and happy and together.

Appendix

In the late 1960s, a rising demand for marijuana in the United States paralleled a significant increase in the amount of marijuana smuggled across the U.S.-Mexican border. To halt the flow of drugs, the Nixon administration launched the much-publicized "Operation Intercept" on September 21, 1969, and imposed a land, sea, and air surveillance upon the 2000-mile Mexican-American border. Included in "Operation Intercept" was a massive car-by-car search at each border station, which slowed down and sometimes halted traffic for many hours, resulting in dwindling trade for merchants in border cities and a serious decrease in tourism to Mexico.

Because of the subsequent economic turmoil and general ill will felt by Mexico toward the United States, "Operation Intercept" lasted only three weeks. Then, in a meeting in Washington D.C. on October 7–10, 1969, U.S. and Mexican officials agreed to replace "Intercept" with "Operation Cooperation." Under the new program, the United States promised to adjust the border inspections to eliminate unnecessary inconvenience, delay, and irritation. In return, the Mexican government promised to increase its efforts to eliminate the production and smuggling of marijuana and other drugs.

From that point on, each government tried to show the other that *its* drug laws and *its* enforcement procedures were doing the job promised. In the early 1970s, Mexico increased its laws against drugs, denied parole to all drug offenders, and lengthened mandatory prison sentences.

Meanwhile, to consolidate and unify various drug enforcement groups in the U.S., the Nixon administration formed the Drug Enforcement Administration (DEA) on July 1, 1973. At that time, the supply of heroin in the United States was decreasing significantly due to production controls in Turkey and the U.S. withdrawal from Vietnam. So confident was the DEA of its projections to President Nixon that he announced on September 11, 1973, "We have turned the corner on drug addiction in the United States."*

While the scope of the DEA's efforts have been international, in recent years its activities have concentrated in Mexico, where its annual budget ranges as high as fourteen million dollars and its staff has been built up to thirty full-time agents. All of this is necessary, the DEA agents contend, to continue arrests and drug confiscations. They point proudly to statistics such as these:

DEA/FOREIGN COOPERATIVE DRUG REMOVALS

Drug (lbs)	1972	1973	1974	1975
cocaine	246	1,011	1,114	1,077
marijuana	106,910	220,326	335,520	1,246,899

Drug Enforcement Statistical Report: Organizing and Training Data. March, 1976, p. 9. (Department of Justice: Washington, D.C.)

But other evidence shows that the DEA has concentrated on the easier arrests of these softer drugs at airports and border stations rather than on the tightly controlled Mexican families who now dominate trade of the hard drugs—heroin and morphine. In fact, DEA statistics show that arrests and confiscations of heroin and morphine have actually *declined* since the formation of the DEA in 1973:

Drug (lbs)	1972	1973	1974	1975
heroin	2,340	1,174	659	750
morphine	1,628	2,934	796	329

Drug Enforcement Statistical Report: Organizing and Training Data. March, 1976, p. 9. (Department of Justice: Washington, D.C.)

*Commentary, April, 1975, p. 46.

This information is based on statistics compiled for fiscal years 1972–1975. Calendar year statistics show the same trend: In 1971, 1,109 pounds of heroin were confiscated; in 1973, after formation of the DEA, the amount dropped to 208; in 1974 it dropped again to 141; in 1975 there was a slight increase to 304.*

Concurrent with the decline in heroin confiscations has been an *increase* in heroin originating in Mexico and used in the U.S. In the late 1960s, the percentage of Mexican-originated heroin used in the U.S. was estimated at from ten to thirty per cent. But by 1975, this estimate increased to *seventy to ninety per cent.* Clearly, whatever the DEA was doing in Mexico was not stopping the flow of hard drugs across the border.**

To most health professionals there is no question that heroin and morphine are far more dangerous than cocaine and marijuana. The relative hazardousness of these drugs is in part revealed by annual numbers of drug-related deaths, which the DEA has tallied and published for fiscal year 1975:

Drug	Total Drug-Related Deaths
heroin/morphine	1,608
barbiturates	1,029
methadone	801
other depressants	602
other stimulants	104
amphetamines	36
cocaine	16
hallucinogens	8
marijuana	1

Drug Enforcement Statistical Report: Organizing and Training Data. March, 1976, p. 38. (Department of Justice: Washington, D.C.)

All of these deaths are of course dwarfed by alcohol, which causes an estimated 30- to 50,000 American deaths annually.***

With statistics such as these, it is difficult to understand why the DEA concentrated on cocaine and marijuana in Mexico. One possible answer is that marijuana and cocaine smugglers—

*Drug Enforcement Statistical Report: Organizing and Training Data, March, 1976, p. 11. (Department of Justice: Washington, D.C.)

**The New York Times, October 28, 1975, p. 9.

***National Council on Alcoholism, June, 1977.

especially the small-time independents—are easier to find, arrest, and incarcerate in Mexico than any of the large, syndicate dealers. Another is that corruption within the DEA itself has involved scores of officials on both sides of the border in sophisticated drug rings—indeed, many cases of such corruption have been documented and brought to trial.* Whatever the reason, the conclusion is clear: despite the increases in funding and manpower, and despite top priorities supposedly given to drug enforcement on both sides of the border, the DEA has not been doing the job it was created to do. It could also be said that rather than "turning the corner on drug addiction," the DEA is now *contributing* to the very problem it was supposed to solve.

Furthermore, the American prisoners in Mexico are not heroin traffickers. When I was in Lecumberri prison, not one of the 160 Americans in the federal district of Mexico was charged with heroin. On August 11, 1976, the State Department gave this breakdown of the Americans in all Mexican prisons on drug-related offenses to Robert Ryan, congressional aide to California State Senator Alex Garcia.

CHARGES AGAINST AMERICAN PRISONERS IN MEXICO

Drug	Possession	Trafficking
marijuana	237	118
amphetamines	2	?
hashish	1	0
cocaine	25	71
barbiturates	2	?
heroin	24	3
others	24	?
TOTALS	296	192

Virtually none of the Americans are imprisoned for trafficking heroin, while half are in prison for possession of marijuana. The Mexicans privately describe these Americans as *chivas espiatorias* (expendable goats), while publicly using their numbers as proof to the United States that Mexico is enforcing its stringent drug laws. The fact that virtually no American, regardless of guilt or innocence, can get out of a Mexican prison after he is arraigned before a Mexican "court" is also used as proof of Mexico's strict

*Federal Narcotics Enforcement: Interim Report on the Committee on Government Operations, U.S. Senate, Permanent Subcommittee on Investigations. Report No. 94-000, 1976.

drug enforcement. Meanwhile, the flow of Mexican heroin increases to the United States as the "Mexican connection" becomes more solidly established.

Yet of the approximately 200 prisoners in the federal district of Mexico City charged with *importación* of drugs in March 1977, not one was a Mexican national. Of course Mexican nationals *are* trafficking in drugs just as much as the arrested foreigners are. But the fact that none of them are caught suggests that Mexican authorities have selectively enforced Mexico's U.S.-pressured laws against foreigners, particularly Americans in Mexico, with a vengeance.

This "get the *gringo*" atmosphere surrounding drug enforcement in Mexico is not only the result of new "get tough" drug laws; it is also a tip-of-the-iceberg indication of the deep hostility with which many Mexicans regard Americans. American tourists are increasingly seen as arrogant, white-skinned oppressors who visit Mexico only to take advantage of its inexpensive cost of living, and this national resentment comes out in many ways. In recent years, American tourists in Mexico have experienced frustrating delays, unexpected red tape, and continuous and ever-present needs for tips and bribes. Reports in newspapers and travel and recreation magazines warn of pickpockets, muggers, hotel burglars, and armed highway robbers who are as attracted to the middle-class, middle-aged American tourist as the *mayors* were attracted to *gringos* like me: we have the money; we owe it to them for what we did to them historically and for what we are today. While the Mexican tourist industry (and even U.S. travel agencies) downplay the dangers to U.S. tourists in Mexico, the fact is that robbery of American tourists has become a major criminal business and an important secondary income for Mexican police at all levels. And instances of harassment, entrapment, and arrests of Americans for real or imagined (in any case, always exaggerated) charges of drug trafficking have soared.

For Americans who do travel to Mexico, the best rule to follow is to stay away from all drugs and invitations to use or buy them. Beware of having drugs planted on you by police or their collaborators. They are often looking for any excuse to confiscate your car or possessions. If arrested for whatever charge, be ready to pay a large bribe immediately to the police: to postpone bribery more than three days most often makes it impossible to gain release. Although immediate bribery payment does not ensure release, refusal to pay *guarantees* confinement in prison. Once inside a Mexican prison, be prepared to pay rent for cell and for other basic necessities. And expect no help from the U.S. Embassy or consulate.

The State Department seeks to assure citizens that U.S. prisoners in other countries are granted the same rights as are nationals of that country. Beyond that, they say that there is little they can do regarding the treatment of U.S. nationals beyond our borders. Torture, however, is—or should be—another matter. In Mexico, prior to mid-1973 when the DEA was formed, complaints of the American prisoners generally concerned violations of their legal rights. But by August of 1973, after the establishment of the DEA, reports by American prisoners of torture and forced confessions were loud and unending. While officials of the U.S. Embassy threw up their hands in helplessness, representatives of other embassies were not so passive. As a result, British, Canadian, and Australian prisoners have not been the victims of physical abuse in Mexican prisons. I quickly learned in Lecumberri to claim that I was a Canadian or Australian whenever an unfamiliar guard was about to assault me—if he believed me, I was not beaten.

The U.S. Embassy has never seriously attempted to exercise its powerful influence on the Mexican government to alleviate the continuing brutality levied by Mexican officials (and DEA agents) against American prisoners. Indeed, evidence shows that some embassy agents have been in league with corrupt Mexican officials and lawyers to exploit the situation for their own benefit. While in Lecumberri, I heard Dan Root advise American prisoners to hire Jorge Aviles-Ortiz as a lawyer because he "is the only one who can get you out." And later I heard many stories from prisoners and their relatives about how Root and Aviles had defrauded them. But it was not until April of 1975 that Jorge Aviles, arrested by the Mexican government on charges of fraud, signed the following statement in the presence of Pierre Boulanger, consul of the Canadian Embassy:

I, Jorge Avilés-Ortiz, Mexican attorney at law, license number 16504, issued by Direción General de Professiones, do hearby swear and attest under no duress or pressure, that the following statement is true and correct:

That on many occasions, for valuable consideration, vice consul of the American Embassy in Mexico City, Daniel D. Root did recommend and refer, myself, Jorge Avilés-Ortiz, to act as attorney for American prisoners arrested at the Benito Juarez airport in Mexico City and incarcerated in the Federal District of Mexico.

April 2nd, 1975

(signed)
    licensiado Jorge Avilés-Ortiz
    Districto Federal, Mexico
Witnessed
    Pierre Boulanger
    Vice consul, Canadian Embassy
    Jose Garcia-G.
    Ayudante del Colonel Cardenas
    Carcel preventiva, D.F., Mexico*

Jorge Aviles was later to retract this statement, but this time no consul from the Canadian Embassy would be present to insure that Aviles did not make that retraction under duress. By this time Dan Root had been quickly transferred out of the U.S. Embassy to points unknown.

There are many witnesses to Dan Root's defrauding of Americans for large sums of money, but virtually all of them are behind bars for seven or more years. And Root's case, although extreme, is not unique. Other accounts of the U.S. Consulate's misconduct toward U.S. prisoners in Mexico have been reported throughout Mexico. It is convenient for the State Department that these prisoners remain behind bars until the statute of limitations on the crimes alleged against Dan Root and others like him have expired.

In February 1977, President Carter endorsed the proposed Mexican-United States prisoner transfer treaty that Mexico had originally suggested in June 1976. Mexico had moved rapidly to ratify this treaty in December 1976. As this book goes to press, the treaty and implementing legislation are before the United States Senate.

The Mexico-United States prisoner transfer treaty is a modest, reasonable proposal that satisfies all of the parties and considerations involved. If implemented, it would allow American and Mexican prisoners the option of voluntarily returning to their respective countries as prisoners to finish their sentences. Within

*Hearings before the Subcommittee on International Political and Military Affairs: United States House of Representatives, *Congressional Record*, April 29 and 30, 1975, p. 12.

their own countries they would have access to parole and rehabilitation.

Recognition should be given to President Jimmy Carter for moving the executive branch in support of this treaty. Also to be commended for their help on the treaty are Senator Jacob Javits of New York, Senator Joseph R. Biden of Delaware, and Congressman Fortney Stark of California.

What is to be done about the drug problem in Mexico? Recently, the DEA has announced plans for a coordinated crackdown on heroin production in Mexico, but the idea appears impossible. A poppy crop can be grown in three months, and many of the poppy producing areas are located in inaccessible central mountains. Furthermore, the U.S.-Mexican border *is* 2000 miles wide, and no amount of air, sea, and land surveillance can ever begin to cover it. If millions of illegal aliens can easily make it across every year, how can the flow of heroin possibly be stopped? Finally, the heroin market is controlled by a small number of large, blood-related Mexican families living on both sides of the border. They are well-disciplined, tightly organized professionals who are not about to deal with anyone outside their own clan.* The DEA's efforts to break up these family rings have been ineffectual, and always will be as long as there is a market for heroin in the United States.

It was the Nixon administration's mistake—and the mistake of every administration thereafter—to believe that *only* tough laws and tougher enforcement measures could conquer this deeply entrenched problem of drug smuggling between the United States and Mexico. As a result the DEA has been at best a band-aid approach and at worst a contributing influence to a problem that will exist as long as there is a demand in the United States for drugs. What the DEA is fighting is more symptomatic of a national malaise of family and cultural disintegration, poverty, and unemployment. Fighting symptoms through one isolated, compartmentalized enforcement approach will probably never work. But if it has any chance at all, it must be integrated into a broad-based program aimed at reducing long-term drug *demand* in the U.S. Until this is effectively done, the drug problem will be here to stay.

*Newsweek, March 15, 1976, pp. 28-30.